ETHICAL INTELLIGENCE

THE FOUNDATION OF LEADERSHIP

How to Get It **Right** in Your Life
and in Any Organization

JOHN T. OPINCAR

Houston, Texas

Copyright © 2016 by John T. Opincar

Cultural Fire Press, LLC
Houston, Texas
www.culturalfirepress.com

Printed in the United States of America

First Edition: November 2016

You may contact the author at john.opincar@boardroompartners.com.

Cover and interior design by Brett Miller, www.bjm-bookdesign.com.

The publisher is not responsible for websites (or their content) that are not owned by the publisher.

Library of Congress Cataloging-in-Publication Data has been applied for.
ISBN: 978-0-9980890-0-3

10 9 8 7 6 5 4 3 2 1

This book is dedicated to the One who said, "I have other sheep that are not of this flock. I must bring those also, and they will listen to My voice and pay attention to My call, and they will become one flock with one Shepherd."

CONTENTS

FOREWORD

♦

The past twenty years of applied ethics work from my base in South Africa have taken me around much of my own country, other parts of Africa, Australia, Britain and the USA. Although much has been achieved in these and other countries to enhance ethical practice, much remains to be done as we seek a better future, a quest that calls for the best possible ethical leadership.

I have been greatly privileged to experience some of the greatest ethical leaders of our time in the persons of Archbishop Desmond Tutu, Nelson Mandela and the Dalai Lama, and to encounter direct descendants of Gandhi, whose 21 years in my country transformed him from a young attorney into a Mahatma, a "great soul."

What I have long been seeking is a book that would map for me and others the qualities of leadership to be seen in these paradigms of moral excellence. *Ethical Intelligence* is the book I've been seeking. It is an exceptionally valuable contribution to the quest for fresh ethical thinking, which can make a significant difference in how we live and work.

Having worked early in my career for an international educational publisher, I know only too well that clarity is a fundamental requirement of good writing. *Ethical Intelligence* scores high in this regard. It is a model of considerate, lucid writing, which in itself is a sure sign that the material being conveyed has been understood with utmost thoroughness. The chapters are helpfully divided into sections and sub-sections, and they are amply illustrated with case studies, references to further reading, handy pull quotes in text boxes, graphics, concluding summaries and practical questions to round off each chapter.

The book contains a wealth of material. In this foreword, I can highlight only a selection of what I have found most valuable in it. A great deal of what others have written about applied ethics is set within the framework of Western thought—mostly philosophical but sometimes reflecting a Western religious orientation. While there is real ethical value in this framework, it is too narrow to serve the needs of an increasingly seamless world of many cultures. I applaud Dr. Opincar's immersion in a much wider, richer and deeper world of ethical wisdom, ranging from ancient China westward to his own country and over a time span of 4,500 years, without neglecting the many important ethical teachings of Western philosophers and faith traditions.

Another limitation of much that has been published about applied ethics is that it often draws on a single discipline, mostly philosophy. *Ethical Intelligence* avoids this limitation by using insights from history, literature, business studies, comparative religion and psychology as well. In addition, Dr. Opincar's account of ethics rests on admirable foundations involving three main sources: extensive studies of published work; a great deal of interview material with men and women in leadership positions; and decades of highly relevant personal. professional, corporate and academic experience.

Another significant strength of the book is the fact that it explores and explains not just what is right and good in business and elsewhere, but also what is wrong and harmful. An example of the latter is his discussion near the end of the book of Adolf Hitler and the nature of leadership.

Dr. Opincar has ensured that his book is highly practical. He achieves this by never losing sight of the "real" world of business and leadership practice, using detailed case studies and his own experiences. I greatly admire the frank way he so often draws his own experiences—mistakes included—into the text, giving it great authenticity.

This remarkable book makes me wish I already had it in hand for my ethics training of anti-corruption workers from around Africa as we seek ways to foster a new kind of leader—one who will practice the ethical intelligence presented here with clarity, wisdom and profound commitment to the greater good.

Martin Prozesky
Hilton, South Africa
September 2016

ACKNOWLEDGMENTS

◆

Thank you to:

My soulmate Linda, who has been an ever-present helpful advisor, critic, encourager, supporter, proofreader, and life partner.

Joel Osteen, Jim Lewis and the Men's Ministry and my entire Lakewood Church family for helping transform this alcoholic's life.

John Maxwell, one of the world's most recognized leadership experts and my leadership mentor for over 30 years. You'll find a lot of John's wisdom in this book.

Debra Engle, my literary counsel, editor, and copywriter, who helped me convert arcane academic writing into the readable prose you find in this book. www.debraengle.com

Michael Vandermark, my dissertation chair and colleague, who provided helpful critiques and guidance whenever asked.

My magnificent team of manuscript reviewers and commenters:

- *Dr. Pamela Allen*
- *Dr. Robert Armbrust*
- *Dr. David Breslauer*
- *Dr. Peggy Determeyer*
- *Mr. James Eickhoff*
- *Dr. Janice Harder*
- *Dr. Paul Harder*
- *Mr. Eric Idehen*
- *Dr. Deborah Hornsby*
- *Dr. Jeffrey Kaplan*
- *Ms. Tammy Maynard*

- *Dr. Ernelyn Navarro*
- *Mr. Paul Nilles*
- *Ms. Celeste Palmer*
- *Dr. Roger Parrott*
- *Dr. Carrie Picardi*
- *Dr. Rich Schuttler*
- *Mr. Michael Slavin*
- *Ms. Jeri Uhlmansiek*
- *Ms. Sherill Whisenand*

PRAISE FOR ETHICAL INTELLIGENCE

---◆---

"This is iron-sharpening-iron work that must be at the core of the best leaders' character and decisions. John pushes us all to do it right, and this book gives us the tools to get there."

Dr. Roger Parrott
President, Belhaven University

"We are all being led or leading all the time, and both sides have great responsibility. John digs deep into the ethical sides of decision making. The book is laced with interesting and powerful stories about how others have met moral dilemmas. Some do what is right, and others don't. It has very little to do with who is a 'good person.' Doing what is right seems so obvious, many of us never give any thought to it. We should. If everyone read this book, the world would be a better place. This book should be required reading for everyone."

Michael L .F. Slavin, author, One Million in the Bank
CEO, U. S. Emerald Energy Company

"Many books simply theorize and proselytize about ethics in business. Not so with this exceptional account of the real life experiences of top level executives who succeeded and failed in the arena of ethical intelligence and decision making. The stories in this book provide a much-needed wake-up call for all of us. Read it now."

Michael J. Vandermark, Ph.D.
Consulting Corporate Psychologist

"Dr. Opincar's book is a roadmap for creating an ethically intelligent life experience, and it is a recipe for success. This is a great book. It should be required reading for everyone."

> Eric Idehen, Founder and CEO
> Cornerstone of Hope Orphanages
> Benin City, Nigeria and Pujehun, Sierra Leone

"This book comes at a time in our country when leaders, organizations and communities are mired in increasing ethical dilemmas. Dr. Opincar skillfully created a book that combines research, history, storytelling and his personal experiences to deepen the readers' understanding of the key concepts and framework. The list of questions at the end of each chapter offers the readers valuable opportunity to reflect on their current beliefs and practices. The stories, case scenarios and reflective questions are great tools for teachers, trainers and leadership coaches to engage individuals and groups in dynamic dialogues about ethical issues and develop skills to enhance their ethical intelligence."

> Dr. Ernelyn J. Navarro, LCSW, BCC
> Board Certified Coach, P.E.A.R.L. Coaching & Consulting
> Adjunct Professor, University of Southern California
> School of Social Work

"Dr. Opincar is a skilled leadership thought leader who has created a composite reflection of the leadership body of knowledge that every leader and manager needs to read. In turbulent times, we need ethical leaders to emulate and follow. John's work is a catalyst that can allow for greater ongoing discussions and ethical practices to increase awareness. Each chapter's 'Questions for You' allow the reader to self-reflect, assess and do even better from that point forward. Read 10 pages a day and grow."

> Dr. Rich Schuttler, International Public Speaker,
> Educator and Best-Selling Author

"In a time of cultural and business ethical controversies and issues, Dr. Opincar uses extensive research on ethical intelligence throughout the ages, along with an effective storytelling style, to marry the concepts of truth required for ethical living in your personal and work life. Moreover, Dr. Opincar's message throughout this book shines a light on a path to understanding true ethically intelligent leadership. You will enjoy the stories and message. Read the book. It will change how you work and play."

Paul Nilles, Executive Vice President, GC3, LLC

ETHICAL INTELLIGENCE FOR A NEW MILLENNIUM PROJECT

————————◆————————

This book is the first in a series of four books, which represent the first fruits of my decade-long Ethical Intelligence for a New Millennium Project. The project had a serendipitous and modest beginning. Sitting in a Phoenix hotel room late the night before my second doctoral residency was to begin in May 2006, I was deciding on the research topic for my doctoral dissertation. I was scheduled to present my proposal to a committee of faculty and fellow doctoral students early the next morning. (Yes, sometimes my work is just in time! Please don't tell my students!)

As I sat there pondering what to research, the term "ethical intelligence" flashed through my mind. My ever-present guardian angel told me that was my topic. I dutifully Googled the term and, among the 300 hits that came up, found very few references that didn't involve spying and espionage. Essentially, there was almost nothing written about the subject.

The subject of unethical behavior among business executives was something that had intrigued me my entire business career. So I quickly assembled a PowerPoint presentation, which I enthusiastically unveiled to my committee the next morning.

The response was less than optimal—well, perhaps, *"Are you insane?"* would be a better description. I was given all the standard reasons why it was a terrible idea. *"The subject is too broad. There is little prior research to build upon. It will take far too long. We already know why these things happen—they're all a bunch of greedy bastards! The subject is way too complex. You're never going to get CEOs to talk to you about such delicate matters. Finding a dissertation chair could take years."*

Well, they were right on that last point. It took over a year and a half to find someone brave enough to chair my dissertation committee.

That Doubting Thomas meeting began a quest that ended with the publication of my dissertation on ethical intelligence in 2012. During those six years, I combed through 45 centuries of ethical intelligence literature (more than 9,000 works). I garnered exclusive interviews with CEOs and other C-Suite executives from the Fortune 1000 (more than a year of outreach), and I analyzed a massive amount of data. This book is the first in the series—the first fruit of all that labor.

This project sows the seeds of a new millennium of ethical intelligence thought, research, education and practice. It's a millennium within which ethical intelligence—an ancient legacy and the birthright of human beings—will again come to infuse human conduct, soothing and healing the aching wounds of conflict. You're on the ground floor of an important movement. Enjoy!

THINGS YOU WISH YOU HAD KNOWN...

---◆---

If you don't read instructions, scoff at users' guides as crutches for the weak-minded or jump into swimming pools without checking the water depth, you can skip this section. Otherwise, I recommend reading the next few pages.

We are all judges. Recognizing and resolving ethical dilemmas is something we do all day, every day. And at the heart of that work is ethical judging. Knowing how to do it right is the path to both inner and outer peace. This knowledge and capability is already built within you. *It's your birthright.*

In this book, I show you how to unlock the vault and reclaim that precious gift— your ethical intelligence.

In this book, I show you how to unlock the vault and reclaim that precious gift—your ethical intelligence.

NOT ANOTHER BOOK ABOUT ETHICS

This book is not about ethics. There are plenty of those already. Yes, we'll talk about ethics, ethical behavior and ethical thought.

But this book is about helping you find life—an ethically intelligent life—and changing your slice of this world for the better.

This book contains a unique and powerful combination of ancient wisdom and the life experiences of senior business leaders as they wrestled with ethical dilemmas. It includes a measure of history and theory wrapped around ethical struggles that have burned in the furnace of life. In this book, I offer you theory because theory is important. But it's theory grounded in the real world. It's a powerful fusion that produces a time-tested roadmap for action.

> This book contains a unique and powerful combination of ancient wisdom and the life experiences of senior business leaders as they wrestled with ethical dilemmas.

WHY READ THIS BOOK?

For centuries, we have been on a slow but accelerating descent into ethical fog. We now live in a world society full of fear, distrust and suspicion, all sustained by a growing tsunami of self-centered and harmful ethical judgments. These judgments exist at all levels and within all areas of human endeavor. Managers and leaders in business, government, medicine, philanthropy, science and even spiritual and religious organizations are no longer believed or trusted. This book prepares **YOU to lead the way forward**. The ancient wisdom and practical knowledge contained in this book empower you to make a positive difference in your organization, department, team, church, family, neighborhood and personal life.

ETHICALLY INTELLIGENT LEADERS ARE THE SOLUTION.
AWAKEN THE ETHICALLY INTELLIGENT LEADER WITHIN.
BECOME A WARRIOR OF HOPE!

YOUR PAYOFF FOR READING THIS BOOK

Once you've read this book, you'll be equipped to:

- *Increase, restore or find peace and serenity in your life.*
- *Elevate your managerial and leadership skills to the highest level.*
- *Know that you're not alone in your quest to do the right thing.*
- *Reinstate, reinforce or reify your honor.*
- *Better understand why the world seems a crazy place.*
- *Become a warrior of hope.*
- *Help others achieve the prior six objectives.*

How This Book is Organized

This book is organized into three parts, each containing four chapters. The parts and chapters build upon one another. Reading them sequentially provides a deeper relationship with and understanding of the material. Here is a brief description of each part:

Part One.
Ethical Intelligence: Our Precious Heritage contains the top four inches of an ocean of information so deep I've written four books about it. If the smidgen of information contained in Part One whets your appetite for more—and I hope it does—I invite you to read the other three books in this series. Four inches of that ocean, however, is all we need for our purposes in this book.

Part Two.
Leadership: Our Current Practice and Problems includes the practical wisdom contained in the ethical judging experiences of the senior business leaders who opened their hearts and minds to me during confidential personal interviews for this book. They

lived those experiences in the crucible of our 24/7/365 volatile, uncertain, complex and ambiguous business milieu.

Part Three.
Ethically Intelligent Leadership: Our Solution shows you how not only to awaken that precious gift—your ethical intelligence— but also how to create a vibrant personal and professional ethically intelligent life and become the ethically intelligent manager and leader today's world desperately needs.

FOUNDATIONS

As you read this book, there two sets of terms and four foundational ideas I want to mention for your consideration before we get started. First, the terms *decision-making* and *judging* don't refer to the same phenomenon. I am making a decision when I consider the merits of one investment option over another or I choose a place to eat lunch. Judging implies and involves weighing the equity of outcomes in relationships. Judging is about people and relationships. It is reserved for relationships between and among human beings.

Second, *Self* and *Other* are philosophical and psychological terms, which can seem off-putting and academic. I use these words throughout the book because they're efficient in conveying precise meanings. The *Self* is the self-aware, thinking you. The *Other* is all else. The *Other* may be an individual, a group or an organization, such as a competitor or governmental agency. *Otherness* is all that is not you.

Finally, there are four foundational ideas for your consideration: human ethical intelligence, human collective unconscious, our primal relationship, and our struggle for Selfhood. We'll discuss these ideas in Part One, but I want to introduce them here because of their importance. First, we lay out the basic meaning of ethical intelligence.

> **Ethical Intelligence.** Ethical intelligence is *the intellectual capacity and framework for judging matters of equity in relationships.* It has four separate but integrated elements consisting of (1) relationships, (2) equity, (3) ethical judging and (4) intellectual capacity and framework. This last element contains seven psychological, neurological, mystical or spiritual structures, as follows: Worldview Window, Heart Refuge, Limbic System, Internal Compass, Ethical Fence, Slippery Slope and Adjudicator. We'll discuss all of this in Part One.

Next, we offer Jung's idea of the human collective unconscious.

> **Human Collective Unconscious.** The idea of human interconnectedness has many names. It was popularized as "the Force" in the *Star Wars* series of movies. Carl Jung named it the human collective unconscious. I like Jung's

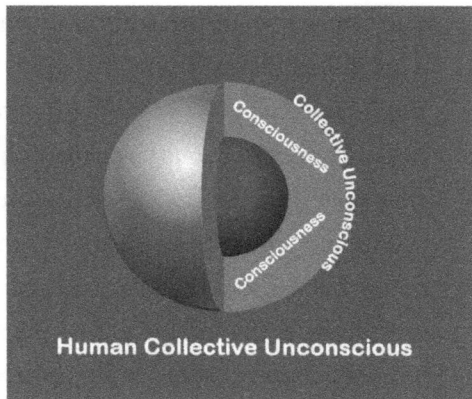

Human Collective Unconscious

description because it's both elegant and consistent with the principles of quantum physics. Jung considered the collective unconscious the common inheritance of humanity, a kind of reservoir of human thoughts and experiences that has existed since the beginning.

This reservoir is available to all of us, and when something happens anywhere, it has happened everywhere. I've captured my personal visualization in the graphic on the previous page. We don't have direct access to this reservoir as we do to our conscious memories, but it's part of our legacy as humans and resides within our psyches, overlaying and interacting with our consciousness. Its contents affect us in subtle ways, and it's an important part of our ethical intelligence. As this book unfolds, you'll see its power and appreciate its significance as you make personal and professional ethical judgments.

Next, and closely related to the idea of the human collective unconscious, is the *Primal Relationship.*

The Primal Relationship. The *Primal Relationship* is the elemental, unique and special connection we humans have to one another—an invisible but real link. In this book, I talk a lot about connections and interconnections. This connection is special, which is why I've italicized it throughout the book. The *Primal Relationship* is the pristine prototype of all relationships. It's important because it's where our ethical intelligence manifests in the real world. Our ethical intelligence lives in our consciousness but shows itself and grows within the *Primal Relationship*, its soil. Flowing from the *Primal Relationship* is our millennia-long struggle for our individuality, our Selfhood.

Our Struggle for Selfhood. It happened at Runnymede, England, on June 15, 1215. King John signed the Magna Carta, the first-ever written description of the individual human rights we all now assume are justly ours—security of property, equality before the law, habeas corpus, regular fair elections, freedom of speech, jury trials and the inviolability of contracts, just to name a few. Given the wide expanse of time humans have occupied this planet, human individuality, or the Self, is a relatively new idea. **In the beginning, there was no me, only us.** Emerging and differentiating the Self from the Other has been and is an ongoing struggle.

I ask you to consider these terms and foundational ideas and keep them in the back of your mind. Together they form the foundation for your ethical intelligence.

THIS BOOK WILL TRANSFORM YOUR LIFE

I've been around the block of life a few more times than I'd care to admit. I've seen careers and lives flourish and then fall apart because of senselessly harmful ethical judgments, including some of my own. I've mentored hundreds of people and changed countless lives for the better.

I challenge you. After reading this book, see if your family interactions and the other important relationships in your life are not better for it. See if you and your organization are not elevated to new levels of performance and rightly earned respect and stature. In the slightly paraphrased words of a former contemporary clothing store CEO, "You're going to like what you see. I guarantee it!"

Finally, at the end of each chapter in this book, I ask you to evaluate your experiences by considering questions—questions that make sense to me based on my life experiences, questions that are designed to provoke additional thought and engagement with the material.

There are answers in this book to questions only you can ask.

I urge you to ask your own questions, because there are answers in this book to questions only you can ask.

INTRODUCTION

◆

> "Don't buy Polycom's stock till I get guidance; want to make sure guidance OK." This is a text that helped send Roomy Khan to prison. After serving her sentence, Khan said "Prison is the easiest part. When you get out and there is nothing there— that's the toughest part."
>
> *Cooperating Witness and Co-Conspirator*
> *Galleon Group Insider Trading Case*

"I stand before your honor today to take full responsibility for my actions ... I know that I was wrong, and there's no excuse for my conduct."

Those were the words of Sanjay Kumar, the former Chief Executive Officer of Computer Associates International, a multibillion-dollar computer software company. Kumar had just been sentenced to 12 years in prison and ordered to pay an $8 million fine for his role in defrauding Computer Associates' investors of $400 million. When compared to his personal net worth, Kumar's gain from this crime was insignificant. From a disinterested observer's point of view, it was a senseless act.

Similarly, Robert Moffat was a straight-arrow 30-year career IBM executive in line to become IBM's next CEO. Yet Moffat exchanged his successful career, his marriage and his children for some pillow talk with Danielle Chiesi, a buxom hedge fund analyst. During their encounters, Moffat whispered inside information about IBM and other firms with which he had special access. The evidence showed he didn't profit financially from the "transactions," but both "pillow talkers" were sentenced to prison terms. Again, from a disinterested observer's point of view, Moffat's actions were senseless.

Over a multiple-decade business career, I saw scores of similar irrational acts, including some of my own. I witnessed incredibly bright and talented people lose their careers, businesses, families and freedom. I lost my first CEO job because I did something that seemed entirely logical and ethical under the circumstances but, in retrospect, was neither. I still feel the humiliation of returning home in a taxicab because I no longer had a company car. I remember walking through the front door of my house and telling my wife that not only had I been fired, but the SEC and IRS were going to investigate me. Fortunately, although stupid and unethical, my activities were not illegal, but the marriage ended anyway.

I should have known better. I was raised in a good family. I was educated at a Jesuit University, nearly becoming a priest. Yet I made senselessly harmful judgments similar to those of Kumar and Moffat. At the time, I chalked it up to youthful inexperience and resumed my career. I moved forward and became the CFO of a New York Stock Exchange company, a trusted consultant to some of the best companies in the world and CEO of several small to medium-size organizations. I was blessed with the opportunity of founding several startups, the last of which was part of the technology incubator at the University of Texas at Austin.

Throughout those subsequent years, my humiliating experience haunted me, and the anguish I saw others experiencing gnawed at my gut. I wanted to know how these things continued happening. Rules, regulations, laws and long prison terms had little apparent deterrent effect. I wanted to know why.

Returning to university in 2005 to pursue my doctorate offered me the opportunity to study these puzzling behaviors as my dissertation research project. This book is about what I learned and how managers and leaders can improve their lives and those of others through ethically intelligent management and leadership.

> Rules, regulations, laws and long prison terms had little apparent deterrent effect. I wanted to know why.

I discovered that much of what we believe today about ethical decision making (judging is the correct description), especially in business, is wrong. Conventional wisdom says a business executive's unbridled quest for money and power results in unethical conduct and is driven by greed and the relentless need to succeed. A contemporary movie, *The Wolf of Wall Street*, is an artifact of those beliefs. As is often the case, conventional wisdom is mistaken.

> Cognition and volition take a backseat to the most primitive part of our brains—the limbic brain, where decisions are made, judgments are formed and emotions rule.

You need to know that greed and the quest for success are *not even on the list* of factors driving business leaders' ethical choices. Cognition and volition take a backseat to the most primitive part of our brains—the limbic brain, where decisions are made, judgments are formed and emotions rule. In this book, I give voice to the forgotten wisdom of the ages and the silence of the C-Suite. I focus a dim glimmer of light into that secret place of refuge to which we all retreat when midnight comes at noon, emotions flow and ethical judging begins.

Based on my glimpse into that secret place, I offer a new way of thinking and acting. I propose an explanation of what happens in the hearts and minds of leaders as they resolve ethical dilemmas. In this book, I demonstrate that rules, regulations, ethics codes and legislation hardly ever pierce the heart and soul of someone driven by cognitive conflict, psychic pain, risk of loss and dire distress. It's time to reconsider long forgotten ancient wisdom and open our minds to the secret proceedings occurring in the minds and hearts of those with the power to harm. This book begins a long-needed critical conversation. I hope you will join the discussion.

The first part of this book describes who we are—members of a marvelous race of creatures imbued with rights and gifts that cannot be taken from us regardless of any form of human governance. Many of us have a gnawing feeling that those rights are being compromised, and most of us have either forgotten or never knew about the gifts. Part One reaffirms who we are, who "they" are, our ethical intelligence birthright and the Neurosynapticware we have that makes it all possible.

PART ONE

---◆---

ETHICAL INTELLIGENCE: OUR PRECIOUS HERITAGE

We hold these truths to be self-evident, that all men are created equal, that they are endowed by their Creator with certain unalienable Rights, that among these are Life, Liberty and the pursuit of Happiness.—That to secure these rights, Governments are instituted among Men, deriving their just powers from the consent of the governed,—That whenever any Form of Government becomes destructive of these ends, it is the Right of the People to alter or to abolish it...

United States of America Declaration of Independence

Welcome to Part 1, a celebration of who we are. Here's what you'll find in this portion of the book:

The first chapter is about who we are, including our claim to recognition as an equal with rights that cannot be eclipsed by any other human or human institution. Chapter 2 is about who "they" are. Should we fear "them?" Chapter 3 is about what we have— our ethical intelligence. And Chapter 4 is about our Neurosynapticware, the elegant package of psychological, neurological, mystical or spiritual structures we possess that enable us to use our ethical intelligence—the *how* of our gifts.

We begin with a look at who we are so that we can establish what is ours.

CHAPTER 1

---◆---

WHO WE ARE
—A GIFTED PEOPLE

The first time that I had been seated behind a curtain in the dining car, I felt as if the curtain had been dropped on my selfhood.

Dr. Martin Luther King, Jr.

In life, we have to establish who we are before we can claim what is ours. For example, we can't simply walk up to a valet parking attendant and claim a car without showing who we are and that the car belongs to us.

In this chapter, we explore four gifts to which we can lay claim as our inheritance simply because we are members of the human race. These gifts include (1) our unfettered claim to recognition and respect and its implications for the Worldview Window, (2) our *Primal Relationship* and its connection to ethical judging, (3) the secret place—the Heart Refuge, our personal inviolate sanctuary and (4) the part of us that makes us uniquely human—our emotions. We begin our exploration in the summer of 1942 with a horrifying story of ordinary men becoming extraordinarily evil in less than six hours.

The trucks were heavily laden with ammunition crates, and the men had been issued extra ammunition magazines.

Summer of 1942. The alarm pierced the early morning darkness and, in short order, the men from the reserve police battalion began climbing onto the waiting trucks. The trucks were heavily laden with ammunition crates, and the men had been issued extra ammunition magazines. The trucks slowly headed out of the Polish town on the way to a small village, some 30 kilometers away. It was a hot and humid July morning, even before sunrise. As the trucks lumbered along the deeply rutted dirt road, the men aboard sleepily thought about their first village pacification assignment.

This reserve police battalion had been in Poland only three weeks, having just completed its training in Germany before deploying in mid-June 1942. These men had been drafted to serve in the German army, but for various reasons were deemed unfit for combat. They were ordinary, mostly older, but otherwise patriotic lower-to-middle-class family men from Hamburg. They were shopkeepers, clerks and laborers. As the German army conquered territories, police battalions like this one followed and backfilled the security function to maintain order and pacify the population.

After a bone-jarring journey, the trucks arrived at their destination. The men climbed out of the trucks and were ordered into formation. Dawn had just broken. The men could barely see the commander in the early morning light. Climbing atop a nearby tree stump, the commander, a grandfatherly individual in his late 50s, addressed his police battalion.

"Men, we have been given an important assignment here today. I can assure you this assignment has been ordered and approved at the highest levels of the Reich. There are approximately 2,800 Jews living in this village. It's our job to remove them. We're going to round up the men, put them on these trucks and deliver them to the nearest rail depot, where they will be transported to labor camps to serve the Fatherland."

The men, who had been groggy, snapped to attention upon hearing the commander's words. A palpable unease filled the morning air. The commander continued.

"That leaves us with about 1,800 women and children who are of no use to us. We have been ordered to execute every one of them by gunshot."

"That leaves us with about 1,800 women and children who are of no use to us. We have been ordered to execute every one of them by gunshot."

Gasps and low murmurs spread through the battalion. Sensing a potential for open rebellion, the commander ordered his personal bodyguards to shoot any man who disturbed the formation.

"I know you may find this shocking and harsh," he said, "but we must remember these are enemy collaborators. They are the reason we are in this war. Besides, they've been robbing us blind for years. It is our duty to defend our homes, our families, and our country. Any of you who feels unable to carry out this task, please step to the side, and we'll assign you a different duty."

Hanging their heads in shame, about 10% of the men stepped aside. The commander gave his final orders.

"I salute those of you who have volunteered to serve the Führer in this difficult but necessary task. Work efficiently and with precision. We must be done by nightfall, and we must conserve our stock of munitions. Heil Hitler!"

The men were then given detailed orders, and the operation began.

Those men who had stepped aside were ordered to round up the Jewish men and teenage boys and transport them to the railway depot. Those who resisted or refused were ordered shot on the spot.

The remainder of the battalion was split into two groups. One group was assigned the task of going door to door and rounding up the Jewish women and children. The second group of men was lined up next to a long and deep recently excavated trench. The ammunition crates were taken from the trucks and lined up behind the men who were standing alongside the trench. The planners had designed the operation for efficiency because it had to be finished by dark.

It was now fully daylight, and the men could see that the village was set into a beautiful wooded area. The heavy morning air had the smell of nearby flowers, and birds were singing a July melody. The men had been instructed to fix bayonets. The bayonets were to be used as aiming devices for the rifles. They also added extra space between the executioners and their victims.

The first group of women and children, stripped of all clothing and jewelry, were marched to the edge of the trench and ordered to turn around and face the gaping trench. Although some of the women were sobbing and the children crying, the men of the police battalion were struck by the eerie calmness exhibited by most of the victims.

The commander called a halt because many of his men were doubled over on the ground vomiting. Some were sobbing profusely.

The executioners had been instructed to shoot the victims in the back of the head, making sure the body fell forward into the ditch. The guns rang out, and women and children began collapsing forward into the ditch. Some of the bullets, however, missed their mark, and exploding heads sprayed the executioners with body fluids. After several rounds, the commander called a halt because many of his men were doubled over on the ground vomiting. Some were sobbing profusely. Upon seeing the spectacle, the commander gave another rousing exhortation and veiled threat to his men and, again, offered a reprieve to those who could not continue. None accepted the offer.

The killing began anew. Wave after wave of women and children, stripped not only of their clothing and jewelry but also their human dignity, were marched up to the edge of the trench and summarily shot in the back of the head. Those who didn't die immediately had to be shot again at closer range. Mothers carrying infants posed an even bigger problem and slowed down the operation because after the mother was dead the infants were killed using bayonets. Ammunition was precious.

By midday, the executioners were drenched in blood, other body fluids, and bits and pieces of bones, skin and hair. The air was filled with the acrid smells of gunpowder, decomposing flesh and death. Because the killing was less efficient than the planners had anticipated, the men were unable to eat lunch, got angry and began complaining. As the day wore on, it became more and more obvious the battalion was not going to finish its work before dark. The anger increased, and the complaints grew louder.

By late afternoon, the killing had slowed even further because many of the victims who had run into the woods had to be chased down, shot, and the bodies then dragged back and thrown into the trench. The executioners began complaining even more because they were going to miss a hot evening meal, and it was now obvious they were going to have to work far into the night to finish the job. The day ended close to midnight. The men were hungry, hot and angry. But this newly initiated reserve police battalion had successfully "pacified" its first village.[1]

I AM JUST LIKE YOU. DO YOU SEE ME, RESPECT ME?

I begin this chapter with this gruesome true story to introduce one of the most important structures of ethical intelligence—the Worldview Window—and to reaffirm the truth that **we are all deserving of recognition and respect.** This story presents the spectacle of ordinary middle-class German family men losing their humanity in a matter of hours. They weren't soldiers They weren't Special Forces. They weren't trained killers. Many could barely hit their targets at point-blank range. Only a few days earlier, these men were living ordinary German middle-class lives, going to work, taking their kids to school and taking care of their families.

How do such ordinary humans transition from vomiting in the morning to complaining in the afternoon while mercilessly killing other humans? Surely some of the Jewish women reminded these men of their wives or grandmothers. Possibly some of the three-or four-year-old Jewish children reminded them of their children or grandchildren back home. These men, who were not trained killers, became soulless killing machines in the space of just a few hours. How does this happen?

I grew up on a small farm in Indiana and, as the oldest son, I was assigned the task of killing a farm animal whenever we needed to fill the freezer. It was always a hard task for me because, inevitably, I would catch a glimpse of the animal's eyes just before shooting it. In that instant, I saw the innocent life I was about to extinguish. I have also been a hunter most of my life, and I, or my family, always ate the game I was fortunate to bring home. In those cases, I always felt a twinge of regret about taking a life. I believe it is unnatural to feel otherwise because we are emotionally wired to value life. Yet the men of Hitler's police battalions somehow severed that wiring in just a few hours.

> I always felt a twinge of regret about taking a life. I believe it is unnatural to feel otherwise because we are emotionally wired to value life.

We have contemporary examples of this apparent rewiring of human psyches. As I write this chapter, we see daily occurrences of suicide bombers slaughtering innocent men, women and children. We are sickened by videos of human beheadings posted on the Internet. We witness public executions of people suspected of being "enemy collaborators." The innocent Jewish women and children were also called "enemy collaborators." Perhaps this term provides an insightful clue into our apparent emotional rewiring.

The elusive explanation of how ordinary men and women leave their humanity at the door led me on the search for a more complete understanding. In his book, *Understanding Ethical Failures in Leadership*, Terry Price proposed the possibility of class exclusion or devaluation. Price believed that if you could exclude or devalue a certain class of individuals as human equals, you could justifiably treat that class of individuals differently than you might treat yourself or others you perceived as human equals. Price proposed this as a possible explanation for human slavery.[2]

This insight, coupled with substantial additional research, my interviews with senior business leaders and my own professional experience resulted in a structure of ethical intelligence I have metaphorically called the Worldview Window. The Worldview Window is a psychological, neurological, mystical or spiritual structure through which the Self (you) views the Other (everyone else) during ethical judging. When we are born, our Worldview Window provides a crystal clear view of reality.

As infants and children, we willingly welcome the world through this window. It's only later in life that our window becomes clouded by our worldview, other prejudices we learn and our experience. If we aren't diligent and careful, our Worldview Window slowly becomes a devaluation window, where we see people as different, not worthy of respect and, as in the case of our preceding story, not worthy of life.

The Worldview Window is the only outward facing structure of the seven ethical intelligence structures. Its corruption enables much of the evil perpetrated today. When the Worldview Window becomes the devaluation window, it seamlessly corrupts ethical judging because it excludes one of the two people (or classes of people) from the ethical judging relationship. An open and clear Worldview Window, as depicted in Graphic 1, implies that the Other (in this case, the woman) is included in the eth-

Graphic 1

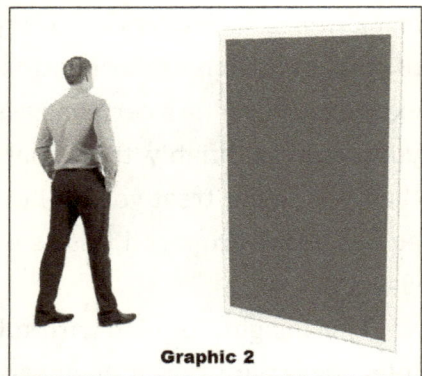

Graphic 2

ical judging deliberations. In other words, the man (the Self) sees the woman through the window and includes her (and/or her class) in his ethical judging deliberations.

A cloudy or closed Worldview Window implies exclusion of the Other (the woman, in this case), as depicted in Graphic 2. The man no longer sees the woman. He may, in fact, see himself in a mirror. In this illustration, the man and the woman are involved in a relationship within which an ethical dilemma has occurred.

If the Worldview Window is open and clear, she is visible, and he renders an ethical judgment considering her as a partner in the dilemma. If the window is closed or opaque with prejudice, distrust and hate, he throws her under the bus because it's only about him. The ethical dilemma dissolves because it's only him. Incidentally, we can reverse the genders in the preceding illustrations, and we get the same results.

Why does this matter? Who cares if my Worldview Window is open and clear or closed and opaque because of prejudice, distrust, and hate? It matters because you have to "see" someone to have a relationship with them. An open and clear Worldview Window is a key component of an ethically intelligent life and meaningful relationships. And relationships are at the core of your ethical intelligence and ethical judging. Let's have a look at them.

RELATIONSHIPS ARE GARDENS. ARE YOURS?

BOOM! BOOM! Little Jimmie's eyes sprang open. His body was tense as a coiled spring. All he could see was pitch-black darkness. He could hear the rain pounding on his window and the roof. The wind was howling. The sound was deafening. Jimmie tried to move but couldn't. Something was holding him down.

Terrified, he started screaming. Suddenly, he heard a soft sooth-ing voice in the distance.

"I'm coming, my sweet son. I'm coming." Jimmie stopped screaming for a moment to be sure of what he'd heard. He lis-tened intently. And, there it was.

"I'm almost there! I'm coming! It was just thunder."

After what seemed an eternity, and even though the room was still bathed in darkness, Jimmie felt his mother's touch. As she scooped him out of his crib and hugged him to her breast, Jimmie sensed his mother's familiar heartbeat and felt safe again.

Jimmie and his mother shared a connection that cannot be broken. It's timeless. Distance has no effect on it. Death doesn't sever it. It's eternal. It's the *Primal Relationship.*

A Pure Loving Bond. The special bond between mother and child is the purest form of the *Primal Relationship.* Within it, there are no doubts, barriers or pretenses. There is only unconditional love and unlimited trust. The child knows the mother, and the mother knows the child. After we leave our mother's protective arms, that *Primal Relationship* doesn't end. Our mother's em-brace is only our first experience of it. As we psychologically and physically separate our Self from our mother, we come to under-stand that the *Primal Relationship* also includes all other humans in a special unbreakable connection.

That connection is central to our existence as humans. It's the most basic connection we share, one to the other. The *Primal Re-lationship* is the essential connection between the *Self* and the *Other.* It has existed since the beginning. It's the model of all re-lationships. It's ageless and necessary. In its pristine condition, its components include love, trust, empathy, caring, respect, sym-pathy, compassion, altruism and intimacy. But it simultaneously births love and hate. It's often contradictory. And we don't yet understand it very well, as demonstrated by the multitude of words written and spoken about relationships every year.

The *Primal Relationship* between the Self and Other has evolved. In the beginning, there was no concept of the Self because it was submerged within the Other, much like the child at first is submersed in the mother. In antiquity, the *Primal Relationship* was an intimate, nonjudgmental and nourishing bond between and among human beings. We all crave that connection— the type of bond we once experienced with our mother.

Recently, I was in the waiting room of a medical clinic. The room was large and very busy. In one corner of the room, I could see three mothers with their young children. It was obvious the mothers didn't know one another, and neither did the children. Yet when one child's eyes locked onto another child's eyes, something magic happened. Each child started smiling, pumping their hands and feet and wriggling in their mother's arms to get free. It was obvious the children wanted to meet and touch. They saw something in each other that sparked that special recognition. That special recognition is the *Primal Relationship*.

The *Primal Relationship* is organic and unique to us as humans. It's the elemental connection between the human you and everything human that isn't you, which also includes organizations comprised of human beings. "Humanness," in this case, refers to the me who thinks about my thinking and the you who thinks about your thinking, which is what the two children immediately knew and acknowledged.

> The *Primal Relationship* is organic and unique to us as humans. It's the *elemental connection* between the human you and everything human that isn't you . . .

The *Primal Relationship* is complex and a bit ambiguous. It's like an onion. The more you peel, the more you find. We're only going a couple of layers deep in this discussion because that's all we need. This connection is simultaneously one-to-one and one-to-many.

One-to-One. A relationship is one-to-one when the human me recognizes the human you. This connection is embodied in a greeting of Eastern origins, Namasté. One simple translation of Namasté is, "The divine in me recognizes and affirms the divine in you." If you're not a believer in divinity, we can translate the greeting as, "The humanity in me recognizes and affirms the humanity in you." In the most primitive and secular terms, that is the *Primal Relationship*.

Here's another example of recognition of this kind of a connection. My wife and I have Standard Poodles. She's been a poodle lover for many years and converted me just a few years ago. If you aren't familiar with Standard Poodles, they are a German breed of dog bred for duck hunting. Poodles are extremely smart and perceptive. Our three Poodles are socialized, and they get along well with other dogs. But when they see another Standard Poodle, they get extra excited. Their ears perk up. Their stance becomes more erect and showy, and their tail wags more energetically. When this happens, it's obvious they sense the "poodle-ness" in the other dog. This is the type of connection we have with one another—it's the *Primal Relationship*.

One-to-Many. The *Primal Relationship* is also a one-to-many connection. I am connected to everyone else. Everyone else is connected to me. We're all part of an interconnected living universe. You can conceive of that living interconnection in any way that fits your personal belief system. The entanglement principle of quantum mechanics—which says that once objects interact, they are connected (entangled) forever—works for me. For Christians, the one body with many members connected by the Holy Spirit is another manifestation of this underlying truth. There are others. The point is, whatever your belief system, it's possible to appreciate this one-to-many interconnection.

As beautiful and simple as it is, however, The *Primal Relationship* is also full of contradictions—the yin and yang, if you will. We yearn for belonging, yet we covet our independence. We want the companionship of living within a community, but we aggressively defend our private space. Often we feel smothered by the demands of the Other, yet we suffer separation anxiety when alone. To most of us these apparent contradictions are mind-numbingly frustrating in their ambiguity and complexity. So we brush them off, which is a mistake. But there's more.

> The *Primal Relationship* is also full of contradictions, the yin and yang, if you will. We yearn for belonging. Yet we covet our independence.

Most of the time, we love our Self. Sometimes, we love the Other. At other times, we love our Self and hate the Other. In yet other instances, we hate our Self but love the Other. And, in some interesting and extreme cases, we hate both our Self and the Other.

The complexity of this connection is one of the reasons we rarely examine it. That complexity is partially due to the intricate mosaic comprising our human nature, which includes our conscious mind, subconscious mind and the collective unconscious. The *Primal Relationship* serves another indispensable purpose. It's the soil within which our relationships grow and flourish.

Relationships Are Soil. Ethical intelligence lives within your consciousness, but it manifests in the real world within the *Primal Relationship*, which is its soil. Soil is the substance from which organisms live, grow

> Ethical intelligence lives within your consciousness, but it manifests in the real world within the *Primal Relationship*, which is its soil.

and obtain nourishment. Your ethical intelligence becomes real and is experienced by the Other only within the *Primal Relationship*. Ethical intelligence reifies and reigns within relationships planted in the garden of the *Primal Relationship*. The potential (the seed) is in your consciousness. The actual permeates your relationships. I know this may sound a bit dense. Let's consider an analogy.

Soil is where plants grow. A seed is a potential plant. The seed only becomes a plant when it's placed in the soil and given an appropriate growing environment. Eventually, the seed blossoms, manifesting itself in the real world as a plant.

Likewise, your ethical intelligence is that seed living in your consciousness. It becomes manifest to the world when planted within its soil, the *Primal Relationship*. Your ethical intelligence becomes real within your relationships.

Why Does It Matter? Before we move on, I want to answer some questions that I've addressed on numerous occasions, and that I've asked myself.

How is this information related to ethical intelligence? Let's recall the definition of ethical intelligence. Ethical intelligence is the intellectual capacity and framework for judging matters of equity in relationships. Being able to identify, articulate and understand relationships is key to living an ethically intelligent life. Ethical intelligence lives in your consciousness, but it manifests in your relationships. *The Primal Relationship* is the prototype for all relationships. Nurturing a flourishing *Primal Relationship* is key to all other successful and meaningful relationships. Without either one, your ethical intelligence has no soil within which to germinate, grow and blossom.

Let me provide an example. For many years I have taught adult undergraduate and graduate business students. During those years, my classes have discussed hundreds of ethics cases. One of the assignments embedded in any ethics case study is the identification of stakeholders and their respective relationships within the case. During these case discussions, I was surprised at how unprepared these students were to identify relevant relationships. Please don't take this as a criticism of the students because it isn't. It's an observation and an acknowledgment of the neglected *Primal Relationship* gardens most of us have. Nurturing and nourishing your *Primal Relationship* garden is critical for awakening your ethical intelligence.

How is this information related to leadership? First, let me say something you're going to hear a lot about throughout this book—leadership is not about you. Leadership is about serving others within relationships. In order to lead someone somewhere, you must first have a relationship with them. That relationship will be based on the *Primal Relationship* because it's the prototype for all relationships. Understanding how to build, cultivate and work within relationships is a prerequisite for leadership.

If I am a practical and down to earth person, not given to putting much stock in these types of "esoteric" ideas and theories, can this book help me? Earlier in my career, I was that practical and down to earth person who thought psychology, philosophy and social science theories were more fictional than real, more along the lines of someone's opinion rather than "fact." I was an engineer interested in hard evidence I could see and measure. I was truly a student of Francis Bacon. If I couldn't feel it, see it and measure it in the real world, it didn't exist. Much later in life, I realized having that mindset was like being a visually impaired person—I was missing some of the most important facets of life simply because I could neither see them nor measure them. I urge you to maintain an open mind as you read this book. I've lived what I'm writing about. I assure you, it's real! And, so is your secret place.

YOUR SECRET PLACE: IS IT PEACEFUL, JOYFUL?

Our country, and perhaps the world, is on the cusp of a spiritual awakening—not necessarily religious, but spiritual. Secular materialism and unbridled scientism dominated the twentieth century, with devastating results. The Holocaust story beginning this chapter is but a small sliver of those results. Millions are seeking internal peace, tranquility and life meaning outside of the material world. Often that quest centers on unseen and scientifically unprovable realms. The evidence of this awakening is everywhere. People are engaging in mysticism, mindfulness retreats, yoga, nondenominational religions traditions and meditation, just to name a few. The lifelong work of the late Dr. Wayne Dyer and his colleague Deepak Chopra are, perhaps, symbols of that seeking.

That seeking is about the place everyone is yearning to find— our secret place—our Heart Refuge. It's a location created by our consciousness that is not seeable with our material eyes. Mindfully knowing about and understanding your Heart Refuge is key to activating your ethical intelligence. And the evidence of the existence of this place is compelling.

We begin looking at some of that evidence as we consider the ancient origins of the Heart Refuge, called the heart–soul in antiquity.

Ancient Origins. According to the ancients, the Heart Refuge is where *you* reside. It's a psychological, neurological, mystical or spiritual structure—take your pick, whatever construct suits your beliefs. In whatever manner you define the *self-aware* *thinking you*, it's where the *self-aware thinking you* lives. Christians and Jews think of the *self-aware thinking you* as the soul. The Greeks called the *self-aware thinking you* the soul-essence. Hindus refer to it as atman. Buddhists call it anatman. And humanists refer to the *self-aware thinking you* as an epiphenomenon of firing neurons. However you conceive of your essence, it lives in your Heart Refuge.

Lau-Tzu talked about the Heart Refuge in the *Tao Te Ching*:
My teachings are easy to understand
and easy to put into practice.
Yet your intellect will never grasp them,
and if you try to practice them, you'll fail.
My teachings are older than the world.
How can you grasp this meaning?
If you want to know me,
look inside your heart.

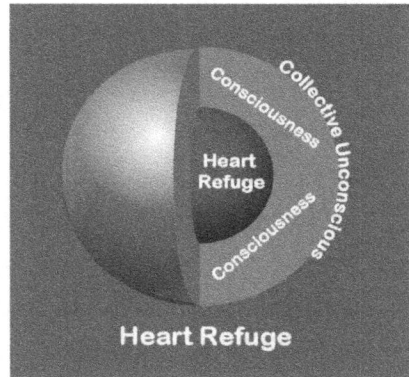

Heart Refuge

The Bible contains dozens of admonitions and commentary on the Heart Refuge. For example, "Guard your heart with all diligence, For from it *flow* the springs of life." Proverbs 4:23

In his book *Seat of Consciousness in Ancient Literature*, Richard Lind, an expert on this subject, summarized the concept of the Heart Refuge elegantly, as follows:

... in every ancient geographical and cultural context the heart was the experiential location of the seat of the consciousness as a whole, in all of its sacred, prosaic and aberrant manifestations, not just of the consciousness of the body as opposed to the head. The heart functioned as the mind of the body as a whole, and was the experiential point of the origin and primary reference point for consciousness in general and for the sacred in particular. The ancient use of the word heart referred both to the physical heart as a subjective localization of consciousness of the body as a whole and to the spiritual heart as the nexus of a sacred space or heavenly dwelling within the body.[3]

That untouchable and sacred place has been called by many names throughout the millennia. Husserl called it the sphere of ownness. Augustine alluded to it as the secret place. Locke named it the sphere of personal jurisdiction. Mill likened it to the inner man. I've called it the Heart Refuge. It's an inherent part of who we are and one of the most important structures of ethical intelligence.

I've included my visualization of the Heart Refuge and its relationship to our consciousness and collective unconscious in the graphic on the previous page. The Heart Refuge is the most intimate and inviolable place or space within the human person. It's a place or space of seclusion void of any uninvited intrusion. It's where the Self retreats and transcends the outside world. The Heart Refuge is our ultimate sanctuary of safety, security, serenity and peace. For millennia, it was inviolable. You—the Self—had complete control over that place. Everyone else—the Other—needed an invitation to enter. Since the dawn of modernity, perhaps beginning in the 18th century, these ancient beliefs have been slowly rejected.

Modern Understanding. The consensus of contemporary neuroscience and neuropsychology is that the modern mind is the seat of consciousness. Many neuroscientists have further reduced mind to brain, proposing specific brain locations as the origin of consciousness. The location is unimportant. Your ethical intelligence works just fine in either case. The important points are knowledge, presence and nurture. Become intimately knowledgeable about your Heart Refuge. Spend lots of time there. Keep it pristine because it's where the *Primal Relationship* connects.

> Become intimately knowledgeable about your Heart Refuge. Spend lots of time there. Keep it pristine because it's where the *Primal Relationship* connects.

For those of us who are a bit less mystical and more material in our worldview, here's an analogy that may help you relate to this and other "mystical" concepts I present in this book. Think of the *Primal Relationship* as a super-sized fiber optic cable connecting you to the humanity network. Further, imagine that cable is connected to your Worldview Window. You then become a node on the humanity network. Your status as "human" is dependent on this connection.

Limbic System, Your Engine Of Life

> I can tell you without any doubt, *this is not what happens in the real world.* Ethical judging is drenched in emotions.

If I were to ask—and I have—any member of the C-Suite of the Fortune 500 how they form their ethical judgments, I would receive this standard answer: "I thoroughly analyze the situation. I may call Legal or look at our code of conduct. I think it through, and then I make a rational choice." Most of us think this way. Because of our enculturation, this is the answer we believe society expects. I can tell you without any doubt, *this is not what happens in the real world.* Ethical judging is drenched in emotions. If you ask leaders to *describe their experiences* or tell stories about their ethical judging, you come away with an entirely different point of view than if you simply ask the direct question I just posed.

The next time you're making an ethical judgment, your emotions are a enormous silent partner sitting next to you on the judgment seat. Emotions permeate every ethical judgment a manager or leader makes. It's the main reason managers and leaders go to prison, and innocent people lose their financial and physical lives.

We start our exploration of the Limbic System with the story of Captain van Zanten, a man celebrated for calm, rational and reasoned judgments.

Mr. Safety. Jacob Louis Veldhuyzen van Zanten was a senior KLM airline Captain, and somewhat of a celebrity at that. He had logged almost 12,000 hours of flight time, including more than 1,500 hours flying the Boeing 747 jumbo jet. In fact, van Zanten had taken delivery of KLM's initial order of Boeing 747 aircraft and had subsequently become not only KLM's most senior captain but also its director of training and safety. He was known throughout the airline industry for his by-the-book approach to airline safety and his impeccable attention to detail. Literally, if you looked up airline safety, you would have seen his picture because KLM had featured him as part of its advertising.

On March 27, 1977, van Zanten was flying a 747 carrying 248 passengers from Amsterdam to the Las Palmas resort in the Canary Islands. The flight was proceeding smoothly and on time— one of van Zanten's trademarks. He was always on time, and he always followed the rules. As the flight approached its destination, the crew received a message diverting the plane to a different tropical island with a much smaller airport. The Las Palmas airport had been closed due to a terrorist attack. Duly following orders, van Zanten landed his 747 at Tenerife, a small island approximately 100 miles off the coast of Morocco. He taxied the plane to the end of the runway to await further instructions.

Tenerife was a small resort island, and its airport was not designed to service planes the size of the Boeing 747. On this day, because of the problems at Las Palmas, this tiny airport was heavily congested with other diverted aircraft including a Pan Am 747 parked right behind van Zanten's plane. It was about 1:30 in the afternoon. As was his practice, van Zanten began laying out a plan for staying on schedule. To avoid disrupting the entire KLM network schedule, van Zanten determined that he had to leave the island no later than 6:30 PM. If he missed that deadline, van Zanten would have no choice but to stay on the island overnight because he would have reached the end of his allowable flight time.

The Dutch had just passed a law mandating rest periods for flight crews, and violating that law was punishable with prison time. So, skipping the required rest period was not an option. The plane had to be airborne no later than 6:30 PM. Besides, there was no place for his passengers to stay overnight on the island. All of the hotels were completely booked. So, to save time, van Zanten required the passengers to remain on board while they waited, and he topped off his fuel tanks even though the flight to Las Palmas was quite short. Normally, KLM would have refueled the aircraft at Las Palmas for its return flight to Amsterdam.

It's easy to imagine the tension building on that aircraft as the passengers and flight crew waited for permission to leave. Cockpit recordings showed the normally calm and collected van Zanten becoming more and more agitated. All of us have had a similar experience. You're running late for a meeting, and you get stuck behind a train crossing. Your composure goes out the window, thinking about how bad it's going to be if you're late. The longer the wait, the more agitated you become. For van Zanten and his crew and passengers, the afternoon wore on and became evening. Finally, the flight crew received word that Las Palmas was open. As the sun went down, a thick fog covered the entire airport. Because of its small size, the airport did not have ground radar, so the planes on the runway were invisible to the tower and to one another.

Undeterred, van Zanten radioed the tower for permission to head for the other end of the runway in preparation for takeoff. He received permission to use the runway itself as a taxiway. Once van Zanten reached the other end of the 11,000-foot runway, he was to turn his plane around and wait for permission to take off. Meanwhile, the Pan Am 747, that was parked directly behind the KLM 747, began its slow trip down the same runway.

In his haste to lift off by 6:30 PM, van Zanten had raced down the runway and was in position to take off much sooner than anyone in the tower realized. In fact, most of the tower personnel were listening to a live soccer match. This was a resort, after all. The tower crew was not accustomed to running on tight and hurried flight schedules.

The KLM flight crew was feverishly racing through the pre-takeoff checklists, and van Zanten was nervously glancing at his watch as it ticked closer and closer to 6:30 PM. The plane reached the end of the runway and made a complete turnaround, readying for takeoff in the direction from which it had just come.

The flight crew radioed the tower that they were ready for takeoff. In addition to the other substandard equipment at this airport, the radio system was often full of static and difficult to use. Many messages had to be retransmitted for additional clarity. Having completed all of the required checklists—part of van Zanten's safety manual—the KLM Boeing 747 carrying 248 passengers and crew waited impatiently, with the engines revving, for final takeoff clearance.

After what seemed an agonizingly long time, the radio came alive with a message. The third officer seated behind van Zanten, said, "What did he say?" With full confidence and determination in his voice, van Zanten said, "He said we're cleared for takeoff!" The third officer said, "We should get confirmation!"

"I am absolutely sure of what I heard", van Zanten yelled as he plunged the throttle to full speed forward. Meanwhile, the Pan Am 747 was still lumbering down the same runway, headed straight for the KLM jet. By the time the pilot of the Pan Am 747 glimpsed van Zanten's plane racing down the fog-shrouded runway straight towards them, it was too late for evasive action.

Because of his fully loaded fuel tanks, van Zanten was having difficulty lifting off the runway. The Pan Am pilot made a desperate turn to the left, but it was too late. The KLM 747's landing gear and tail section sheared off the top of the Pan Am 747. Both planes exploded into flames, and van Zanten and everyone aboard his aircraft perished. Miraculously, 61 people aboard the Pan Am 747survived, including the entire flight crew. But, in the end, 588 people died in what is still the worst airline disaster in history. Ironically, when word of the horrific disaster reached KLM headquarters in Amsterdam, KLM executives began trying desperately to locate van Zanten so they could dispatch him to take charge of the investigation.

Powerful Hidden Forces. Although tragic in its consequences, van Zanten's story is similar to dozens of career-ending episodes I've seen in my business career. The common theme in the stories is a seemingly rational person doing something that is completely irrational—or, shall we say, stupid. Fortunately, over the last decade, a significant body of research has accumulated on the subject, helping us understand why smart and talented people act stupidly.

Chief among these researchers are two brothers, Ari and Rom Brafman[4], and Dan Ariely[5]. Most of the theory about irrational behavior I've included in this discussion is taken from their groundbreaking research. Among many other similar cases, the Brafmans studied the van Zanten incident. From their research, they isolated three hidden but powerful, psychological/emotional forces, including *loss aversion, germinal judgment/value attribution,* and *diagnosis bias.* Here, we focus on loss aversion, the most powerful and pervasive of the three.

> Humans often go to extreme, often highly irrational—some might say deranged —measures to avoid losing something.

Loss aversion is our fear of loss. Humans often go to extreme, often highly irrational—some might say deranged—measures to avoid losing something. Murdering your estranged spouse comes to mind. Forging documents to cover up a mistake or lying or stealing to keep your job are others.

Loss aversion is simply avoiding a loss, which is what drove Captain van Zanten's disastrous lapse in judgment. Aside from maintaining his personal on-time record, he knew any slippage in his schedule would've cascaded throughout the KLM system, costing millions of dollars. As it turns out, humans are very loss averse. And the larger the perceived loss, the more irrational we become in its prevention. This powerful hidden emotional

> As it turns out, humans are very loss averse. And the larger the perceived loss the more irrational we become in its prevention.

force—fear of loss (actually an entire family of fears)—has profound effects on our ethical judging.

Losses—A Royal Family of Five Fears. Fear of loss is ever
present in our lives. As we've seen, much of it is hidden and silently influences our thought lives. As I analyzed the data from
the stories I heard, I isolated what I call the royal family of five
fears. Here are the five, with each fear ranked in order of power
to motivate. Preface each item on this list with, "Fear of losing ... "

1. Reputation, prestige, power
2. Job or career
3. Money
4. Credibility or face (avoiding shame)
5. Freedom (as in going to jail)

The fear of losing something is not only a powerful motivator, but it operates outside of our conscious awareness. In other words, it's hidden from view. We may consciously believe that
we're rationally analyzing a situation, when in fact, *our limbic
brain is undermining our analysis in the background.* In the end, we
form a judgment we believe was a reasoned and rational choice,
but it was actually a combination of reason, rationality and fear.
An ethically intelligent person understands this dynamic and consciously cultivates constant awareness. Let's have a closer look.

Although the fears on this list appear self-evident, there are
some nuances that I want to mention. The greatest nuance, applying to all five, is that these are not goals of attainment but
fears of loss. The other nuance that applies to all five of these
fears of loss is actually a continuum with substantial overlap of
categories. For example, losing your job or career can also result
in money loss.

Reputation, Prestige, Power. The fear of losing reputation, prestige and power was the motivating force most commonly mentioned by business leaders I interviewed as they described their ethical judging experiences. This result was not surprising to me because I know how difficult it is to reach a significant senior leadership position. The fear of losing all of the perquisites that go with that position is highly motivating—substantially greater than losing your personal freedom by going to jail. This fear of loss was head and shoulders above the others on this list.

Job or Career. The fear of losing your job or career was almost always mentioned in connection with losing reputation, prestige and power. This is also not surprising because reputation, prestige and power normally flow from your job or career. This fear of loss is important in our culture because many of us create our Self's identify and derive our self-worth from what we do for a living. In our society, losing your job or career is almost always seen as a sign of failure and significantly diminishes your self-esteem.

> Many of us believe that money is at the root of all flawed ethical judging. It isn't. In fact, it's not even close to the reality.

Money. Many of us believe that money is at the root of all flawed ethical judging. It isn't. In fact, it's not even close to the reality. Don't get me wrong. Fear of losing money is a powerful hidden motivator. Remarkably, this fear is most pronounced when the money is not yet in our possession. In other words, our fear of losing *potential* money is often greater than our fear of losing money we already have. I realize this is a bit counterintuitive and possibly confusing. So here's a real-world example.

Raj Rajaratnam was the billionaire founder of the Galleon Group, a New York-based hedge fund management firm. When he was arrested for insider trading, his net worth was estimated at $1.5 billion. Yet he was convicted of insider trading as a way to avoid losing a mere $20 million investment. You can do the math. This very bright guy risked going to prison (he's currently serving an 11-year sentence) to avoid what some would call "lunch money" compared to his total wealth. The fear of losing potential gain is very powerful indeed.

Credibility or Face (avoiding shame). This fear of loss may also seem counterintuitive because, in Western society, shaming and losing face are significantly diminished motivators. When we think of shaming and losing face, we tend to focus on other cultures, especially Eastern. Based on my research results, we should understand what a powerful motivator losing professional credibility and being publicly shamed remains in our postmodern culture. This fear of loss is also closely aligned with the fear of losing reputation.

Freedom (as in not going to jail). The fear of incarceration is present and powerful, but definitely a distant fifth place. This result was also not surprising to me. Over the past 80-plus years, we have imprisoned thousands of senior business leaders. Yet we see the same serious ethical lapses continuing year after year. Although important, this fear of loss is not nearly as motivating as the other four, which is one of the reasons more laws and regulations are not the answer.

The royal family of five fears is always with us. Like a hidden force field, they permeate our ethical judging—claiming an uninvited position next to us on the judgment seat. But the five fears are not the only ingredient in the ethical judging emotional soup. When we are adjudicating ethical dilemmas, emotions are our constant companion. For that, we can thank our Limbic System.

Our Limbic System. The Limbic System of our brain is one of the most primitive but important. It's the seat of our emotions and **where judgments are formed.** The Limbic System is highly interconnected to other segments of our brain including the nucleus accumbens, the brain's pleasure center. Even though connected to the prefrontal cortex, the center of rational thought, the Limbic System is not involved in "rational thought." Instead the limbic brain is *pure feeling.* Although responsible for learning and long-term memory, the Limbic System does not "think"—it only feels and is in control of the endocrine system (our hormones—remember the term "raging hormones"), autonomous nervous system and our sense of smell, which is why smells are so important to memory recreation.

This is important because I want you to understand your prefrontal cortex, your rational mind, is not the engine of your mental life. It's merely a brake on the real engine—the limbic brain—the *feeling* you. The philosopher, Hume, said, "**In the face of passion, reason is impotent.**"

Your limbic brain drives your life. It's your center of motivation. It may "consult" with other parts of the brain, but it makes the final judgment without thinking—it only feels. Your limbic brain is also the way you connect with other people. Goleman and other researchers coined the term "limbic lock" to describe an unseen process where my Limbic System connects with your Limbic System. Goleman used the metaphor of two modems syncing up as a way of describing this function. (Yes, I know. No one uses those kinds of modems any-

> Your rational mind is not the engine of your mental life. It's merely a brake on the real engine—the limbic brain...

> Your limbic brain drives your life. It's your center of motivation. It may "consult" with other parts of the brain, but it makes the final judgment without thinking—it only feels.

more. But the analogy fits.) The easiest way for this "syncing up" process to occur is through laughter, which may explain why many speakers start out with a joke. It helps them connect with the audience.

I've validated this theory many times in practice. In speaking to an audience, if I can get them laughing with me, I can sense the connection and subsequent engagement. This is also a technique that I've used successfully in my teaching. If I can get a classroom of students laughing together on the first night of class, the emotional togetherness of the group throughout the remainder of the course is remarkable. Emotion, especially laughter, helps people connect. Ah ha! There's that word *connect*. Remember, the *Primal Relationship* is a connection.

Following Your Feelings. Our emotions are central to who we are as human beings. They transform our lives from mere existence to transcendence. Our emotions lead us into deep valleys. They also drive us to climb the highest mountain peaks. None of us would desire living life without them. Lord Tennyson said, "'Tis better to have loved and lost than never to have loved at all."

That is my message to you. Fully embrace your emotions. But do it with *crystal-clear constant conscious awareness*. Emotions drive our lives. Purposeful emotions become passions. Passions enable us to scale great heights and realize our dreams. There's nothing wrong with following your feelings.

As we end this chapter, I want to briefly return to the opening story about the wanton killing of human innocents. I began the chapter with that story because it encapsulates who we are—or, more importantly, who we can become—when we don't use our ethical intelligence. We are a gifted people possessing a box containing all of the tools we need for coexisting with one another while leading ethically intelligent lives full of purpose, passion, peace and the pursuit of happiness. This book is the key that opens that toolbox and the activator of the tools within.

◆

Chapter Highlights

- Cloudy or closed Worldview Windows are everywhere.
- We are hardwired to value life. Cloudy or closed Worldview Windows short circuit that wiring.
- Cloudy or closed Worldview Windows enable unethical, often evil, behavior.
- The *Primal Relationship* is the elemental connection between the human you and everything human that isn't you.
- The *Primal Relationship* is the essential connection between the Self and the Other.
- The *Primal Relationship* has existed since the beginning. It's the archetype of all relationships.
- Mindfully knowing about and understanding your Heart Refuge is key to activating your ethical intelligence.
- Your Heart Refuge is where the self-aware thinking you lives.
- The Heart Refuge is our ultimate refuge of safety, security, serenity and peace.
- We are predictably irrational and regularly engage in stupid behavior.
- There are hidden psychological/emotional forces responsible for our stupid behavior.
- Your emotions are a ginormous silent partner sitting next to you on the ethical judging seat.
- Ethical judging is drenched in emotion.
- We act out of fear more than we realize.

Questions for You

- Do you know the names of the people who clean your office every night?

- Do you hire only from "name" schools?
- Do you feel a deep bond or connection to your mother? Why or why not?
- Have you ever watched young children play together? Do you see the pristine *Primal Relationship* manifest in that play?
- When was the last time you visited your Heart Refuge?
- Do you meditate or have quiet time every day?
- Are you unplugged from the humanity network?
- Can you judge your actions fairly?
- Would you rather be led by an emotionless, rational leader or a leader who shows and acts on his or her emotions?
- How do you react to the admonition, "Whatever you do, don't get emotional in this meeting?"
- Do your emotions run your life?
- Do you agree with Hume that, in the face of emotions, rationality acts only as a brake?

Endnotes

1. Browning, C.R., Ordinary Men: Reserve Police Battalion 101 and the Final Solution in Poland. 1998, New York, NY: HarperPerennial.
2. Price, T.L., Understanding Ethical Failures in Leadership. 2006, New York, NY: Cambridge University Press. 224.
3. Lind, R.E., Seat of Consciousness in Ancient Literature. 2007, Jefferson, NC: McFarland & Company, Inc.
4. Brafman, O. and R. Brafman, Sway: The Irresistible Pull of Irrational Behavior. 2008, New York, NY: DoubleDay.
5. Ariely, D., Predictably Irrational: The Hidden Forces That Shape Our Decisions. 2008, New York, NY: HarperCollins Publishers, Inc.

CHAPTER 2

◆

WHO "THEY" ARE— OUR SILENT THUNDER

> So far as I can grasp the nature of the collective unconscious, it seems to me like an omnipresent continuum, an unextended Everywhere. That is to say, when something happens here at point A which touches upon or affects the collective unconscious, it has happened everywhere.
>
> *Carl Jung*

We look over our shoulders. We glance the other way when passing a stranger on the sidewalk. We lock and sometimes double-lock our doors. We question others' motives. We don't trust the stranger at our door. We buy firearms for protection. We feel it deep in our spirit, a *subtle unease*, a *continuous stressor.* I call it silent thunder. It's real. But, most of us simply dismiss it and go on with our lives because we question such inner "feelings."

In this chapter, we explore how the *collision* of two powerfully intertwined currents of history and a growing countervailing current are producing this silent thunder within us.

Current One: Human-on-Human Carnage. The first intertwined current is the unprecedented human-on-human carnage that began around the turn of the 20th century. It is slowly poisoning our collective unconscious, producing a form of subtle mass paranoia.

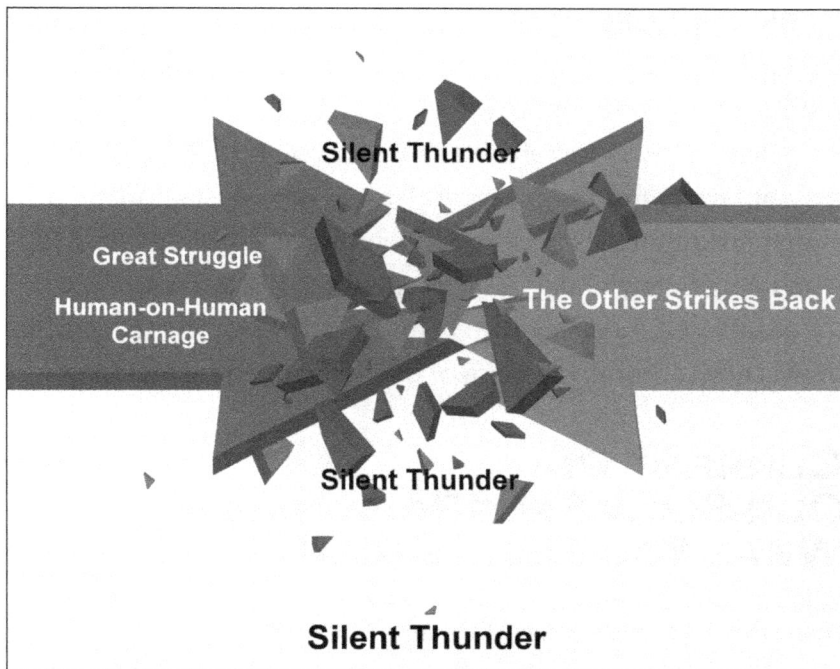

Silent Thunder

Great Struggle

Human-on-Human Carnage

The Other Strikes Back

Silent Thunder

Silent Thunder

Current Two: Great Struggle. The second intertwined current began in antiquity and has recently crested. Current two is humanity's struggle to differentiate itself (the Self) from the Other, which I call the Great Struggle.

Countervailing Current: Other Strikes Back. The Other Strikes Back countervailing current began with Woodrow Wilson and is also just now assuming tsunami-like proportions, manifesting as Hostile Otherness.

The silent thunder we feel is the ongoing aftermath of this collision, an aftermath we all need to understand because it *has poisoned and continues to poison our ethics.* I've included my depiction of this collision and its aftermath in the Silent Thunder graphic.

We begin our exploration with a familiar movie scene.

"What is it, Obi-Wan?" Luke asked.

Obi-Wan replied, "I felt a great disturbance in the Force, as if millions of voices suddenly cried out in terror and were instantly silenced. I fear something terrible has happened."

What Obi-Wan Kenobi felt in that scene from *Star Wars* was the obliteration of the planet Alderaan. He felt the horrific pain of that instantaneous mass extermination of billions of lives. Obi-Wan immediately understood. He doubted neither his sanity nor the reality of the searing pain in his spirit. We say art reflects life. That scene captures the truth of the first current of history.

CURRENT ONE: OUR SLOW SELF-POISONING— WHAT YOU FEEL IS REAL.

Over the last 115 years, humans have violently killed more than 220 million fellow humans—as many people as constituted the entire population of Earth at the time of Charlemagne. It's as if an asteroid struck the Earth in the year 800 and snuffed out all life. The horrific terror-filled screams of those exterminated humans has mushroomed into an Alderaan-like explosion contaminating the human collective unconscious, the way a nuclear blast poisons large areas of the earth.

> Over the last 115 years, humans have violently killed more than 220 million fellow humans.

Just like Obi-Wan, we all sense it, some more keenly than others. But most of us dismiss that faint thunder in our spirits, that kind of knowing in our gut, because we no longer believe in such things. *Star Wars* is fiction. *I can't feel someone else's pain, can I? C'mon. Be real. This is all too New Agey for me. If this is true, how does it work?*

That's a great question. Let's consider Jeri's journey.

"Jeri are you ready? Bill, the spelunking guide asked.

"I think so," Jeri replied. "I've been looking forward to doing this for a really long time. I must say, though, now that we're standing at the mouth of this cave, this is a bit scary. Maybe, I should do this some other time."

"It's nothing to fear. I guide people all the time," Bill replied.

"Why are we wearing such light clothing?" Jeri asked. "I always thought caves were dark and cold."

Bill laughed. "This cave is different. It has warm outcroppings inside. And, no, we're not on top of some kind of volcano. There's nothing to fear. This is not Mount St. Helens."

"Do I look like I'm dressed and ready to go?" Jeri asked. She was wearing shorts, a sports bra, tank top, baseball cap turned backward and hiking boots.

Bill looked her over and said, "Everything looks good! You might want to fasten the adjustable headlamp on top of your cap before we enter the cave. It can get dark very quickly."

"Okay. Done. Let's get started."

With that, they entered the cave. At first, it was a slow, steady descent over an easily navigable passageway. After about a quarter of a mile, the rate of descent increased, the passageway became more difficult and they began feeling the heat and humidity rising.

"This feels like a sauna," Jeri said, "and these rocks are really slippery and hard to walk on. And it's a lot darker in here than I thought it would be."

Bill remained silent, and they continued to make their way forward. After another long and difficult walk, they could see a faint light in the distance.

"This is really strange," Bill said. "I've never seen the light that bright in all the times I've been here."

"Well, that's what makes this an adventure, isn't it?" Jeri said.

Suddenly they walked into a wide opening in the cave. It was a large domed-shaped room. The air was much less humid, and the temperature was cooler. The walls were glowing, giving off an eerie, soft, pulsating light.

"Wow, you didn't tell me about this treat!" Jeri said. "Why didn't you mention this to me?"

"I can't reveal all my secrets now, can I?" Bill replied.

"I kind of like it here," Jeri said, "and this is a good place to rest."

She found a flat rock and sat down to marvel at the spectacle before her. Meanwhile, Bill faded away to the perimeter of the dome to examine the rocks embedded in the wall. After a short while, he walked over to where Jeri was sitting and sat down beside her.

Bill said, "I like this place, but it feels a bit spooky in here."

Jeri said, "You know, you're really starting to scare me."

Just as the words left her mouth, a foul-smelling liquid dripped from the ceiling and splashed right onto Jeri's right shoulder, looking kind of like a pigeon dropping.

Jeri jumped up and screamed. "What is this stuff? It stinks to high heaven and it's stinging my shoulder! Get it off me!"

Bill leaped to his feet and, using a bottle of water, rinsed her shoulder. "Yeah, I see this stuff all the time. Look how it damages the rocks."

Everywhere the liquid had dripped, it had left an indelible stain and pockmarks in the rock. Just about the time both of them calmed down a bit, the walls came alive with a jumble of images. It was like watching hundreds of movies on a Jumbotron all at once. Jeri screamed again. She tried to run but couldn't. Her eyes were fixated on the moving images, and she was mesmerized. She couldn't look away.

Jeri said, "This is amazing. I can see myself sitting on my Papa's lap while he told me one of his stories. Over there, I can see myself graduating from college. Over here, it looks like I'm watching a war movie, and all those people are being executed. Oh no! That guy just beheaded that woman, and there's blood everywhere. Bill, where have you brought me?"

Before Bill could answer, another drop of the foul-smelling liquid from the ceiling landed on Jeri's left shoulder. It smelled like a mixture of sulfur, chlorine and burning human hair, and it stung her skin. Jeri looked to her left, trying to locate Bill. Before she could find him, another series of images burst forth on the cave walls. The scenes included a nuclear explosion. The blast impact reached a group of horrified onlookers whose bodies seem to melt right before her eyes.

On another wall, Jeri could see hordes of shrunken naked humans marching into what looked like a large warehouse. Once inside the warehouse, the doors were closed and locked. After a few moments, the ceiling began spewing a liquid. It looked like a large community shower. Instantly, the liquid burst into a fireball of flames. The deafening shrieks and screams of humans burning alive echoed throughout the entire cave.

By this time, Jeri was shrieking and sobbing and calling for Bill. She felt Bill's arm around her shoulders, and he softly said, "Remember, I asked you if you were ready for this journey."

Jeri said, "I thought I was. But this is not what I expected! Where are we?"

Bill said, "We've journeyed into your subconscious mind. The dome enclosure you see is the collective unconscious. It surrounds your subconscious mind. We all carry this with us. The images that randomly flashed before you are the collective experiences of humanity—good, bad and indifferent. That foul-smelling liquid that you feel dripping on your shoulders is the poison humans have injected into the collective unconscious by their heinous acts toward one another. It slowly drips into your subconscious mind."

"I'm done with this place. Get me out of here!"

"Jeri! Jeri! Jeri! Wake up! Please stop screaming!"

Jeri opened her eyes and saw her husband next to her in bed, shaking her trying to wake her up. Jeri breathed a sigh of relief. "I was having a very bad dream."

"I'll get you a glass of cold water," her husband said. As she lay there wet with sweat, her heart pounding in her chest and struggling to catch her breath, Jeri dared ponder Bill's words. Her mind was flooded with questions. "Can this possibly be true? Do I always carry these horrific images with me? Is there really something dripping into my subconscious mind? What effect is all of this having on me?" Jeri's husband bid her good night, and she slipped back into a fitful slumber.

This is my personal and fanciful visualization of the inner workings and interactions of the collective unconscious and subconscious mind. It's also a reflection of my personal journey. I hope that C. G. Jung would approve.

I opened this discussion with a dramatization of the collective unconscious and its interaction with the subconscious mind because it's a complex and foreign phenomenon for our rational minds to grasp. Fantasy and imagination help stretch our minds around the idea, just as a good story brings clarity.

Our rational minds demand hard solid evidence—something we can see with our eyes and touch and feel with our hands. But your subconscious thoughts have a profound influence on your thought life, especially in your relationships with others—more specifically the *Primal Relationship*. We all carry subtle reminders of what's happened to us as a race of human beings.

Do I think most of us have periodic visions of past memories that are not personal to us? No. Do I have a specific memory of something that happened at Auschwitz? No.

But like you, I've seen movies, documentaries and horrifying images, and I've read books, some so graphic they made me ill. I don't have a direct experience, but I do have a deep-seated relationship with the sorrow and horrors of that place and what happened there. You do as well. It's part of who we are. We're all connected. Understand the influence of the collective unconscious as you make ethical judgments in your life. But I can assure you that what you feel is real. I call it Violative Paranoia.

Violative Paranoia. A common dictionary definition of paranoia is "A mental condition characterized by delusions of persecution, unwarranted jealousy or exaggerated self-importance, typically elaborated into an organized system. It may be an aspect of chronic personality disorder, of drug abuse or of a serious condition such as schizophrenia in which the person loses touch with reality." Okay, we're *not* talking about this type of paranoia.

Ours is much simpler—*suspicion and mistrust of people or*

their actions without evidence or justification. This is the type of paranoia most of us feel, and it's the result of a drip here and a splat there—the poison Jeri experienced—into our subconscious minds. It's caused by the relentless leakage of the toxic poison into our subconscious mind from our collective unconscious.

This directly affects the level of safety, serenity and peace we feel within our Heart Refuge. We feel violated, but we're not sure how or why. As long as humanity continues pouring toxic poison into our collective unconscious, the seepage will continue, and our Violative Paranoia about the Other will continue.

You Have Doubts About This Idea. That's okay. Six years ago, I had doubts too. Later in this book, you'll see what senior business leaders told me about this subject. In the meanwhile, just know that Violative Paranoia subtly infects the *Primal Relationship*, which has indirect but important effects on ethical judging. Remember, ethical intelligence is a holism. We must be aware of and pay attention to all of its aspects. So what are we to do?

Short of some miraculous change in the behaviors of humans, stopping the flow of this poison is not going to happen. Our imperative, then, is to understand that we're not crazy. Our task is to appreciate what is happening and acknowledge the subtle but *real* influence this phenomenon has on us. We can run from the Violative Paranoia, which is what most of us have been doing. But we can't hide from it. Its corrosive consequences are dissolving the goodness inherent in the *Primal Relationship*. As a result, our world is a much less satisfying place, and our societal institutions are suffering.

> We can run from the Violative Paranoia ....
> But we can't hide from it. Its corrosive consequences are dissolving the goodness inherent in the *Primal Relationship*.

If we are truly interested in changing the way things are, denial is not an option. Recognize that the terror of that last slashed throat is now a subtle part of you, as are Auschwitz and Hiroshima and the latest school shooting. You may have little control over what is pouring into the collective unconscious, but you have complete control over your response to it. That response shouldn't be fear. It should be recognition.

Acknowledging the reality of what is happening is the first step. If you're a normal, healthy human, and you feel someone is out to do you harm, you may very well be right. Remember, we're talking about awareness, not fear. Pay attention to those feelings. You're not crazy. You're human, and your equipment is working as designed. Let me repeat that: **You're human, and your equipment is working as designed.** Remember the *Primal Relationship*? That special connection brings you information. You're designed to receive that information. Don't blow it off simply because you don't yet understand the transmission mechanism or because you can't physically see it working.

Most of us have listened to a radio during our lifetimes. Radios work by picking up a signal broadcast by a radio station. We understand the transmission method because engineers have explained it. Yet we can't see the radio waves nor feel them even as they are passing through our bodies. Similarly, we're receiving transmissions from that special connection, the *Primal Relationship*. Perhaps someday we'll understand that communication mechanism as well as radio waves. In the meanwhile, our ignorance of the broadcast mechanism doesn't make the signal any less real.

That's the first current. Now we move to the second.

CURRENT TWO: THE GREAT STRUGGLE POSSESSIVE SELF'S TRIUMPH —"IT'S ALL ABOUT ME!"

Recently, at a crowded McDonald's restaurant in New York City, four teenage girls brutally assaulted another teenage girl. The assault continued for several minutes. It was so brutal, most news outlets refused to air the video. The other patrons in the restaurant not only offered no assistance but instead busily recorded the incident on their cell phones and took selfies of themselves using the beating as a backdrop. Eventually a restaurant employee called the police.

Our "selfie" society proclaims the Self is the indisputable, imperious and victorious member of the Self/Other relationship. Societal consensus says there's no longer any doubt. It's all about me. That's the more obvious point.

The more subtle observation is that it's not only all about me, but I'm also not particularly interested in what happens to you, the Other, either. It's a disturbing ambivalence rooted in Violative Paranoia. Psychologists call this the possessive self. I call it evidence of a contaminated *Primal Relationship*.

We've reached the historical apex of a great struggle—the Self's quest to escape the dominance of the Other. As a result, we think today's version of the Self is normal or what it has always been. From time to time, we may think it's a bit overdone, but it's all most of us have ever known.

So let's have a quick look at how we got here. How did we so rapidly inflate this self-esteem bubble? Because we're examining 45 centuries in just a few paragraphs, this survey is necessarily cursory but sufficient for our purposes. There are, however, two points to keep in mind. First, in antiquity there was *no* concept of

Self. Second, our self-esteem bubble has inflated only in the past 50 years—a tiny sliver of the preceding 4,500 years!

The Great Struggle. *In the beginning, there was no me, only us.* That statement is a simple summary of the ancient condition. There was no individual concept of Self. The Self was subsumed within the Other, much like an infant is subsumed in the mother. Over the next couple of pages, we're going to review the Self's 45-century struggle for emergence from the Other. In the nearby graphic, Great Struggle: Evolutionary Periods, I've depicted my understanding of this emergence broken into four historical periods, which divide the discussion that follows.

I know this seems a bit detailed and dense. Why should you care about this? Because it's all about the connection—the *Primal Relationship*, which is the soil within which your ethical intel-

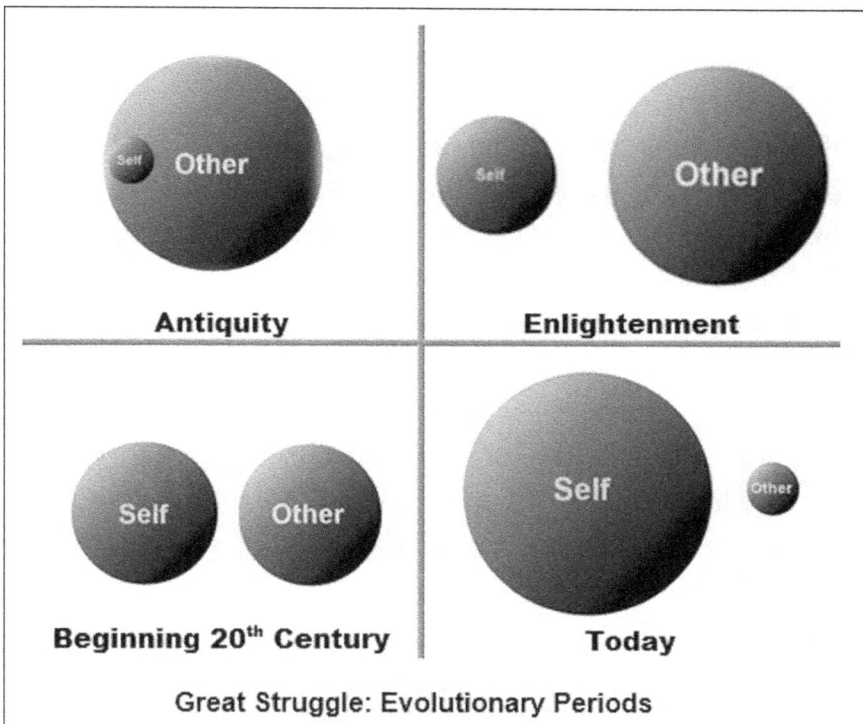

Antiquity

Enlightenment

Beginning 20th Century

Today

Great Struggle: Evolutionary Periods

ligence manifests itself. Understanding a bit of the history of the *Primal Relationship* will greatly assist you in your journey.

Antiquity (2550 BC). I realize it's a bit difficult for our postmodern minds to grasp the concept of *togetherness,* as depicted in the graphic on the previous page. The Self is part of the Other and has no separate existence. What made this possible was that ancient humans saw themselves as part of a much larger interconnected community or universe. This level of togetherness is completely foreign to us postmodern Westerners.

C. G. Jung studied ancient Egyptian civilization and partly based his concept of the collective unconscious on the artifacts and writings of this early race of humans. Within the ancient Self/Other relationship, the community or tribe was all that mattered. The needs, wants and desires of individual community or tribal members were of *secondary or no importance.* The individual Self had no identity apart from the community. He or she was subsumed into the whole. The needs of the many *always* outweighed the needs of the one.

> Within the ancient Self/Other relationship, the community or tribe was all imperative.... The needs of the many *always* outweighed the needs of the one.

Greece (200 BC). We fast-forward to Greece around 200 BC. Here, more than two millennia later, we find a hotbed of activity swirling around the concepts of Self/Other. We see the first real evidence of an emerging Self. But, recall that Socrates relinquished his life for his Selfhood. Among the Greeks, there was still substantial disagreement about the desirability of this emergence.

Plotinus wrote in *The Six Enneads*, "Whatever it is, then, that has caused souls to forget God their father, and, although sharing in the world and belonging completely to him, to be ignorant both of themselves and of him? The beginning of their wickedness was their audacity, their birth, the first "otherness" and *the wish to belong to themselves*. When they had appeared in this world, they took pleasure in their free will and made much of their self-movement. They ran along the opposite path and put a great distance between themselves and the God."[1]

The debate and the struggle continued for another 1800 years, but we see more rapid progress with the onset of the Enlightenment.

Enlightenment (1550). By the time of the Enlightenment, the Self had been slowly emerging from the Other's dominance for more than four millennia. There are reasons for this slow emergence, not the least of which was the Divine Right of Kings and the authoritarianism of the Church. Denying an individual's Selfhood was an excellent means of control. Both the Monarch and the Church found it much easier to control subjects who were denied the right to think for themselves. One of the great battles of the Enlightenment was the quest for individual self-determination and Selfhood. Martin Luther and those who followed demanded—and even died for—their right to Selfhood.

The religious reformation ignited by Martin Luther and the scientific revolution sparked by Francis Bacon fanned the flames of the human quest for self-determination and freedom from the Other. The English-speaking Western world was the battlefield from which arose the intellectual giants who created the necessary theoretical frameworks for modern democracy. This democracy was built on an understanding of the incontrovertible right each human person has to Selfhood—the right to self-governance, self-will, self-determination and freedom from the oppression of the Other.

The separation of the Self from the Other accelerated significantly in the Western world after the Enlightenment. It significantly picked up speed within the young United States of America, whose founding documents reflected the aggressive Selfhood intellectual underpinnings of such writers as Bacon, Hume, Locke and Smith. Within the USA, puritanical personal responsibility and fierce self-reliance were championed and vigorously pursued. The Self was now equal in stature to the Other and quite resistant to the Other's domination and control.

Beginning 20th Century. At the beginning of the twentieth century, the Self's 45-century-long struggle for self-determination and freedom had reached a new promised land and was on the cusp of an important turning point in history. The triumph of puritanical personal responsibility and fierce unrestrained self-reliance had resulted in the emergence of the United States of America as the preeminent future world superpower. The unfettered personal freedom to pursue happiness and property had resulted in a material prosperity unprecedented in world history. In fact, it may be what makes the United States of America that "exceptional" place frequently discussed.

The successful emergence of the Self and its pursuit of personal freedom was an anomaly in world history. *It had never happened before.* As we've seen during our brief historical tour, the Self had always been subordinate to the Other. The Self's battles for freedom had been bitter and frequent, including the US War of Independence, extending to the French Revolution, and the British struggles for freedom from the Crown and the Divine Rights of Nobles. The newly independent Self was revolutionary, an unnatural occurrence in the grand sweep of history, and mostly within Western culture. But revolutions frequently spawn counterrevolutions and counterrevolutionaries.

In the early twentieth century, the Progressive movement in

the United States and the Socialist and Communist movements in Europe sought to reestablish the old "natural order" of the world—that men and women should not be free in their persons and their property. A great centuries-long battle to reestablish the enslavement of the Self to the Other was joined. In Europe, the results were revolutionary, quick and deadly.

In the United States, the Progressive movement has been evolutionary in its reimposition of the Other's control over the Self. The Self, however, has not surrendered to the Other's aggression. The Self has fought fiercely to retain its hard-won independence from the Other, especially in the Western world. Currently, we find a distrusting, destabilized and destructive détente between the Self and Other.

Today. Today, we find ourselves in an apparent contradictory set of circumstances. We know that it's all about me. The possessive Self is exultant. We find evidence of it everywhere, as illustrated by the stories included in this chapter. The Self is now everything. It's clearly the dominant partner in the Self/Other relationship. The relationship of the Self to the Other appears an inverse image of that which existed in the beginning. We, won, right? Why, then, is there a subtle but perceptible, pervasive and persistent doubt?

You feel it. I feel it. We have this unsettled feeling in our guts that the "victory" is just a battle that is part of a larger war—one that's not yet won. So, as a counter-offensive, we've created the self-esteem bubble. It's a reaction to the deep-seated unease we feel about our "victory"—and it's manifest in our selfie culture. You may think that a selfie is just a vain attempt a self-glorification. It isn't.

So what does a selfie mean? A selfie is a loud and continuing proclamation to the Other containing an unmistakable message.

The next time you see someone taking a selfie, listen. You'll hear these primal screams:

- *Here I am.*
- *I matter.*
- *I am not some anonymous member of a faceless crowd.*
- *I don't have to apologize for my existence.*
- *I am worthy to breathe this air.*
- *You can't ignore me.*
- *You can't turn me into a nobody.*
- *I have rights you can't take away.*
- *You can't just push me around.*

Aside from the few showoffs among us, why do we feel compelled to engage in this activity? Why do we feel it necessary to continue giving the Other the finger with selfie after selfie? It's because the *Primal Relationship* has been contaminated by our struggle escaping from the Other's domination.

Think of the ancient *Primal Relationship* as a pristine mountain lake we shared with the Other. We could plainly see each other—the connection between us was crystal clear. Now, after 45 centuries of struggles, the lake is cloudy. We can still see each other, but the connection is no longer flawless. It's ambiguous. It's like looking through a dirty window or foggy shower door. I can see you holding something, but I have to ask, "Are you holding a gift or a gun?" This ambiguity has created an aftermath. Let's review just how far and fast that aftermath has propelled us.

Bookends of Time. It was New Year's Day 1901, and Sally Frost was standing on the platform in Atlantic City waiting for the train. She dressed demurely so as to conceal her blossoming womanhood. Sally was a shy 15-year-old who looked 20. The train lumbered into the station. Sally boarded and quickly took a seat in the front of the car. Sitting a few seats back was Sam Sprague, whose friends described as a debonair gentleman of the world. Sam fancied himself a ladies' man. He took note of the empty seat next to Sally and quickly moved to sit close to her.

Smiling broadly, smoothing his glistening black hair and straightening his high-collared jacket, Sam glanced over at Sally. The train's conductor noticed Sally's agitation with the attention accorded by her new seatmate and quickly came to Sally's rescue. Just before the conductor reached the couple, Sam looked intently into Sally's eyes and romantically said, "I think it may rain today." The conductor was incensed and had Sam arrested. Shortly thereafter, a magistrate's court found Sam guilty of "flirting" and sentenced him to six months in the county jail for the crime of "gazing intently into Sally's eyes while speaking with romantic feeling."

Fast-forward to the present.

Recently, I was listening to the morning news on the radio. The newscaster told the story of two young men who broke into a pickup truck and stole a MacBook, iPad and about $5,000 in cash. The truck belonged to an independent construction contractor who used it in his business. After a few days, the contractor began seeing selfies and other pictures appear in his iCloud account. Apparently, the thieves were using the stolen iPad for taking selfies, and they were recording videos about the theft. Here is an approximate transcription of one of the videos.

"Hello, America! My name is Dorian. My brother's name is Dillon." Dillon is standing behind and to the right of Dorian. Dillon says, "Thass right!" while he waves $100 bills around. Dorian says, "We're the money team!"

Dillon says, "Thass right!"

Dorian goes on, "And, we're here to show you dumb shits what a real hustle looks like!"

While Dorian talks, Dillon is mumbling in a low voice, "You don't see no stinkin' ones, fives, tens, or twenties here, do ya?"

Dorian goes on, "This is how it's done. Smash and grab what you need. Just go out and do it. The only thing that matters is you and yours!"

The contractor posted the video on Facebook, hoping someone might recognize either one of the thieves. After a short time, clues started coming into the Facebook page. Finally, one person posted, "Yeah, I recognize that idiot. He went to the same high school I did. He was a loser then. It looks like he's still a loser now." From all of the Facebook posts, the police were able to identify and arrest both of the thieves.

These two vignettes metaphorically capture the nearly silent invasion of our sacred space over the past 115 years. They are bookends of time. One captures a more innocent time when casually violating somebody's personal space and privacy was forbidden and punishable with jail time. The other is symbolic of the time in which we live. Someone's private space and property are there for the taking.

> Sam's violation of Sally's privacy has gone from crime to commonplace, symbolic of our violated Heart Refuge. It represents the loss of an ancient inheritance.

Sam's violation of Sally's privacy has gone from crime to commonplace. It represents the loss of our ancient inheritance. We've gone from "Don't crowd my personal space or gaze into my eyes without my acquiescence" to "I'll just watch you undress by hacking into your webcam."

Dorian and Dillon embody the rise of the possessive self, all about, me, me and me. Whatever happens to you is secondary as long as I and me are okay. You have more than you need. So I'll just smash and grab and take what I need. It's now all about looking out for number one.

What does this have to do with your business or life? Here's an example:

A few years ago, one of my public-company-board-member clients called and asked me to meet him for lunch at a certain restaurant. I couldn't understand his choice of restaurants because this particular place was an open space and very loud, especially during lunch. We sat down at a table, and the din was so overwhelming we had to practically shout into each other's ears—so much so, my voice was scratchy after that lunch.

I asked him why we were meeting in such a large, loud and public place (especially since he was a member of a number of private exclusive clubs). He said he had become greatly concerned about his privacy, and he wanted to talk about sensitive matters in a place where the conversation couldn't be heard and recorded.

"You know that people have directional microphones that can record a conversation all the way across a room, don't you?" he said. "That wouldn't be possible here."

This is a senior executive not given to flights of fancy. He was genuinely concerned about his loss of privacy. I hear this concern about privacy loss more and more frequently with each passing year.

In fact, the loss of our sacred inviolable internal space was evident in all of my interviews with senior business leaders. The number one overriding theme arising from those interviews was what I have called perceived Hostile Otherness, something we'll discuss shortly. Or, in the words of one CEO, "The bastards are out to get you!" The effects of this loss are not benign. It tips the balance in our ethical judging. As we journey through this book together, you'll see the truth of this emerge.

But, there's more than just the two intertwined currents.

COUNTERVAILING CURRENT: OTHER STRIKES BACK

During the 115 years that serve as bookends of time, another parallel sequence of events has simultaneously unfolded. We experience the effects of this sequence earlier and earlier in life, as Jimmy Williams discovered.

Jimmy is an enterprising 10-year-old. He wanted a pair of Michael Jordan's latest shoes. His mother agreed to buy the shoes for him if he earned and saved at least half the cost. So Jimmy set up a lemonade stand in his front yard and started eagerly serving customers. After several hours of brisk business, a police car pulled up in front of Jimmy's house.

Two police officers got out of the car and walked up to Jimmy's stand. Jimmy eagerly awaited the opportunity of serving the officers ice cold lemonade. Just when he was about to pour lemonade into two cups, one of the officers handed Jimmy a piece of paper. The police officer explained that it was a citation for operating a food business without a license. The police officer further explained that Jimmy had to close his lemonade stand immediately, and once he paid the $200 fine and obtained the necessary licensure from the city, he could reopen and continue serving his customers. As he was leaving, the police officer mentioned that the license only cost $300, which was twice the cost of the shoes Jimmy wanted.

Here's another example:

Recently, sections of the country had extreme snowfall. Most municipalities now require residents to shovel their sidewalks within a specified period of time or face fines. Noting this requirement, two young men began offering their services as snow shovelers. Both young men were detained by police for shoveling snow without a license.

In 1950, only 4.5% of workers required a license to practice their craft. Today, more than 20% of workers must first obtain a license before they can offer their services to the public. Don't get me wrong. There are good reasons certain professions need licensing—medical doctors and dentists come to mind. But, really—snow shoveling? Welcome to our increasingly oppressive regulatory culture.

> In 1950, only 4.5% of workers required a license to practice their craft. Today, more than 20% of workers must first obtain a license ...

Since Sally met Sam on that New Year's day in 1901, the Other has engaged in a consistent, continuous and relentless assault against the Self. The evidence of this assault is everywhere. I could regale you with pages and pages of examples taken from current news sources, but I won't. They're not hard to find. Our individual rights are under attack from many sources. You know it and I know it. We feel it in our guts. Here are a couple more personal examples. I'm sure you could identify several of your own.

Several years ago, I was leading a small information services firm. One day, our receptionist—yes, at one time we did have such people—frantically called me and said there were armed government agents in our lobby. Could I please come out and take care of them? I proceeded to our lobby, and I encountered five armed IRS agents. I asked the nature of their business, and they responded that one of our employees was behind on her taxes. They were there to seize her personal vehicle for unpaid taxes.

I responded that I would be glad to make a room available where they could have a discussion with the employee in private. The lead agent then shocked me by pulling back his coat, putting his hand on his pistol, and asking me if I was planning to resist! I looked at him and said, "You're joking, right?" He wasn't.

> ... putting his hand on his pistol, and asking me if I was planning to resist! I looked at him and said, "You're joking, right?" He wasn't.

Our employee peacefully and voluntarily came and gave the vehicle keys to the agents. The *five armed agents*, then, called a tow truck and towed the employee's car away. The employee was able to retrieve the car a few days later because it was leased. She had no equity in the vehicle that could be applied towards her unpaid taxes. The IRS knew this but conducted the "raid" anyway as a way of intimidating and embarrassing our employee. It was also a way of letting us all know "who's in charge these days."

Recently, a colleague related a story to me about the enforcement of school truancy laws in his school district. He has his own business and works from his home. One day his high school honors-student daughter was at home in bed ill with the flu. Around mid-morning, five police cars pulled up in front of his home. The officers who came to the door said they were there to arrest his daughter for truancy. He was so shocked, he started recording the incident with his cell phone. The officers then told him he would be arrested unless he turned off his phone. They apparently didn't want their abusive activities documented.

Unfortunately, these are not isolated incidents. And it's not only government. Anyone who has ever dealt with a health insurance company over denied or unpaid claims can attest to getting the "who's in charge these days" feeling in their gut. It's also not concentrated in any one social economic sector. My two examples involved upper middle-class individuals. Here is that same manifestation in Corporate America.

HOSTILE OTHERNESS— "THE BASTARDS WILL GET YOU!"

It was early summer 2010, and my office phone rang. The caller asked, "May I speak to John Opincar?" I responded,

"This is he speaking. How can I help you?"

The caller said in a threatening tone of voice, "My name is Jeff Woodson, Vice President of Security for Large Financial Corporation. Earlier today you left a voicemail for Cheryl Richards, Chief of Staff for Walter Hazelett, our CEO. I am calling to determine the nature of your business and the reason for leaving the voicemail message."

Although I had left a very detailed voicemail message about the nature of my call, apparently Cheryl Richards had not listened to it. She'd simply forwarded it to the corporate security department for handling. Mr. Woodson summarily told me their executives didn't talk to outsiders, and if I called again, he would refer the matter to law enforcement as harassment. This was my introduction to the perceived Hostile Otherness theme.

Perceived Hostile Otherness was an enduring theme throughout my interviews with senior business leaders. It was not always addressed in direct statements, but it was a pervasive and powerful background undercurrent.

Yes, I know. These are wealthy executives working for multinational organizations employing legions of lawyers and security experts who shield them from these problems. What's the big deal? How does it relate to ethical intelligence?

It's true. Organizations of all types and sizes hire lawyers and other experts who deal with both internal and external hostility, spending hundreds of billions of dollars annually in the process. Although that seems a significant waste of resources, that isn't my point.

My point is this—the people in these organizations engage in ethical judging every day. Ethical judging occurs within relationships. Perceived Hostile Otherness poisons the soil within which those relationships live, transforming them into toxic relationships. As we've previously noted, ethical intelligence manifests within a relationship, which is its soil. We know that when we grow something in toxic soil, the resulting fruit is toxic, which is the result we see—toxic or harmful ethical judgments.

> Ethical judging occurs within relationships. Perceived Hostile Otherness poisons the soil within which those relationships live, transforming them into toxic relationships.

Love Canal Relationships. Love Canal has been called one of the worst environmental disasters in United States' history. The Love Canal was a toxic waste dump located in Niagara Falls, New York, upon which the city of Niagara Falls and others built homes and schools. In the late 1970s, the 22,000 tons of toxic wastes previously buried at Love Canal had permeated the soil and began making people sick. The aftermath of this disaster and others led to the creation of the so-called "Superfund Act," the passage of which created the methodology and funding for cleaning up environmental disasters like Love Canal. These sites, of which there are hundreds, are now called Superfund sites.

I introduce the Love Canal disaster because it provides us with a suitable metaphor for discussing toxic ethical judging relationships. We all can understand and relate to the idea of toxic soil and the aftermath flowing from that soil— sickness, serious diseases resulting in loss of life and significant property impairment and loss. Sometimes the aftermath and its root cause goes unnoticed or unidentified for years, sometimes decades. Then, years later, we have hundreds of Superfund sites and thousands of Brown Field sites, all of which contain soil unsuitable for plant growth or human use. This is where we are today with ethical judging.

Year after year, decade after decade, we've watched a tragic parade of the results of toxic ethical judging—Waste Management, Enron, WorldCom, Tyco, Bre-X, Siemens, HealthSouth, Freddie Mac, AIG, Lehman Brothers and Saytam, just to name a few of the most recent failures. We've created ethical judging Superfund sites and brown fields—ethical judging relationships made so toxic by perceived Hostile Otherness that it's impossible for ethical intelligence to manifest itself.

How does this work? Remember that, during ethical judging, you, the Self, are the sole arbiter of the equities of outcomes in the ethical dilemma relationship between you and the Other. If you distrust the Other, hold suspicions about the Other, fear the Other or hold the Other in contempt, your ethical judgment is most likely compromised or clouded, and the outcome is more likely inequitable and unjust—and, *in your favor*! It's like allowing the victim of a crime to sit on the jury. In this case, however, the victim is not only sitting on the jury but also acting as the judge and prosecutor.

This is the root cause of many flawed ethical judgments and the source of much unethical behavior. If I *think* (or perceive) you're out to screw me over, my ethical judgements about the equity of outcomes in our ethical dilemma relationships will be quite different than if I were't suspicious. If I weren't convinced you were going to cut my budget proposal by 13%, I might not add an extra 16% to counter your cut. So let's have a look at this in action.

Elegantly Ethical. Mandy's multinational manufacturing firm needed to locate a new facility in a foreign country. Although the facility would bring much-needed employment opportunities for the local populace, it was not necessarily welcomed by all the townspeople. They were concerned about traffic congestion, potential pollution and changes to the fabric of the community and its culture. More importantly, and in keeping with cultural customs, the provincial governor was expecting a respectful "licensing fee." As it turned out, a competitor who was not headquartered in the USA and not subject to the Foreign Corrupt Practices Act (FCPA), had offered such a cash "licensing fee" for the right to build a competing facility.

Mandy's firm made a counter proposal to the provincial governor. In lieu of paying the cash "licensing fee," Mandy's firm agreed to make significant infrastructure enhancements within the community where the new facility was proposed. These improvements included building new streets and roads surrounding the facility and the construction of a town hall park.

This allayed some of the townspeople's concerns, and it was taken as a sign of cultural respect. Mandy's firm also agreed to build a new school named in honor of the provincial governor, which was received as a gesture of respect. This was an ethically intelligent solution to a difficult problem that accomplished the final objective without violating provisions of the FCPA.

How does this relate to ethical intelligence? Two points:

First, understand that your connection to the Other is no longer crystal clear. The *Primal Relationship* has been compromised. What you think you're perceiving as hostile intent from the Other may be the result of the ambiguity, suspicion, contempt and the black hole of trust now present within the *Primal Relationship*.

> What you think you're perceiving as hostile intent from the Other may be the result of the ambiguity, suspicion, contempt and the black hole of trust now present within the *Primal Relationship*.

Second, awareness and discernment are an ethically intelligent person's best friends.

Once you understand and recognize your inherent suspicions and mistrust of the Other, learn how to add value to the Other *based on the Other's value system.* Consider the ideas of awareness, discernment, mindfulness, respect for insignificance, compassion and empathy as we move forward. You'll find they are essential ingredients in creating an ethically intelligent organization and personal life.

Green Fields Vs. Brown Fields. We're going to visit two different fields. Close your eyes and imagine taking an early morning walk through a meadow. The grass is green and moist from the overnight dew. There's a soft breeze caressing your face and carrying the fragrant scent of flowers and newly mowed grass. The bees are busily making their rounds, and the birds are softly serenading you with their special music.

You come upon a pristine babbling brook whose sounds mesmerize your consciousness and your heart. Slowly, these disparate instruments of nature unite into an operatic aria fitting for royalty. The moment engulfs your spirit and refreshes your soul, and you become one with creation. This is the green field relationship within which your ethical intelligence manifests and flourishes. Planted in such a place, your ethical intelligence produces just and elegantly equitable ethical judging outcomes.

Let's take our second walk. Close your eyes and imagine taking an early morning walk through a field where a lead acid battery manufacturing plant once stood. There is no grass, and the dirt is a mix of blast-furnace-like ashes, small bits of black plastic, lead shavings and a shimmering yellowish powder. There are no birds singing. In fact, the field is completely lifeless. The early morning breeze off the river carries the stinging stench of burning tires. You come upon a ditch filled with what appears to be a mixture of water, oil and foamy chemicals. The only sound you hear is the din of morning traffic coming from the nearby freeway. This is a brown field. I don't have to describe what doesn't grow here.

Both of these fields exist—the former outside of Gunnison, Colorado and the latter not far from the Detroit River. I have visited both, the former many times and the latter only once. The first is a green field, obvious to anyone who visits. The second is a brown field, so classified by the Environmental Protection Agency.

Both of these fields also exist metaphorically. I have visited both metaphorical fields, the former a few times and the latter many times. So have you. Your relationship with your spouse, significant other and children hopefully lives in a green field or some gradation of a green field. Many relationships with the IRS are brown fields.

Today, we find ourselves making judgments about equitable ethical dilemma outcomes within some variation of these two relationship soil extremes. Let's consider the metaphorical soil contents of each type of field. A soil analysis of the metaphorical green field shows trust, truthfulness, empathy, compassion, respect, sympathy, altruism and intimacy present in varying percentages.

A soil analysis of a metaphorical brown field shows distrust, disrespect, deception, suspicion, fear, cynicism and contempt. Within which field might your ethical judging be unbalanced or skewed in your favor? Bias in this situation may be unavoidable, but at least understand, recognize and acknowledge the bias and its effect on your ethical judging.

Now you understand the influence perceived or real Hostile Otherness has on ethical judging.

Perceived Hostile Otherness has transformed pristine green fields, where our ethical intelligence thrives and produces excellent ethical judging fruit, into scorched earth brown fields where our ethical intelligence falters and yields ethical judging Franken fruit that is shrunken, emaciated, and harmful to all who consume it. If we combine perceived Hostile Otherness with Violative Paranoia, we have two powerful converging forces intruding into our Heart Refuge and influencing our ethical judgment. We'll continue this discussion in Part Three where we lay out our Roadmap for creating an ethically intelligent life.

> Perceived Hostile Otherness has transformed pristine green fields into scorched earth brown fields where our ethical intelligence falters and yields ethical judging Franken fruit...

◆

Chapter Highlights

- You're not crazy, you're not alone—and what you feel is real.
- Your Heart Refuge (that sacred place where You reside) is no longer sacrosanct.
- Your loss of inner peace isn't an illusion.
- The possessive self (it's all about me, me, and me) is in full bloom, and for reasons that may surprise you.

- Today, the Self is the indisputable, imperious, and victorious member of the Self/Other relationship. Or, is it?

- We've created a self-esteem bubble!

- It took 45 centuries for the Self to escape the dominating grasp of the Other.

- As long as humanity continues pouring toxic poison into our collective unconscious, the seepage will continue, and our Violative Paranoia about the Other will continue.

- We can run from the Violative Paranoia. But, we can't hide from it. Its corrosive consequences are dissolving the goodness inherent in *Primal Relationship*.

- We all now swim in a sea of possessive individualism engulfed within a fog of militant Otherness.

- Difference is not necessarily hostility.

- Your ethical intelligence manifests within the soil that is the *Primal Relationship*.

- Hostile Otherness has transformed relationships into Love Canal relationships, within which a black hole of distrust prevails.

Questions for You

- Does the brutal extermination of 220 million fellow humans since 1901 give you a moment of pause?

- How often is your Heart Refuge violated?

- When you close your eyes and relax, is your mind quiet and peaceful?

- Is it all about you? Why? Why not?

- Where does my Selfhood begin and yours end?

- How much is too much self-esteem?

- Do you believe you have the exclusive rights to the fruits of your labors?

- Where do you begin and I end?

- Do you exist to serve society (the Other)?

- Do you trust the government and other institutions? Why? Why not?
- Where does Hostile Otherness end and your loving family begin? Do you ever have a difficult time finding the dividing line?
- How many of your relationships are brown fields? Why?

Endnotes

1. Plotinus, The Six Enneads of Plotinus. 270/2007, Charleston, SC: Forgotten Books Publishers.

CHAPTER 3

---◆---

WHAT WE HAVE—
THE SOLUTION

> In the beginning, it was consciousness…identified as a Reality…understood on the highest level as Absolute Consciousness, which is transcendent and yet the source of all consciousness in the cosmic realm including our own.
>
> *S. H. Nasr*

"Hey, Joe, got a minute?"

"Sure. C'mon in, Jack," Joe replied. "Do you wanna close the door?"

"Nah! I've got some great news!" Jack said.

"What's that?" asked Joe.

Jack could hardly contain his excitement. "Seein' how this project is really crankin' up and all the overtime I'm gettin', I stopped by the Ferrari place over the weekend and ordered a brand new Ferrari! I'll be pickin' it up tomorrow!"

"Wow ... that must've set you back a few bucks!" Joe quipped.

"Yeah, they have some great zero-interest bank financing, and my down payment is only $50,000," Jack said. "Well, I better hustle! I don't wanna miss the bus out to the blast site." With that, Jack headed for the construction trailer door.

Joe was a construction superintendent overseeing a large road-building project. Jack was one of his large equipment operators, but he also had explosives experience. Just two days earlier, Joe was on a conference call and was told the funding for the project had been reduced by 40%. As a result, Joe was going to have to lay off 40 of his crew members at the end of this week, and Jack was on the layoff list.

As is the case in most situations like this, Joe was warned he couldn't tell anyone about the reduction in force until the human resources folks showed up on Friday with the final paychecks and the paperwork. Even though he was sworn to secrecy, Joe was uncomfortable with what Jack just told him. "Poor bastard's going to lose his life savings!" he thought.

This is a paraphrased story that one of the COOs I interviewed related to me from early in his career. He was conflicted. How could he let this young guy buy an expensive car when he knew he was going to lay him off in a few days? On the other hand, if Joe said anything, he would lose his job.

I've presented this scenario to a number of my adult MBA students, asking how they would have handled the situation. Many have been unconcerned. They've said they would carry out the instructions they were given without a second thought. Others, however, have been as disturbed as Joe. Some of the students have said they would take the risk and confidentially confide in Jack. Others have simply been stumped.

One scenario, several different answers. Let's have a more detailed look at the story within the context of ethical intelligence.

ETHICAL INTELLIGENCE

When we examine the scenario, we find four elements:
1. Relationships
2. Equity

3. Ethical judging
4. Intellectual capacity and framework

Relationships. A relationship is a connection, association or involvement among or between people. Discerning the relationships embedded within an ethical dilemma, such as the one we're considering, lies within the purview of your ethical intelligence. In fact, *perceiving the existence* of an ethical dilemma is one of the prime responsibilities of a functioning healthy ethical intelligence.

In this case, some of my students didn't see any ethical dilemma. Personally, I do see an ethical dilemma, and perhaps you do too. Let's assume there's an ethical dilemma and talk about the embedded relationships.

There are potentially a large number of relationships, but we're going to keep this simple. Joe has a relationship with his employer, and he has a relationship with Jack. Joe may recognize one, both or neither of these relationships. If Joe recognizes neither, there is no conflict or dilemma, and nothing further is required. Assuming Joe recognizes one or both of the relationships, we move to the second element, which is an equitable outcome in the relationship(s).

Equity. One of the definitions of equity from the Merriam-Webster dictionary is "fairness or justice in the way people are treated." Although there are other definitions, this one suits our purposes. Joe has to identify the equity of the potential relationship outcomes. There are two sets of outcomes: In the relationship with his employer, Joe either keeps or loses his job. In the relationship between Joe and Jack, Jack either loses his down payment or not.

Ethical Judging. This is a somewhat mysterious phenomenon happening in our Heart Refuge and involves the other structures of ethical intelligence: Limbic System, Internal Compass, Ethical Fence, Slippery Slope, Worldview Window and Adjudicator. Joe will adjudicate the equity in the perceived relationships through ethical judging and within his intrinsic intellectual capacity and framework.

Intellectual Capacity and Framework. This is our mental ability for holistically evaluating what passes through our senses and then processing that information through the structures of ethical intelligence. This intellectual capacity and framework for judging matters of equity in relationships is built into all of us. It's part of our legacy as humans. It's the foundation of our ethical intelligence.

Ethical intelligence is the intellectual capacity and framework for judging matters of equity in relationships.

My formal definition of ethical intelligence is *the intellectual capacity and framework for judging matters of equity in relationships.* It has the four separate but integrated elements we've just covered. The fourth element, intellectual capacity and framework, contains seven structures, as follows:

1. Heart Refuge
2. Limbic System
3. Internal Compass
4. Ethical Fence
5. Slippery Slope
6. Worldview Window
7. Adjudicator

This elegant creation lives in our consciousness, which is encased within and subject to our collective unconscious. Ethical dilemmas involve a relationship between or among human beings—people like you and me, or in philosophical terms, the Self and Other. As we've seen, resolving that dilemma involves establishing equity between or among the people involved in the relationships. You, the Self, using ethical judging, are the **sole arbiter** of that equity. The phenomenon plays out where the sentient/sapient you lives—within your Heart Refuge.

I know this sounds complex and complicated. It is, until it's explained. In fact, another term used to describe ethical intelligence, especially by Aristotle, is practical wisdom. We'll begin unpacking this beautiful but cryptic gem in this chapter. Before we begin that task, however; let's look more closely at another ethical dilemma.

TOWER OF ETHICS BABEL

The maître d' has just seated you at your favorite table at Bella's, one of the finest Italian restaurants in the city. You like this secluded table way off in the corner because you can sit with your back to the wall and see the entire restaurant, even though it's dimly lit. You're waiting for your wife to join you because today marks one year since you became chief engineering officer of a prestigious Pentagon contracting firm. And what a year it has been!

Business is booming, and you work for one of the most well-respected CEOs in the business. General Jessop is a retired four-star officer, a graduate of West Point, a decorated combat veteran, married for 35 years to his high school sweetheart, active in the arts and local charities and extremely well connected.

He runs the company with a tight fist and demands that everyone adhere to the ethical standards he learned at West Point. It also doesn't hurt that you're now able to afford a vacation home in Aspen, and that your wife was finally able to quit her job and stay home with the family. Life is good!

As you actively scan the restaurant looking for your wife, you see General Jessop seated in a secluded booth with a very attractive young woman who looks vaguely familiar to you. The young woman is not General Jessop's wife. As you continue to watch the couple, you're hopeful your gaze doesn't catch the General's attention. But you can't believe what your lying eyes are telling you. After all, General Jessop is known as a straight arrow, a man of integrity.

Maybe the young woman is the general's niece. Perhaps she's a granddaughter you've never met. You're just sure it's something very innocent. But then she leans over, begins kissing the General's cheek and starts nibbling on his ear while gently stroking the inside of his calf with her foot. The cuddling gets so heated, you can feel your face beginning to flush. Then it hits you. You've met that woman before at a social gathering. She is a highly placed Pentagon contracting officer. General Jessop introduced her as a special friend to the company. It's now obvious how "special" she is.

You finally look away. But your mind is flooded with thoughts, questions and emotions. *Is this why our company has such a huge backlog of Pentagon contracts? What happens if this "relationship" becomes public knowledge? This restaurant isn't exactly a private place. What would knowledge of this do to the General's family? He has three sons who are high-ranking military officers. He serves on the boards of some high-profile charities and raises a lot of money for them. What about Anne, his wife?* You're so engrossed in your thoughts, you don't see your wife walk up to the table.

This is a small snippet of a much larger and more complex true story. It's a case study I use in my adult MBA classes, an exercise that elicits widely varying opinions and emotions about the potential embedded moral and ethical dilemmas in the story. Some students see nothing wrong with any of the behavior contained within the vignette. Some even applaud the General's moxie. To those students, it's just the way business is done these days. Besides, who could complain about getting rich while simultaneously attracting that kind of attention from a beautiful woman half your age?

Other students, however, find serious moral and ethical lapses in the scenario and want to string up the General from the nearest tree. I'll let you decide which camp the men and women fall into (just kidding). The point is, all of us reach certain conclusions after reading the scenario. Regardless of our conclusions, there is a process through which we reached them. That process is ethical judging. We judge General Jessop's behavior. Some of us find him guilty of ethical malfeasance. We detect potential betrayal, conflict of interest and abuse of power. Others of us not only find him innocent but admire his business acumen. For some of us, it's not as simple as knowing "right from wrong."

One of the COOs I interviewed told me, "I don't need our ethics code to know the difference between right or wrong. I learned that from my parents long ago." Another COO told me, "It all depends. Sometimes, finding where right fades to wrong is nearly impossible."

One CEO said, "I think it's wrong to take a pencil or paper clips home. The value of the item is not important." Yet, another CEO said, "Yeah, we know some of our lower-level employees steal from us, but we overlook it unless it becomes a big problem. After all, we don't pay 'em a lot of money."

All four of these senior executives lead Fortune 1000 companies whose names you would recognize. How do these widely varying ethical judgments happen? Here's my explanation:

Ethical judging is at the heart of ethical intelligence, but it's not simple. Ethical judging has clear cognitive and volitional components, but it occurs in the most primitive part of our brain—the limbic brain, the seat of all of our emotions. Take an ethical dilemma and wrap it in love, hate, jealousy, fear, lust and loathing, and you have a combustible cocktail that is as unstable as a beaker of nitroglycerin.

Return for a moment to General Jessop sitting in that darkened booth next to a smokin' hot woman. If you are a typical man, you understand how compromised your rational reasoning faculties might become—especially with such a woman caressing your calf and nibbling on your ear after you've shared a bottle of wine. But wait! Couldn't the General have avoided putting himself into that sweaty booth and compromising situation in the first place?

The answer to that question is easy. Yes. The problem is, we've created a Tower of Ethics Babel, which impeded the General's use of his ethical intelligence. Our human ethical intelligence is one of our greatest gifts. It is as much a part of us as our hearts or personalities. Unfortunately, for many of us, it has lost its vitality like an old pair of scissors left for years outside in the elements. The scissors are no longer usable because of rust and corrosion, but that doesn't make them any less a pair of scissors. Perhaps that was the case with General Jessop and so many others who have found themselves in similar circumstances.

I don't blame General Jessop—or anyone else, for that matter. This is not about blame. It's not about judging others. It's about stripping away centuries of corrosion and neglect and showing

> The problem is, we've created a Tower of Ethics Babel, which impeded the General's use of his ethical intelligence.

the way forward. We've all been subject to the same maelstrom of forces. Our postmodern chutzpah has darkened our inner vision and nearly silenced our still small voice, which many have called our conscience. It is, in fact, our Internal Compass that calls us to account and is a vital component of our ethical intelligence.

> Our postmodern chutzpah has darkened our inner vision and nearly silenced our still small voice, which many have called our conscience.

We've been unwittingly, but slowly and silently, descending into this ethical fog for many centuries. Part of that explanation involves our beliefs about human consciousness.

LIVING A LITTLE OR LARGE LIFE

Consciousness is the alpha and omega of ethical intelligence. The link between ethical intelligence and consciousness is the "I am" of human existence. Live a little life that is bounded by you, or live a large life that includes everyone. Let's explore what I mean.

This abbreviated exploration will include the Egyptians who built the pyramids, Vedic culture and Hinduism, the Buddha, the Zhou Dynasty of China, ancient Greece, and early Christianity. We could include many others, but these are sufficient to make the point. As you read, consider the qualities that stand out to you as part of ethical judging.

Egyptians. In the beginning—which for us is approximately 2550 BCE, or about when the great pyramid at Giza was finished—we find evidence of a belief in an interconnected, conscious and living universe. Those ancient Egyptians knew they were connected to one another. They understood that their consciousness intersected with and was inextricably intertwined with all others. They shared a common understanding.

Ancient Indian Culture. This culture has always believed in a living interconnected universe. Hindu Scripture speaks eloquently about the river of consciousness that flows through and connects us all. In his search for a unification theory of physical science, Irwin Schrödinger, one of the giants of quantum physics, studied the Vedic traditions. Within those traditions, Schrödinger found a way of thinking that helped him create his quantum theory.

The Buddha. Buddha's philosophy of life resonates with the idea of the universal consciousness and the interconnection of all of us. Eknath Easwaran captured this idea beautifully: "To the Buddha, the universe is a vast sea where any stone thrown raises ripples among billions of other ripples. Karma raises ripple effects within personality and without, for both are in the same field of forces. When we pursue our own self-interest, we are adding to a sea of selfish behavior in which we too live."[1]

The Zhou Dynasty. This is considered one of China's golden ages, when peace, progress and prosperity prevailed. Near the end of that dynasty, two prophets walked the land—Confucius and Lao-Tzu. They called for a return to the Tao, which they described as a never-ending stream of consciousness that flows through all things and returns to the origin of all things. Qualities that originate in the Tao are harmony, interconnectedness, order, flow, holism and vitality. This flow is also call Qi, pronounced "chee." If you've ever heard of Feng Shui, Qi is its chief component. Carl Jung was a student of the Tao, and he loved to share this simple illustrative story:

There was a terrible drought in the part of China where Richard Wilhelm, China expert, author and friend of Jung, was living.

After the people in the area had tried all the ways they knew of to bring rain, they sent for a rainmaker. This interested Wilhelm, and he was careful to be there when the rainmaker arrived.

The man came in a covered cart. He was a small, wizened old man who sniffed the air with evident distaste as he got out of the cart, and asked to be left alone in a small cottage outside the village. Even his meals were to be left for him outside the door.

No one heard anything from him for three days. But then, not only did it rain—it snowed, which was unheard of at that time of year.

Impressed, Wilhelm sought out the rainmaker and asked him how he could make rain, and even snow. The rainmaker replied, "I have not made the snow. I am not responsible for it."

Wilhelm insisted that there was a terrible drought until he came, and then after three days they even had quantities of snow. The old man answered, "Oh, I can explain that. You see, I come from a place where the people are in order. They are in Tao, so the weather is also in order. But when I got here, I saw the people were out of order and they also infected me. So I remained alone until I was once more in Tao and then, of course, it snowed."[2]

I understand why Jung so loved that story. Although the rain-maker got himself back into Tao, the people were not. So, their condition touched him. What you do touches me. And, what I do touches you. It's inescapable. This truth is now so real to me I am completely unable to relate to that day long ago when it wasn't. I now watch with sanguinity as many postmodern "realists" try to persuade me that the earlier incarnation of me was right after all. But there are more believers in this ancient truth.

The Greeks. The ancient Greeks bequeathed an immense legacy to humanity. In *Timaeus*, Plato related his version of creation and the resulting universe. He believed the earth was a living organism made animate by a mystical universal (world) soul. Plato wrote that the divine Creator had infused the universe with the laws of mathematics, and that all of creation included the beautiful symmetry of geometry. Plato believed the universe was a seamless interconnectedness between all forms of existence, including the human soul.[3] That idea flows forward into Christianity.

> Plato believed the universe was a seamless interconnectedness between all forms of existence, including the human soul.

Christianity. A foundational belief of Christians is the triune God, consisting of the Father, Son and Holy Spirit. The Holy Spirit is a force that lives within us, flows through us and connects us to one another and God. I could cite numerous passages from both the Old and New Testament of the Bible reflecting the concept of Karma and the interconnected consciousness that concept implies, such as the idea of reaping what you sow. The ancients believed—and most Eastern philosophies and religions still do—in an interconnected living universe. In the postmodern West, that is now not necessarily the case. Remember, we're not judging here, just explaining.

SLOW DESCENT INTO ETHICAL FOG

The four centuries that began coincidently with Martin Luther affixing his 95 theses on the door of the church of the Castle of Wittenberg on Halloween 1517 are among the most significant in human history. During those 400 years, fundamental changes in religion and its relationship to believers, the emergence and domination of human reason, and the rising role of science and technology changed humanity's view of the cosmos, itself and the interrelationships of both. The Enlightenment transformed the world. One of those transformations was a new way of understanding the universe, which opened the door to destructive, but real, unintended consequences.

Mechanistic Universe. Isaac Newton and others completed the model of a mechanistic universe, a universe based upon a mathematical model in which randomness was absent. Despite Newton's religious beliefs and good intentions of using the model to show the dominion of God, the actual effect became, over time, the opposite. Humanity now had a new universe, complete with mathematical equations, to compete with the living interconnected universe of antiquity.

This ushered in a new way of thinking—a thinking method that says we can understand all phenomena simply by reducing such phenomena to its smallest components, known as reductionist analysis. One of the unintended consequences of reductionist analysis was a slow withering of ethical intelligence and the increased use of reductionist analysis in the study and practice of ethical judging.

By the beginning of the twentieth century, science and the reductionist way of thinking had triumphed. We believed that, by using the scientific method, we could reduce all phenomena to its smallest component. We were convinced we had the holy grail for understanding everything. The ancient wisdom bequeathed humanity by the prior four millennia was airily dismissed as superstition or old wives' tales. We became servants to scientific theories, mathematical models and equations. We became haughty, and we administered the final blow.

We transferred human consciousness from the heart to the head. Science convinced us that consciousness was

We became servants to scientific theories, mathematical models and equations.

merely the result of firing neurons, a phenomenon arising solely from the electrical currents in our heads. The ancient notion of a shared consciousness was thrown on the scrapheap of history. We concluded that my consciousness was mine alone. There was no universal consciousness of which you and I are members. There were no interconnections. My actions couldn't and didn't affect you. There was no ocean into which I was casting stones and creating ripples that washed over you. We were all isolated and insulated containers.

Then, along came quantum physics and the quantum enigma. **Quantum Enigma.** Max Planck discovered the quanta in 1900 and lit the fuse of an explosion that rocked the scientific world, especially Newtonian physics. When fully formulated by the late 1930s, quantum physics had seriously undermined Newton's model of the universe.

Then, along came quantum physics and the quantum enigma.

Using quantum mechanics, we began to uncover scientific evidence supporting the ancient idea of an interconnected living universe underpinned by consciousness. For particles, atoms and molecules to exist, a conscious observer is required. *Conscious observation creates reality.* This is the quantum enigma. Consciousness is inextricably bound to the creation of all that is real. Sir James Jeans summarized it this way, "The universe begins to look more like a great thought than a great machine."[4]

In the late 1940s, two researchers, Thouless and Weisner, coined the term *psi* as a way of referring to psychic experiences, which, if true, gives credence to an interconnected conscious universe. In 2006, Dean Radin, using the entanglement principle of quantum mechanics, proposed an explanation of a range of phenomena called by various terms, such as extrasensory perception, precognition, telekinesis, clairvoyance and psychokinesis.[5]

Einstein called entanglement "spooky interactions." Rosenblum defined entanglement as "any two objects that have ever interacted are forever entangled. The behavior of one instantaneously influences the other. An entanglement exists even if the interaction is through objects having interacted with a third object. In principle, our world has a universal connectedness."[4] In his book, Radin chronicled almost 50 years of experiments involving psi phenomena. He established, at least to my satisfaction and that of other scholars and scientists, that psi is real and a vitally important aspect of our life experiences.

We do, in fact, live in an interconnected living conscious universe. Your consciousness intersects with mine, and mine intersects with yours. It's not some ancient legend or superstition. And, here's the important point: it affects our ethical judging.

Embracing Our Heritage

This discussion is important because consciousness is where your ethical intelligence lives. It draws its sustenance from consciousness much like we draw our breath from the atmosphere in which we live. And the way in which you view your consciousness has profound implications for your understanding of your ethical intelligence. We have moved far away from humanity's ancient understanding, and the results are visible everywhere—laws, regulations, rules, ethics codes, values statements and codes of conduct, none of which work very well.

Our shriveled and corroded ethical intelligence has reduced us to checking off ethics code boxes. We have accepted the idea that our individual consciousness is merely generated by and occurs only within the synapses of our brains, disconnected and affected by anything else. Incidentally, we now understand that the phenomenon occurring in our brain's synapses is governed by the laws of quantum, not classical physics. We fail to see that the stones we throw into our own consciousness cause ripples far and wide. This affects our ethical judgment and leads to little lives.

I am proposing that we reverse the unintended consequences and reclaim our precious heritage. When we understand that your consciousness and my consciousness are part of the same ocean, we expand our horizons and opt for living a large life.

> When we understand that your consciousness and my consciousness are part of the same ocean, we expand our horizons and opt for living a large life.

I opened this chapter with two true stories of ethical dilemmas, and I laid out the different interpretations and proposed reactions of a group of professionals to those stories. The diversity of ethical outcomes reflected in my students' and senior business leaders' reactions, however, is emblematic of the ethics babel in which we find ourselves trapped. There is a way for us to end this babel and emerge from our ethical fog. The answer lies within us. We need to reclaim our ancient heritage—that ancient cryptic gem living in our consciousness, our ethical intelligence.

In the next chapter, I will show you how our Neurosynapticware enables us to use this gift.

———————◆———————

Chapter Highlights

- We live in an interconnected, living, conscious universe.
- Your consciousness intersects mine and mine yours.
- What I do affects you, and what you do affects me.
- Ethical intelligence is the intellectual capacity and framework for judging matters of equity in relationships.

- Ethical judging is the way in which we establish that equity.
- Ethical judging is a mystery that occurs in our Heart Refuge and involves the other structures of ethical intelligence—Internal Compass, Ethical Fence, Slippery Slope, Worldview Window and Adjudicator.
- We have allowed our ethical intelligence to wither into dormancy.
- We can reclaim this hidden gem and change the world.

Questions for You

- Are you able to quickly recognize ethical dilemmas?
- Can you discern the relationships embedded within an ethical dilemma?
- What's an example of a time when your actions affected others?
- Do you believe there is an objective right or wrong? Why or why not?
- Does the graphic violence portrayed on the Internet bother you? How?
- Have you thought about the difference between decision-making and judging?
- Can the CEO of your organization make decisions that ruin your day, week and life?
- Can what you do in secret affect others?
- Can you dump a stone into your consciousness and not create waves that wash over your spouse or children?

Endnotes

1. Easwaran, E., The Dhammapada. 2nd ed. 2007, Tomales, CA: Nilgiri Press / The Blue Mountain Center of Meditation.

2. Hannah, B., Encounters with the Soul: Active Imagination as Developed by C.G. Jung. 1981, Boston, MA: Sigo Press.

3. Plato, Timaeus, in Plato: Complete Works, J.M. Cooper and D.S. Hutchinson, Editors. 360 B.C.E./1997, Hackett Publishing Company, Inc.: Indianapolis, IN. p. 1224-1290.

4. Rosenblum, B. and F. Kuttner, Quantum Enigma: Physics Encounters Consciousness. 2006, New York, NY: Oxford University Press, Inc.

5. Radin, D.I., Entangled Minds: Extrasensory Experiences in a Quantum Reality. 2006, New York, NY: Paraview Pocket Books.

CHAPTER 4

$\blacklozenge$

HOW WE USE IT— OUR NEUROSYNAPTICWARE

A mystical, spiritual, or synaptic place, where the conflict between right and wrong produces a righteous fire of truth within which dilemmas are purified of the dross of pretense and presented as pristine essences.

From the writings of Augustine, Husserl, Locke and Smith

This chapter is about the elegant package of psychological, neurological, mystical or spiritual structures we possess that enable us to use our ethical intelligence—the *how* of our gifts. These are the structures of ethical intelligence: Worldview Window, Heart Refuge, Limbic System, Internal Compass, Ethical Fence, Slippery Slope and Adjudicator.

We discussed the Worldview Window, Heart Refuge and the Limbic System in Chapter 1. We're going to explore the remaining elements of this elegant package in this chapter. We begin with the Internal Compass, our source for ethical True North.

FINDING TRUE NORTH

Most of us believe in the existence of some form of an internal human compass. It's sometimes called the moral compass, moral core or personal ethics compass. If you Google the term, you get multiple millions of hits. It was the fourth most dominant theme arising from my interviews with senior business leaders. Most of the senior business leaders I interviewed mentioned his or her Internal Compass. Here are some representative comments.

> "I don't know if I'm right or not. I'd like to think everyone has the potential to have that ethical compass. But I think for most people it's instilled in them at a young age—doing the right thing, being honest. And for others it's not a high priority. Or they may even come from a culture where that kind of behavior is not something that's valued."

> "So, it was difficult because, in that particular instance, we had an investigation. And this is what I meant about consternation. We had a legal investigation of this individual's conduct. We went through a bunch of crap. The investigators couldn't come up with anything illegal, okay. But yet it was wrong. You knew it was wrong. It felt wrong. It set the wrong tone. So I don't know that he legally did anything that could have been held legally wrong, okay. But in my mind and according to my moral compass, it was wrong."

I've defined the Internal Compass as a psychological, neurological, mystical or spiritual structure that contains a metaphorical internal human cognitive, psychological, moral or ethical compass used for making ethical judgments. I know that definition is quite a mouthful, but it includes all of the elements we need. All of us will have a different vision of our Internal Compass. Most of our senior business leaders described interactions with their Internal Compass as a "knowing," which is similar to the Cambridge dictionary definition: "a natural feeling that makes people know what is right and wrong and how they should behave."

Regardless of how we visualize our Internal Compass or its location within our human person, its functioning is driven by the core values and principles we've accumulated over a lifetime. Our core values and principles may have been rationally learned and internalized, but their activation is powered by our emotions. Or, another way to put this is to ask a question. Are our core values and principles dispassionately stored in a database, or has that storage also been accompanied by emotional passion, along the lines that memories are stored with complete context?

For example, I may dispassionately "know" that stealing is wrong. And when I see theft, it may or may not move me to action. If I'm tempted to steal, I may or may not resist the temptation. If, on the other hand, I not only "know" that stealing is wrong but also infuse that stored knowledge with heartfelt emotion, I'll be compelled to react with action when I see theft. And when I'm tempted to steal, I won't. You may think I'm splitting hairs. I'm not. These are critical distinctions. I was surprised by how prevalent these distinctions were as I listened to the stories senior business leaders told me.

Senior Business Leaders Speak. As an example, we take the case of Gwen, a Chief Administrative Officer, as she describes the functioning of her Internal Compass. In Gwen's case, shades of gray and complicated contexts are not part of her Internal Compass. Her compass operates in stark black and white. The question I asked was, "How do you resolve ethical dilemmas?"

"I guess some issues would be more visible internally or externally to people, and it may make a difference in how it's viewed. Right? If you took a pencil home, that's still bad. It's not yours so you shouldn't do it. It's wrong even though it's just a pencil. And you can't say it's just a pencil because that pencil could become something else.

"But you're not going to get the kind of bad press you're going to get if you bribe an official. I think both actions are wrong. And they are equally wrong. But one, I think, hurts the company a whole lot more than the other from the standpoint of the visibility it could get. But they're both wrong. So I think your answer is—things are either right or they're wrong and they're equally right or wrong. Some will have more visibility than others."

Now we have the case of Roger, whose enculturation occurred in a foreign land, and his career took him to some of the most hostile places on earth exploring for oil and gas. Roger is a man hardened by life's circumstances and his chosen profession, but he possesses a kind and gentle demeanor and forgiving heart. His Internal Compass is more flexible. For six years, he led worldwide exploration operations for one of the largest energy companies in the world. His approach to resolving ethical conflicts was to protect life, look inside to his Internal Compass and search for the rightness.

"How do I resolve ethical dilemmas? I'm looking at the situation and asking the question: Is there any chance whatsoever of an injury or death? If the answer is yes, then it's not acceptable. After that, one reaches inside to look for rightness, and it's very, very hard to find the answer. Finding where right fades to wrong is oftentimes nearly impossible."

Rick is the Chief Compliance Officer for a Fortune 500 natural resources company. Rick is also a lawyer with deep experience as a federal regulator. He has a keen sense about doing the right thing and is sensitive to nuance.

> "How do I approach ethical issues? Whenever I think about it, I just consider what my mother would say because she's the source of my moral compass. I tell people that. But that doesn't always work because your mom might be a crook! Ha, ha, ha! I also use the newspaper or online test. Would it be something I would be embarrassed about if it was published? If it's a question about my own personal conduct, that's the way I approach it.
>
> "If it's something one of our senior executives wants to do, like add some expensive C-Suite perquisites or fiddle with some executive expense account policies, I pose a different question: Suppose we publish your proposed perqs or expense account policy changes in the annual proxy statement to shareholders? That usually ends the conversation!"

Why does this matter, and what does it have to do with ethical intelligence? The short answer is it matters a lot, and it lies at the heart of ethical judging.

Why It Matters. Your Internal Compass is either infused with *knowledge or belief*. You can transform information into knowledge upon which you may or may not take action. But belief lives in a transformed state already infused with emotion and passion, and it's always poised for action. Let's make this real. Would you rather lead a team that has excellent *knowledge* about your vision and mission or a team that actually *believes* in your mission and vision? I thought so.

> Would you rather lead a team that has excellent knowledge about your vision and mission or a team that actually believes in your mission and vision?

There are two vital points.

1. As a manager or leader, you must understand your team members' worldviews because such understanding provides insight into the contents of their Internal Compass. Some have called this a measure of the content of character. Different worldviews yield Internal Compasses pointing to different True Norths. Posing the same ethical dilemma to two different team members may yield surprisingly different ethical judgments.

Oh, you say, that's not a problem for you because you have an organizational code of ethics and a stated set of organizational values. That's great! It's an excellent first step, but it's insufficient. I'm sure with all the training you provide, your team members know the content of your organizational code of ethics and your values statement. I have two questions for you: One, is it knowledge or belief? Two, when employees are confronted with an ethical dilemma, which set of values is going to prevail—the organization's or the team member's?

2. As a manager or leader, you must know whether your team members' Internal Compasses are based on knowledge or belief. Oh, you think this is not important because each team member signs a statement of agreement every year assuring you of their devotion to the organization's code of ethics and values statement. This may result in great legal protection for your organization, but it should give you little piece of mind. Team members who have merely intellectualized your organization's code of ethics and its value statement will always act out of knowledge, not belief. I know that's a surprising and upsetting revelation. Remember, ethical judging is drenched in emotions.

Your Internal Compass lives in your Heart Refuge. It's one of the most important structures of ethical intelligence because it's crucial to ethical judging. It doesn't work alone, however. It works in close tandem with another structure of ethical intelligence— the Ethical Fence, which we cover next.

WHERE RIGHT FADES TO WRONG

A ray of morning sunlight poked through the gap in the drawn hotel room curtains and struck Marty on the cheek. At first, he swatted at the warmth on his cheek. Then he gradually opened his bleary and bloodshot eyes. He stared at the ceiling for a few moments and didn't recognize the color. His bedroom ceiling was blue. This ceiling was gray. Marty opened his eyes a little wider and didn't recognize anything about the room. His once sluggish heart gave way to a quickened beat! "Where in the hell am I?" he thought.

Marty sat up in bed and noticed a human form under the covers next to him. It was too large to be his wife. He gingerly lifted the covers and glimpsed a shapely nude female form. He quickly dropped the cover and thought, "Whew. At least it's not a guy. Wait! Oh shit! What have I done?"

Marty jumped out of bed. His feet hit the soggy carpet. He realized he was as bereft of clothing as the form in the bed, and he immediately surveyed the room. With a pounding head, he nervously thought, "Damn! This room's a mess. How'd I get here? How'd all this clothing get scattered like this? Where did all those empty champagne bottles come from? Someone must've had quite a party here!"

Just then, the form in the bed said seductively, "Oh, Marty. Please come back to bed. We're not done yet. You promised ..."

Then it hit him. He recognized that voice. It was Missy, his smokin' hot assistant!

"Oh shit, shit, shit! I'm in real trouble. How did this happen?

About that time, Missy vaulted out of bed, threw her arms around Marty and started kissing his neck and caressing his chest hair. She whispered, "You never told me to stop. I guess we never reached your line in the sand! Wherever that line is, I'd like to keep looking for it! I love playing in your sandbox!"

Suddenly, Marty remembered the prior evening. The whole office went out for drinks, and Missy was sitting next to him in the booth. She playfully stroked his thigh and kiddingly asked him if it bothered him. "Oh my God!" he thought. "She accepted my challenge! I told her there was a line I would never cross. Now I'm in a shitload of trouble!"

"A penny for your thoughts," Missy said.

"I don't remember much from last night," Marty said. "I must've blacked out."

"You poor man. How could you forget? We had such a wonderful time. We drank champagne. Then we had some uh, uh, uh ... We drank some more champagne. And more uh, uh, uh ...! Then, you passed out."

"I'm sorry. I just don't remember!"

"Well it's only 6:30," Missy said. "We've plenty of time for encores. Maybe it'll help bring back your memory!"

"That's okay. I'll take your word for it. I'm good for now."

"I thought you'd be too tired for a three-peat," Missy said. "So I made a video on my phone as a keepsake."

Instantly, Marty's foggy mind became as clear as a fresh mountain stream. "Video?" he thought. "I'm a dead man."

Seeing the angst on his face, Missy said, "Don't worry. Our secret is safe. Maybe sometime next week I can look for that line again. I'll even give you a key to my place."

I'll let you and your imagination continue this all-too-common scenario to its logical and tragic conclusion. Many strong and disciplined senior business leaders have fallen into Ethical Fence quicksand. You crowd the Ethical Fence or line time after time. Then, BOOM! You're in the quicksand. I'll admit, I've crowded the line. And I know dozens of colleagues who have suffered the same fate. Marty thought he knew where his line in the sand was, but that line was easily washed away by a river of alcohol, which is an all-too-common eraser.

In this scenario, we see four elements: First, Marty said he had an Ethical Fence or line in the sand. Second, he claimed to know its location. Third, Marty implied he had the wisdom to maintain a safe distance from the Ethical Fence. Fourth, he was prideful enough to think his rationality could withstand the tsunami of desire his Limbic System was about to unleash. Pit your rational mind against your limbic mind, and limbic wins every time!

We also have the issue of rational impairment—in this case, alcohol—but it could also be drugs or other conditions. At first glance, rational impairment may seem an effective excuse. But we know it isn't. Our actions are driven by emotions. And our rationality is an insufficient brake on those emotions. Wherever Marty thought his Ethical Fence was, he'd already crossed it when he climbed into that booth next to Missy. In fact, we could make the case that he'd already crossed the fence when he walked into the bar. We'll come back to that idea later. First, let's look at the meaning of this idea.

Meaning. The Ethical Fence is a psychological, neurological, mystical or spiritual structure that contains a metaphorical fence separating ethical from unethical behavior, or right from wrong. Many senior business leaders refer to this concept as a "line in the sand" or just "a line." The location of this line is a result of a functioning Internal Compass. The location of the fence or its brightness results from the distinction between knowledge and belief. Knowledge typically implies many shades of gray rather than a clear demarcation between black and white. Passionate belief yields not only a bright line or clearly visible fence but also an easily recognizable DMZ well ahead of the fence.

> The Ethical Fence is a psychological, neurological, mystical or spiritual structure that contains a metaphorical fence separating ethical from unethical behavior, or right from wrong.

A DMZ, or demilitarized zone, is a military term that has entered our everyday lexicon. The DMZ is a cleared and marked section of the territory preceding a sovereign country's borders. It's an area that warns of the approaching border. Some senior business leaders described the DMZ as a well-lit area with flashing lights and alarm bells, with the flashing lights becoming brighter and the alarm bells louder as the fence loomed. The flashing lights and alarm bells were described as a "gut feeling," a "queasiness" or "an increasing discomfort." Many credit their Internal Compass with knowing the exact location of the Ethical Fence or line. Here are some descriptions.

> Passionate belief yields not only a bright line or clearly visible fence but also an easily recognizable DMZ well ahead of the fence.

"I know when I'm getting close to the line. It's hard to explain where it [the warning] comes from. My gut starts to hurt. This little voice says, 'I wouldn't go any further,' or 'You should stop right now.' The times when I didn't pay attention I got into trouble."

"First, let me say that I don't need our ethics code or statement of values to know the difference between right and wrong. I learned that at home before I was six years old. My dad had some very persuasive techniques, if you know what I mean. I never even get close to the line because I knew how important staying way the hell away from it was in keeping me out of trouble. I still remember Sister Mary in elementary school walking around with that ruler. If you got out of line, she rapped you on the knuckles with it."

"I think it's easy to step across the line. There've been many times in my life when finding where right faded to wrong was nearly impossible. We operate under so much pressure. The senior vice president is all over your ass, you have four kids at home to feed and a house with a big mortgage— sometimes you can't see the line until you're on the other side. You look around and hope no one finds you there."

Even though the line or Ethical Fence wasn't directly mentioned by all of the senior business leaders I interviewed, it was clear everyone had a point in ethical judging beyond which they wouldn't go. As in Marty's case, they weren't always successful. We all have a sense of where right becomes wrong, but the strength of and familiarity with that sense are different for all of us. Before we returned to Marty's case, let's have a look at the ancient pedigree of the Ethical Fence or line concept.

Ancient Origins. The Ethical Fence or line structure has roots in antiquity. Socrates spoke of an irresistible pull that distinguished right from wrong, supposing it a protective barrier preventing the ethically intelligent person from making an inappropriate ethical judgment. A passage from the *Sunnah* clearly articulated the idea of an Ethical Fence.

> What is lawful is clear, and what is unlawful is clear. There are other things in between that are doubtful. Many do not take them into consideration. Whoever avoids that which is doubtful truly has saved his faith and himself. Whoever is involved in doubtful things will sooner or later fall into sin. It is like a shepherd who grazes his sheep near a private garden: sooner or later the sheep will enter the garden.

Plato said that good was beautiful. Aristotle proposed that ethical behavior contained within it an inherent beauty. Nearly two millennia later, Freidrich Schiller, a German philosopher, poet and playwright, agreeing with Plato and Aristotle, concluded that humanity could not behave ethically through the powers of reason alone. Schiller proposed that aesthetics enable humans to discern the location of right versus wrong even while under the intoxicating influence of emotions—his version of the Ethical Fence.

Many doctors of the Christian church, including Aquinas and others, have spoken of avoiding the "occasion of sin," a metaphorical place similar to the DMZ, which warns of the impending demarcation between right and wrong. I am quite conversant with this line of thinking. As an undergraduate male attending a Jesuit university, we received abundant instruction and cautionary advice about avoiding places of temptation such as strip clubs, toga parties, anywhere alcohol mixed with scantily clad females or even dates with "accommodating" coeds. Few of us listened— and many proved the validity of the theory, much like Marty.

The Prophet was right. Sooner or later the sheep enter the garden, or we cross over the Ethical Fence, especially if we're oblivious to its location. Know where it is. Recognize your DMZ. It's important that ethically intelligent people understand the operation of the Ethical Fence and its intrinsic relationship to the Internal Compass. Your Internal Compass tells you the location of the Ethical Fence or line. Discernment creates your DMZ, which many have called their comfort zone.

Comfort Zones. We all know about comfort zones. We hear about them in business, sports and entertainment. Normally, comfort zones are described as limiting, barriers or a place from which we should depart if we want to ever get ahead. Google the term "comfort zone" and you'll get almost 20 million hits. The vast majority of those hits are exhortations to leave your comfort zone. Here's a representative comment: "Greatness is found beyond our comfort zone. We know this and yet we find it difficult to take the step." I'm going to give you contrary advice.

Within the context of the Ethical Fence and the DMZ or comfort zone that precedes it, it's important for you to *never leave that area*. This presupposes that you know its size, composition and boundaries. There are dozens of definitions for comfort zones sprinkled throughout dictionaries and other reference materials. Here's mine: A comfort zone is an arbitrary psychological area within which you maintain a sense of security, and outside of which you experience great discomfort.

We all have a comfort zone that precedes the Ethical Fence or line. Some of us have no idea how large it is, where the boundaries lie and what it looks like. And we often pay the price by blowing right through the fence or running right over the line. Most of us have a vague idea how large our comfort zone is. But the boundaries are a bit fuzzy, and its appearance is ambiguous.

The ethically intelligent, though, know exactly how large the zone is, recognize its clear and bright boundaries and know exactly what it looks like. Give these folks an ethical dilemma, and they can tell you precisely how far they are from the Ethical Fence or line. It's my hope that all of us will be in this latter category by the end of this book.

Once you possess this kind of holistic knowledge about your comfort zone, *stay there!* It's designed to not only protect *you* but also those who are affected by your ethical judging. During my interviews with senior business leaders, it was easy to see who had figured this out and who hadn't. Here are some samples of comments from those who "got" it.

> Once you possess this kind of holistic knowledge about your comfort zone, *stay there!* It's designed to not only protect you but more importantly those who are affected by your ethical judging.

"I just had a gut feeling I was too close."

"When I'm beginning to hug the line, I feel a queasiness."

"I get an increasing discomfort the closer I get. That tells me it's time to back off."

"I know where the line is, and I stay as far away as possible."

"It's kind of like pornography. I know it when I see it. That's when I know to stop."

"I don't need a gauge because I never get close enough to the line to feel any discomfort."

Now that we've covered the basics of the Ethical Fence or line, let's analyze the pickle in which Marty found himself and see if we can find his line in the sand. (Perhaps we'll have more success than Missy.)

Marty's Pickle. Marty climbed into that crowded booth and slid over next to Missy. Apparently several others were present and presumably were imbibing copious amounts of adult beverages. Missy stroked Marty's thigh and posed a question loaded with sexual innuendo. Marty responded with his "I have a line that I never cross" comment. The next time we hear from Marty, he's waking up in bed with Missy, and he claims no memories of what transpired between the stroke on the thigh and the surprise in the motel room bed.

I don't know about you, but I don't think it takes a genius to imagine all of the steps that resulted in the final outcome. So where did Marty cross the line? Was it the next caress of his thigh? The next several drinks? The inclination to stay behind in that booth with Missy as the other co-workers left one by one? Was it getting a room? Was it ordering the champagne to the room? Was it walking into the room with Missy?

I don't think we need to continue our list. Wherever Marty's line is, as we say in Texas, I think we crossed it way back yonder! Early in our careers, when we're young and less experienced, we tend to have a much higher regard for our rational mind's ability to overcome the onslaught of our limbic system. I think that attitude is reflected in Marty's prideful statement about his line in the sand. As a result, our DMZ or comfort zone is usually much smaller, if it exists at all. We arrogantly believe that we can hug the Ethical Fence or line, much like walking on a slippery river bank and thinking we'll never fall into the river. After a few drenchings, we come to realize we aren't the superhero we think we are, and we begin to take more seriously the wisdom of the ages.

The admonitions of people like Father Jim, one of the faculty members at the Jesuit university I attended, begin to make a lot more sense. So does the Prophet's observation that sheep grazing too close to a garden eventually end up in the garden. It's then that we consider creating a large DMZ or comfort zone. We understand the wisdom in knowing where the Ethical Fence is located and staying as far away from it as possible. It's much harder to fall into a river if you're 100 yards from the bank.

So, what's the point of Marty's story and our discussion? The point is fourfold. First, nurture and care for your Internal Compass because it establishes the location of your Ethical Fence or line. Second, create a DMZ or comfort zone that fits you and the way you think. Visit your DMZ often and make sure the alarm bells and the flashing lights work every time. If you don't have alarm bells and flashing lights, I suggest you consider installing them.

Third, never ever leave your DMZ or comfort zone for any reason. Fourth, don't become involved in activities or behaviors that move you from the outer limits of your DMZ or comfort zone ever closer and closer to your Ethical Fence or line. In other words, don't pride yourself on your ability to "hug the line" because you will ultimately fall into the river. That's what happened in this next story.

Gateway to Prison. Jack was the CFO of a Fortune 1000 company that manufactured and sold high-tech equipment worldwide. During the economic downturn that followed the terrorist attacks on 9/11, Jack's firm began experiencing a decline in the rate of growth of its revenues. Jack's company was led by a young, hard-charging, aggressive, take-no-prisoners CEO. The company's culture was similar to some Japanese and South Korean organizations, in which the workday begins with pep rallies and other teambuilding activities.

Although the senior leadership team earned reasonable salaries for their level of experience, more than 50% of their total annual compensation was tied to company stock options and annual grants, whose value was directly pegged to the company's stock price. Consequently there was continuous pressure to meet or beat the Wall Street estimate of their quarterly earnings. Otherwise, the stock price would take a big hit, and annual compensation would decline substantially.

Toward the end of one quarter, it became obvious the company was not going to meet the Street's estimate of their earnings-per-share. The CEO came to Jack and asked him to find a way to make up the two cent shortfall they were about to report. In other words, the Street was expecting $0.27 per share earnings, but they only had $0.25 per share. The CEO suggested keeping the sales ledger open for three or four days at the end of the quarter, which would compensate for the missing two cents per share. Jack was skeptical of proceeding with this plan. But he wanted to be a team player, and everyone was counting on him for their annual bonuses. We pick up my conversation with Jack here.

"I verified the CEO's calculations to make sure that keeping the sales ledger open for four days after the quarter-end would yield the two cents we were missing. And then I had a heart-to-heart talk with our vice president of sales to make sure that he was going to produce enough sales in the next quarter to cover this adjustment. He assured me that his team already had enough in the pipeline to cover a measly four days of sales. So I kept the sales ledger open for four days, and we hit our earnings-per-share number.

"Then we approached the end of the next quarter, and the economy was still sputtering along. This time we were going to be three cents per share short. So, we had a replay of the prior conversation between me, the CEO and our vice president of sales. Except, this time around, I was going to have to keep the sales ledger open an extra eleven days into the next quarter—four days to make up for the last quarter and seven days for this quarter. I told both the CEO and vice president of sales that this adjustment was getting me very close to my line in the sand.

"The economy continued declining. The next quarter was going to be short nine cents per share. So the CEO and vice president of sales wanted me to continue the practice of moving sales from one quarter to another. This time around, we had some very heated arguments about when this was going to stop because in order to cover the prior two quarters and this quarter, I was going to have to keep the sales ledger open almost an entire month. This meant that our quarterly revenues were going to be overstated by almost 26%. I told them I wouldn't do it.

"Then the problems and the pressure really started. The CEO badgered me with the threat of disclosure of prior quarter adjustments if I wouldn't go along with this adjustment. We had already filed fraudulent 10Qs with the SEC. The CEO told me that he was absolutely convinced we would pull the irons out of the fire in the fourth quarter because it was always the company's best quarter. Not thinking I had many options now that I had already come this far, I made the adjustment.

"Of course, you know the end of the story. We had to restate three quarters of financial statements, and our stock price went into the toilet. We had multiple shareholder lawsuits, and the SEC launched an investigation into our accounting practices. When the SEC examiners found the adjustments I had been making to the sales ledger, they filed criminal charges against me, the CEO and the vice president of sales. The CEO and the vice president of sales conspired together and got plea deals. They got fines and probation. I went to prison."

> Never ever leave your DMZ or comfort zone. If you do, know that in the end, you're going to be left holding the bag.

The moral of this story is plain and clear. Never ever leave your DMZ or comfort zone. If you do, know that in the end, you're going to be left holding the bag. Never ever begin a process that incrementally moves you from the outer limits of your DMZ or comfort zone ever closer to your Ethical Fence or line. Hugging your Ethical Fence or line never works. Eventually, you end up in the river or, as in Jack's case, prison.

What happened to Jack is also described as making a small, seemingly insignificant germinal decision that places you squarely on the Slippery Slope, which is our next subject.

PASSPORT TO PRISON

"Hello, this is Frank."

"Hi, Frank. Marcia here. I've got a small favor to ask."

"Hi, Marcia. I'm at my son's baseball game, and I can barely hear you. Sure, what is it?"

"Okay, I'll speak up. You know how you've agreed to reimburse me for expenses I incur on Lion Capital's behalf?"

"Yeah, sure."

"Well, I'm out making a financial planning presentation to a group of college students today, talking about the importance of underwriting firms like Lion."

"On Saturday?"

"Yes. It's the only time we could get this group in one place at the same time. I've agreed to buy lunch for everyone here. It's going to cost about $335. I can put it on my personal credit card and submit an expense report, like we're doing right now. But it would be so much more convenient for me if you could get me a company debit card. That way, it'd be easier for everyone."

"Not a problem. I'll get right on it first thing Monday."

"Thanks, Frank.! I promise you won't regret it!"

One year later:

"State Treasurer's office. Bonnie speaking. How can I help you?"

"Hi, Bonnie. Frank here. Is Marcia available?"

"Sure, Frank. I'll put you right through."

"Hi, Frank! What can I do for you on this beautiful day?"

"I've got a report on my desk from my CFO showing your debit card usage last month was over $12,000!"

"I'm sorry, Frank. I should have said something. I had a

lot of expenses last month."

"Marcia, we can't sustain these kinds of expenditures. It just doesn't look good!"

"Frank, I'll make sure this doesn't happen again. I'll also make sure you make it up on the next bond deal!"

Six months later:

"Hi, Frank. I just wanted to let you know we've awarded Lion Capital the contract to underwrite the upcoming $2 billion financing for the State Road Commission. Congratulations!"

"Marcia, that's great news! Thanks for the business!"

"Frank, I also wanted to give you a heads up that I'm going to have some heavy expenses these next few months. Have a great evening!"

Six months later:

"State Treasurer's office. Lilith speaking. How can I help you?"

"Hi, Lilith. This is Frank Fleming. I need to speak to the State Treasurer."

"She's in a meeting with the governor. I'll see if she can talk."

"Thanks, Lilith."

"Hi, Frank! I've just got a sec. What do you need?"

"Marcia, I have another report from our CFO showing you used your debit card for over $50,000 last month. We're going to cancel the card!"

"Frank, that sounds a lot like a threat! We've got a great mutually rewarding relationship here. I'd hate to see it jeopardized over something this petty. Anyway, I've got to go. The governor is waving at me. I'll call tomorrow."

Two years later. The doorbell rings at Frank's home.

"Jenny, would you answer the door? I'm taking dinner out of the oven."

"Sure, Daddy... it's for you!"

"Hi, what can I do for you guys?"

"Are you Frank Fleming?"

"Yes, I'm Frank Fleming. What's this all about?"

"Mr. Fleming, my name is John Lavis, and this is Bill Morrow. We're special agents for the FBI. You're going to have to come with us."

With that knock on the door, Frank reached the bottom of his Slippery Slope. A snap decision to give a client a debit card, which he thought at the time was trivial, morphed into one of the largest state bond underwriting scandals in his state's history. Frank was charged with an assortment of crimes, including bribing a public official. Over a multi-year period, Frank's bond underwriting firm, Lion Capital, had earned tens of millions of dollars of fees underwriting his state's municipal bonds. Marcia had used her Lion Capital debit card to the tune of $300,000. Both Frank and Marcia were sentenced to substantial prison terms.

The idea of the Slippery Slope is well embedded in our culture. People reference the Slippery Slope having only a vague idea what it is and how it actually works. For example, we've had a debate about the connection between marijuana and hard drug use for almost as long as I can remember. Those who oppose legalization of marijuana cite the idea of the Slippery Slope, meaning that if someone begins using marijuana, they're automatically on a Slippery Slope to hard drug usage. That pop-culture Slippery Slope is not the one we're talking about in this chapter.

The marijuana assertion may or may not be true, and its validity is irrelevant in this context. I offer it as an example to not only demonstrate the ubiquity of the idea but also the ignorance that surrounds it. In the pages that follow, I will show you the real meaning of the Slippery Slope and how getting off is nearly impossible once you've made the fateful decision to begin the journey. So, let's open the hood and take a look.

Under the Hood. As I listened to the stories from senior business leaders and vicariously coupled their stories with my experiences, it became clear how pervasive and destructive the Slippery Slope is. I can recall dozens of colleagues whose professional and personal lives were ruined by the Slippery Slope. As in Frank Fleming's case, most people who find themselves whizzing down the slope at an increasing rate of speed are shocked at the revelation. Also, as in Frank Fleming's case, those who are watching the metaphorical trees zoom by as they speed down the Slippery Slope can see no way of exiting without catastrophic consequences. So, let's take a look at how this sneaky structure works.

> ...those who are watching the metaphorical trees zoom by as they speed down the Slippery Slope can see no way of exiting without catastrophic consequences.

Slippery Slope. The Slippery Slope has three elements, all working synergistically, subconsciously and destructively. Each of these elements is so simple and bound into the mosaic of human psychology, we hardly ever think about them, much less pay attention to them.

The first element is a perennial human characteristic—false hope. The second element is a germinal or original decision bias, a very devious but ever-present factor in the human psyche. The third element is paying attention to details or, as most of the senior business leaders called it—sweating the small stuff. Let's examine each of these in detail.

False Hope. This is a difficult element for me to talk about because I am a very optimistic and hopeful person by nature. And I coach people to always have hope and eternal optimism about changing their circumstances. False hope, though, is an unrealistic expectation for future improvement in circumstances that will justify actions that are not in keeping with current reality. False hope often is used to justify short-term actions inimical to long-term success, as we saw with our CFO Jack who went to prison for thinking things would turn around. His false hope—or possibly more correctly stated, the false hope of his CEO and vice president of sales—led to devastating long-term outcomes.

If we dig a little deeper into the idea of false hope, we find some unsettling circumstances. We also need to remind ourselves that we're talking about ethical judging. Ethical judging is all about determining the equity in outcomes in relationships. So it's perfectly acceptable to have false hope for yourself. If your expectations for changes in your circumstances proves wrong, you haven't harmed anyone else. But if your unreasonable expectations are part of determining the equitable outcomes in a relationship—within ethical judging—then we have to apply a different standard. Making an original decision, within an environment permeated with false hope, is usually a mistake.

Germinal (Original) Decision Bias. Germinal decision bias describes a situation in which the original decision is followed by a long series of further choices, without much additional thought or analysis. For instance, a person chooses to drive a particular make of car, and without an external interruption, will probably continue to drive that make of car because humans like coherence in our decision making.

Choosing a brand of car is an innocuous germinal decision, but other decisions can have life-changing consequences, as

Frank Fleming discovered. As we have seen, a germinal decision may be the entry point of a Slippery Slope.

We're all guilty of this. We all have our own window on reality. And we're inclined to justify and defend decisions we've made based on that window. Many of us are so stubborn that we'll discard overwhelming evidence that shows we made a wrong choice simply because it was *our* choice. Unfortunately, this is a common human condition. We've all known people who would never admit they were wrong. no matter how much proof you might offer to them. In most cases, this is harmless behavior, and we laugh it off or make jokes about it. When it enters into our ethical judging, however, it often becomes harmful behavior. Here's an example.

> Many of us are so stubborn we'll discard overwhelming evidence that shows we made a wrong choice simply because it was *our* choice.

Zack was CIO of a retailing organization. Prior to becoming CIO, he was a developer and sales consultant for a premier worldwide cyber security company. We'll call it Supreme Security, a totally fictitious name. When Zack became CIO of this large retailer, he replaced its entire cyber security system with Supreme Security's cyber defense suite of software. During the first year he was CIO, the retailer's outside auditing firm detected some weaknesses in the cyber defense software. At great expense, the defect was rectified.

The CEO and the board of directors were concerned about the audit's findings. They pushed Zack to reevaluate the firm's cyber security needs and make whatever changes were necessary. Blinded by his loyalty to his old firm and his original decision bias, he hired Supreme Security to conduct the reevaluation study. Much to no one's surprise—including Zack's, because he knew he was right—the study found no deficiencies in the retailer's cyber security. Knowing how internally explosive the issue was, the external audit firm relied on the Supreme Security study in their annual audit. The audit report said nothing negative about cyber security.

Four months after the second annual audit had been finished, the retailer had a cyber security breach, exposing 3 million customers' sensitive credit card and personal information to hackers. As you might expect, Zack was fired, and the retailer has been unsurprisingly suffering from the security breach. If you were to ask Zack if this episode was a case of unethical behavior, he would be shocked. The idea of ethics never entered his mind. He'd simply made a business decision that didn't work out.

I hope you see this case as I do. Zack engaged in seriously flawed ethical judging that harmed millions of people.

The moral of this story is: Don't be hardheaded. Don't ignore evidence simply because it contradicts your original thought process and decision. Be ethically intelligent and admit when you're wrong. And take immediate corrective action even if it hurts your pride and lowers your elevated self-esteem. Believe me, you'll get over it. Consider how different the circumstances might have been if Frank Fleming had jerked that debit card the very first time it was abused.

> ... don't be hardheaded. Don't ignore evidence simply because it contradicts your original thought process and decision. Be ethically intelligent and admit when you're wrong.

Or consider how different Alecia's life would be without Zack's hardheadedness. Alecia is a single mom. She had the misfortune of using her credit card to buy Christmas toys for her children. Her credit card information and credit file were exposed by the cyber security breach at Zack's previous company. Now

Alecia's credit is ruined, despite the credit monitoring services Zack's previous company provided. Alecia's identity was stolen, and many of the items in her credit file are extraordinarily negative. Now, despite all her efforts at clearing her good name, she has found it difficult to get a job.

Unfortunately, too many senior managers and leaders, including Zack, don't sweat the small stuff.

Sweat the Small Stuff. Sweating the small stuff is an attitude that ascribes an elevated level of importance to otherwise seemingly insignificant events or problems. Specifically, this attitude prescribes an urgency toward addressing insignificant or small problems before they morph into larger issues.

This is an area where I often get a lot of pushback from managers and leaders. One CEO said to me, "I'm responsible for over 5,000 people. It's impossible for me to know the details of what's going on."

This was my response: "Would you rather hear about it from Jim Cramer on CNBC? Or read about it in the *Wall Street Journal?*"

Another senior manager told me, "I lead a team of over 200 brokers. It's virtually impossible for me to know everything they're doing."

My response: "Would you rather explain how one of your brokers was manipulating the market to a grand jury?"

Knowing details and micromanaging the people on your team is unrelated to the idea of sweating the small stuff. Former Mayor Giuliani was not out counting windows as he implemented community policing. He established a spirit and a tone of handling small problems before they become large problems.

Here's a comment from a CEO who gets it.

"People start lying about small things. That opens the door for a lot of bigger things. Unanticipated and hidden things—things you don't always see. If it's acceptable to lie to a customer, then it becomes acceptable to lie to one another, as well as the executives. That becomes acceptable behavior, and you open Pandora's Box. Then people start lying to me!"

I hope you see the complete understanding of the Slippery Slope in this CEO's comment. Smoldering sparks become fires. Left unattended, a small fire becomes a raging inferno.

Sweating the small stuff is attitudinal—it's something that should permeate your entire organization.

If you, as a manager or leader, sweat the small stuff that occurs within your sphere of authority, those who report to you will do likewise.

> ...never let any problem that comes to your desk just lie there and marinate. Pounce on it and fix it.

Early in my career, one of my mentors told me to never let any problem that comes to your desk just lie there and marinate. Pounce on it and fix it, he said. He also told me to never run away from problems. They only get worse. Run *toward* problems. No matter how bad you think it is, it could get worse.

Now let's deconstruct Jack's journey to prison so we can integrate and evaluate all the Slippery Slope's elements.

Deconstructing Jack's Journey to Prison. Before we leave this subject, I want to devote a few paragraphs to looking at

Jack's story. If you'll recall, earlier in this chapter we heard the story of how Jack, CFO of a Fortune 1000 company, went to prison because he allowed himself to step onto the Slippery Slope. Unfortunately, accounting professionals are often subjected to tremendous pressures to engage in questionable financial manipulations. In fact, if you look at the statistics, financial officers lead the list of those charged with these types of crimes, with CEOs in a close second place. In today's quarterly fixated-equity markets, Jack's quandary is not all that unusual. The pressure to perform is backbreaking. Here's how one CEO described it.

> "Well, I think it's just the short-term nature of the demands for results every quarter. Now we have Wall Street analysts forecasting our earnings to the *penny* ... a one-penny shortfall and your stock price goes down 5 to 10%. So I think the short-term quarterly demand for results is a strong driver. Sometimes I think, *'Man, if I do that it will trash the quarter!'*
>
> "But the truth is like, okay, so what? It's either this quarter, the next quarter, the next quarter—some quarter is going to get trashed, so you might as well just get it over with, if that's the way it is. So I think just having a longer view is necessary. And sometimes you just need to be a little older, maybe, or just a little less strung out financially, perhaps, to make those calls.
>
> "Sometimes it's not easy. We would all rather not have to come up with the bad news, but most things don't solve themselves. Most problems don't get better by putting them off, and most of the time you'll be better off just getting it behind you.

"It's not always obvious when you're under pressure—a lot of money is involved, you're personally financially at risk, you're strung out financially, you're trying to make some stock option number, or other pressures are weighing on the situation. I think it's better to take a longer-term view most of the time."

Unfortunately, Jack's CEO didn't take this approach. Perhaps his financial risk profile weighed heavily on his mind. As we begin to take a look at this situation, let me remind you of the family of five fears. We see these fears playing out in this story. Notably, we notice the driver of the unethical behavior is money not yet owned. The potential money loss these participants were trying to avoid in this unethical scheme was related to stock options and bonuses the participants had not yet earned. It was future money. Let's examine Jack's false hope.

The circumstances surrounding Jack's hope weren't conducive to the hope's fulfillment. The economy was in the beginning stages of a recession. Jack's firm was earning a profit, but that profit wasn't meeting Street expectations, which included a sustained growth rate. If Jack had thought about it rationally, he would have reached the conclusion that expecting the economy and his firm's prospects to improve enough over the next several quarters not only to maintain the profitability rate but also increase it was highly unlikely. Rationally, Jack's hope was truly false. But, as we've seen, rationality takes a backseat to emotions.

Although Jack's decision wasn't trivial, he caved in to the emotional pressure of wanting to be a "team" player. So, unfortunately, Jack stepped onto the Slippery Slope, made the adjustments and filed fraudulent reports with the SEC. The economic and sales improvement didn't pan out, and Jack was faced with the second quarter of "adjustments." This time, he resisted and told the CEO and vice president of sales that he had reached his "line in the sand." Yet Jack made the adjustments and filed another set of fraudulent reports with the SEC.

By the time the third quarter came around, Jack was really racing down the slope. Even though he strenuously resisted, Jack watched the metaphorical trees whizzing by and decided he had no hope of exit. Then, in a turn of events that always happens in these cases, Jack was blackmailed by his CEO with the threat of exposing "Jack's" fraudulent scheme. Unless Jack had audio recorded the conversations and/or written CYA memos to the file, he was totally exposed, because it was his word against the CEO and vice president of sales. Once you're on the Slippery Slope, exiting is nearly impossible.

We wrap up our look at ethical judging as we consider the ultimate and final arbiter of the equity of outcomes in relationships—the Adjudicator.

OUR NEED TO SWEAT

Harry S. Truman became the 33rd President of the United States on April 12, 1945, after President Roosevelt's death. Within four months, he would become the only person in history to order the use of nuclear weapons to kill other humans. In this section, we're going to accompany him into his Heart Refuge. Once inside, we're going to suffer alongside President Truman in his Sweatbox as he deliberates. We'll have an intimate front-row seat to one of the most important and controversial ethical judgments ever made. Before we vicariously experience that fateful deliberation, I want to set the stage by discussing ethical judging and the Sweatbox.

Ethical Judging. The essence of ethical intelligence is ethical judging. The word "essence" is a philosophical word with complex meaning. Although I've used the word in conversation and writing for de-

> The essence of ethical intelligence is ethical judging.

cades, its full meaning eluded me. We could say that the essence of something is "the quality that makes it what it is." This is still a bit too dense for me. So I propose this, a layman's understanding of the philosophical word "essence:" the essence of something is what remains after you strip away all of its externals. It's the core reality.

Here's an example.

A gasoline-powered automobile has, of course, a gasoline-powered engine, meaning that it's an engine powered by the fuel we call gasoline. When you open the hood of a modern automobile, you see an aggregation of devices, belts, hoses and wiring. These are all necessary for the engine to perform. From this view of the engine, you're seeing the engine and all of its externalities—all of which are necessary, but not the essence of the engine. The externalities are necessary for the engine to achieve its purpose.

As you begin stripping away all of those externalities, eventually you'll isolate a very few number of components. Those components form a closed chamber into which a gasoline/air mixture is injected and then ignited into a small explosion, which is the engine's essence. So the essence of a gasoline powered engine is the continuous explosion of gasoline/air mixtures. Or, as it's commonly called, internal combustion.

Similarly, when we open the hood and look at ethical intelligence, it has an aggregation of components, most of which we've discussed. Once we strip away all of the externalities, we reach a human person weighing the equity of outcomes in a relationship. This "weighing" phenomenon is ethical judging. It occurs within our secret place—our Heart Refuge.

Within the Heart Refuge, we find an Internal Compass, Ethical Fence, Slippery Slope, a large capacity cable connected to our Limbic System and the Sweatbox containing the Adjudicator. Here's a summary of the ethical judging process: First, we check our Worldview Window. If that window is closed and appears as a mirror, all we see is ourselves,

Within the Heart Refuge, we find an Internal Compass, Ethical Fence, Slippery Slope, a large capacity cable connected to our Limbic System and the sweatbox containing the Adjudicator.

and there is no further processing necessary because no one but our Self is involved. This is a rare condition for an ethically intelligent person. Your Worldview Window should always be open and clear. You should always be able to clearly see the Other in your relationships.

Once we've looked through our open and clear Worldview Window and established the relationships and the Others involved in the dilemma, we move to our Internal Compass. Our Internal Compass shows us the equitable outcome of the ethical dilemma. Most ethical judging stops at the Internal Compass because it usually yields a yes or no answer. For example, "Yes, it's okay to put that personal expense on my company expense report." Or, "No it isn't." If we can't get or don't like the directive from our Internal Compass, we might check out the Ethical Fence.

My Ethical Fence and comfort zone or DMZ may enable me to find where right fades to wrong, or where a dim light became pure darkness. Others may make the decision to completely bypass the Ethical Fence by never leaving their comfort zone. A deliberation might proceed as follows.

I'm on company business and, as a result, I've incurred an expense that's most likely a personal expense. Because it is, by definition, a personal expense, and even though I'm conducting company business, I leave it off my expense report. Someone else who wants to test their comfort zone, might say "Yes, this is normally a personal expense, but I am conducting company business. Therefore, I put it on my expense report."

Prior to making this type of "trivial" determination, the ethically intelligent individual will go check the Slippery Slope and ask additional questions. A primary question is, "Once I make the decision to include personal expenses on my expense report whenever I'm conducting company business, is it a practice I can justifiably continue? Where do I draw the line with this practice?"

If there is no realistic place to draw a line, it's safe to conclude you're about to step onto the Slippery Slope. My advice is—stay off the Slippery Slope!

If, at this point in our ethical judging process, we're still not sure of the correct judgment, we have to go see the Adjudicator in the Sweatbox. Or, if we're pretty sure, but we don't like the emerging ethical judgment, we go to the Adjudicator and see if we can get a judgment more in line with what our emotions are demanding. Remember, ethical judging is drenched in emotions. Here's an example deliberation:

"I probably shouldn't be watching this movie on my iPad at work. But it was just released, and I really want to watch it right now. I'm having a slow work day anyway. And I helped Jerry with his computer problem this morning. So I've done my good deed for the day. Let's go see if the Adjudicator will agree with me, and let me watch this movie right now while sitting at my desk in my office pretending that I'm working."

As I first envisioned the Adjudicator, I saw it as an electronic black box in which we input information. Then some unknown but complex algorithmic process analyzed the information and spit out an ethical judgment. That was the engineer, accountant and statistician in me suffering an ill-informed vision.

The Adjudicator is nothing quite that slick and modern. In fact, it's something quite old and much more useful—a sweatbox fashioned after the Native American Sweat Lodge, containing a totally transparent process.

Sweatbox. The concept of a sweatbox reaches around the world and is used in many cultures. Sweatboxes can be found in many dissimilar cultures such as Scandinavia, Africa and South America. They are also part of an ancient Native American tradition. Generically, a sweatbox is a place for peaceful regeneration of mind, body and spirit. The one common element that appears in all instances of the sweatbox is sitting in a sauna-like setting and perspiring profusely. Beyond that, local traditions take over, and we find all kinds of flavors of the sweatbox.

Some traditions maintain complete silence allowing for meditation and prayer. Others allow for participant interaction and spiritual direction from the leader. Some traditions regard the "sweat" as a closed event, meaning participants stay until the event ends. Other "sweat" traditions permit participants to come and go as they please, even designating a surrogate "sweater."

We've chosen a modified Native American "sweat" tradition as the most meaningful and appropriate metaphor for that structure within our Heart Refuge, where we find the Adjudicator.

The Heart Refuge Sweatbox, where the Adjudicator reigns

and renders ethical judgments, is a structure within which sauna-like conditions persist. But the heat and humidity isn't the result of pouring water over hot lava rocks. Rather, it's the result of the explosively emotional proceedings within. Remember, ethical judging is drenched in emotions. Whether any particular Sweatbox is host to prayer, meditation, learning or healing is a function of the Adjudicator, who is always the Self—the sole owner and occupier of the Heart Refuge.

Whether any particular sweatbox is host to prayer, meditation, learning or healing is a function of the Adjudicator, who is always the Self—the sole owner and occupier of the Heart Refuge.

If the Adjudicator believes in Divinity, Divinity may enter the Sweatbox. If the Adjudicator believes in angels and other spirit guides, those entities may also enter the Sweatbox. The environment within the Sweatbox is a direct reflection of the worldview and beliefs of the Adjudicator. In other words, your Sweatbox may look like mine from the outside, but on the inside, it may be completely different. Rendering ethical judgments is a singularly personal experience.

Of the hundreds of ethical judging experiences I could have used as examples, I've chosen one of the most well-known, controversial and profound ethical judgments ever rendered—Harry Truman's use of nuclear weapons. Few of us will ever face the gravity of Truman's ethical dilemma. But it provides a graphically prototypical example of what happens to all of us in the Sweatbox. Many of the senior business leaders I interviewed, who had life-and-death ethical dilemmas to resolve, would closely identify with Truman's experience. So, here it is.

Truman's Ethical Sweat. Harry Truman was a very down to earth and practical man. He was called plain spoken, meaning he spoke his mind clearly and without mincing words, often using what many considered "salty" language. Truman was referred to as "Give 'em hell Harry." He famously said, "I never did give them hell. I just told the truth, and they thought it was hell." Truman loved history and thought it the best teacher. He was a Christian who revered the Ten Commandments and the New Testament.

Truman was born, grew up and lived most of his life in Missouri. His formal education beyond high school included two years at a law academy. He never practiced law. Prior to entering politics, Truman owned and operated a clothing store. Although he could have run for a third term as president, he remarked that if two terms were sufficient for George Washington, they were sufficient for him.

When he and his wife Bess left the White House in 1953, they drove themselves and their belongings back to Missouri. After serving as president, Truman refused to accept payment for any of his speeches, considering it unseemly to profit from his public service.

Truman became president in 1945, after the death of Franklin Roosevelt. He inherited a raging war in the Pacific theater. After four long years of constant war hardships and a seemingly unending stream of dead American soldiers in flag-draped caskets, the American people were weary of war, sick of the sacrifice, angry, vengeful and ready to end the war using whatever means necessary. Truman had served on the front lines in World War I, barely escaping death on several occasions. As with most front-line soldiers, he had seen friends and comrades killed on the battlefield. Death and destruction were

...it's important to understand how utterly personal and lonely ethical judging is. It's a reflection of you, which includes your worldview. When you're in the sweatbox, it's only you.

not strangers to this commander-in-chief. He brooked no romantic fantasies about the spoils of war.

> Truman had said the atomic bomb was the most terrible weapon ever known in human history.

This background matters because it's important to understand how utterly personal and lonely ethical judging is. It's a reflection of you, which includes your worldview. When you're in the Sweatbox, it's only you. There is no phone-a-friend facility available. You are the Adjudicator, the jury, the defense attorney, the prosecutor and the defendant. Depending upon your belief system, you may summon the Divinity, angels, spirit guides, or any other sages meaningful to you. But in the end, it's only you. So this is not a history lesson. I'm providing this background so that you can appreciate, visualize, and empathize with the ethical judging session we are about to witness.

We join Truman on the evening of August 3, 1945. Truman was returning to the United States after attending the Potsdam Conference, which consisted of all the Allied leaders deciding how to end the war in the Pacific. It was the second day at sea for Truman, who was traveling on the USS Augusta. He'd retired to his quarters and prepared for the most difficult deliberations of his life.

> Truman ... stopped at his Worldview Window for one last look. The window was open, and he could clearly see the men, women, and children, civilian and military to whom he was about to issue a grisly death sentence.

Previously Truman had said the atomic bomb was the most terrible weapon ever known in human history. He was most reluctant to use it. On July 25, 1945, he had issued a formal written order for dropping the atomic bomb on or after August 3, 1945, but he had not yet given the final order. He entered his Heart Refuge at 22:09.

Although Truman had a deep visceral dislike for the Japanese emperor and military because of what they had done at Pearl Harbor and Bataan, Truman was a good man. So he stopped at his Worldview Window for one last look. The window was open, and he could clearly see the men, women, and children, civilian and military to whom he was about to issue a grisly death sentence. It would have been so much easier if the window had been closed. But like many of his predecessors, especially Washington and Lincoln, Truman was an ethically intelligent man. He knew those he was about to kill were his human brothers and sisters.

Knowing this judgment would be rendered in the Sweatbox, Truman bypassed his Internal Compass, Ethical Fence and Slippery Slope and entered the Sweatbox. Everyone was already there ready and waiting—hot, ill-tempered and sweating. I present this fanciful dramatization of Truman's ethical judging using a well-established research methodology coupled with my own empathy and compassion.

Adjudicator: "Mr. President, are you ready?"

Truman: "Yes."

Adjudicator: "Do you have an opening statement?"

Truman: "I do."

Adjudicator: "Proceed."

Truman: "I come here with great sorrow but firm resolve. There's already been too much death and destruction in this war. I inherited a military policy of deliberate civilian destruction. I don't think children should suffer because of mistakes of their elders. But, like me, my countrymen are sick of this war. They want the shortages to end. They don't want to receive any more condolences from me because their son or daughter has died on some ungodly battlefield. Our best and brightest sons and daughters are being wantonly sacrificed to feed this war machine. I will end this war. If using this weapon will do it, I will use it!"

Adjudicator: "Are you ready?"

Prosecutor: "I am."

Adjudicator: "You may proceed."

Prosecutor: "Mr. President, I find your opening statement most self-serving and hypocritical. Do you really expect us to believe your only motive for using this new weapon, which will kill hundreds of thousands at once, is to stop the killing and end the war by killing even more? Isn't it more about your reelection and scaring off the Soviets?"

Truman: "So, what are you? A f**king idiot? My reelection campaign is three years off! Sure, I don't want those treacherous Soviets getting involved in the Pacific theater. And I don't want that lying son-of-a-bitch Stalin sitting at the negotiating table with us. But my only concern is no more American deaths."

Prosecutor: "Okay, how many American lives will be saved by using this weapon?"

Truman: "My generals have given me an estimate of up to one million soldiers."

Prosecutor: "But don't you have other estimates showing the saved American lives as low as 140,000?"

Truman: "Those are estimates of people who have an ax to grind. We just took Okinawa with 50,000 American casualties, 90,000 dead Japanese soldiers and 100,000 dead civilians. And that was just an island. I don't think we can invade mainland Japan and lose only 140,000 soldiers. Those bastards are lying to me!"

Prosecutor: "So you're willing to kill hundreds of thousands of innocent Japanese to save a few hundred thousand American lives? What kind of a man are you?"

Truman: "F**k you!" Are you even a man?"

Adjudicator: "Mr. President, that is not a responsive answer."

Truman: "Well, then, f**k you, too!"

Prosecutor: "Okay, let's move on. Mr. President we've brought your Worldview Window here. Look at the mother holding that infant. Are you going to incinerate them?"

Truman: "Yes, I will if necessary. Show me the damned Emperor and his bloodthirsty generals. Then you'll see who needs incinerating!"

Prosecutor: "Mr. President, look through the Worldview Window again. Are you going to kill that entire classroom of orphans?"

Truman: "I will if it saves American lives. Remember Pearl Harbor!"

Prosecutor: "Do you want to be known as a war criminal?"

Defense Attorney: "Don't answer that question. No one here can charge you with a war crime."

Jury, in unison: "You bet your sweet ass we can!!"

Prosecutor: "Mr. President, you said you inherited a military policy that included murdering civilians. In fact, isn't it true that your firebombing of Tokyo has already killed 500,000 civilians? So why don't you have the balls to change the policy?"

Truman: "You really are a f**king idiot. I can't change that policy now. It works! We firebombed Dresden, and we got an unconditional surrender!"

Adjudicator: "But those lives are on the head of Roosevelt. Our interest here is in saving your ass from Hell."

Truman: "I'm already in hell! I'd be impeached for changing that policy. Besides, it works."

Prosecutor: "Your Ten Commandments say thou shall not kill."

Truman: "The Good Book also says an eye for an eye. Remember Pearl Harbor. They attacked us, remember?"

Adjudicator: "Why not just let the war go on as is? Your generals say it will be over by Christmas, anyway. The Japs are out of food, ammo and fuel. Just wait 'em out!"

Truman: "Hell no! If I can save just ten more American lives, it's worth it. Didn't you see what happened on Okinawa? Civilians joined in the fighting. Women with pitchforks and knives charged our troops. Children with grenades strapped to their bottoms charged our lines. Our troops had to mow 'em down!"

Prosecutor: "So you admit our troops are actively killing innocent civilians?"

Truman: "You people really are out of your f**king minds! It's part of the Jap culture. Death is preferable to defeat! The Emperor has already promised 80 million Japs will come at us if we invade their homeland! What more do you need?"

Jury leader: "Why are we here? You've already passed judgment."

Truman: "You're full of shit! My heart aches with despair. I see dying children everywhere. When I'm awake I see them. When I go to sleep I see them. Their eyes are barren. Their fragile bodies hardly able to stand. I can't escape the dying children! I thought I could find solace here."

Adjudicator: "Mr. President, it's unseemly for a President to cry in public."

Truman: "Go to hell! This is my Heart Refuge. I'll do whatever I damn well please here!"

Jury Leader: "Again, Mr. President, why are we here?"

Truman: "We're here to pass final judgment on those miserable bastards who attacked us at Pearl Harbor, force-marched 78,000 of our soldiers to death on Bataan and, so far, killed 140,000 of our soldiers in combat! Their soldiers' souls shout from the grave for retribution. Their families shout at me for recompense in blood. I must answer those shouts!"

Prosecutor: "What cities are you going to bomb?"

Truman: "Hiroshima and Nagasaki, both engaged in making war materials."

Prosecutor: "So you're just going to drop the bomb and kill whoever is there?"

Truman: "Yes!"

Prosecutor: "I rest my case, and I ask the jury for a verdict of 'no.'"

Adjudicator: "Jury, have you reached a verdict?"

Jury: "Yes, and it's unanimous."

Adjudicator: "Jury leader, please read the verdict."

Jury foreman: "The verdict is 'no.' Furthermore, if the weapon is used, we find the defendant guilty of war crimes against humanity."

Adjudicator: "Mr. President, what have you to say?"

Truman: "Go to hell!"

Adjudicator: "So you will defy our verdict? Suppose your defiance costs you your eternal soul?"

Truman: "That's the sacrifice I must make. If I can save one American life, I'll make that trade. It's called leadership."

No Regrets. Truman emerged from his Sweatbox at 23:38, on August 3, 1945. During the voyage back to the United States, he engaged extensively with the Augusta's crew. Pictures show him laughing and at ease. Truman never regretted his gut-wrenching ethical judgment.

> Against his own self-condemnation, Truman rendered an ethical judgment that challenged humanity's sensibilities.

Against his own self-condemnation, Truman rendered an ethical judgment that challenged humanity's sensibilities. On August 6, 1945, an American B-29 bomber dropped an atomic bomb on Hiroshima. The blast instantly incinerated 70,000 people and obliterated more than four square miles of the city center. On August 9, 1945, another American bomber dropped an atomic bomb on Nagasaki, instantly incinerating 40,000 people. On August 10, 1945, Japan offered to surrender.

Truman's cabinet objected to some of the surrender terms and urged him to drop a third bomb, this time killing more than 100,000 people, mostly children. Truman had reached his atomic Ethical Fence and refused. Nonetheless, the Emperor and his generals signed an unconditional surrender on the deck of the USS Missouri on August 14, 1945, ending World War II.

Nuclear weapons have never been used again on humans. Even during the darkest days of the Korean conflict, when our troops were being slaughtered by the thousands, Truman refused to use nuclear weapons again. We now have conventional weapons more powerful than the atomic bombs dropped on Japan. We also now have nuclear weapons that are hundreds of times more powerful than the atomic bombs dropped on Japan. Hopefully, Truman's atomic Ethical Fence will continue standing.[1,2,3,4,5,6]

Our Need to Sweat. Most of our ethical judging doesn't occur in our Sweatbox. It's easily dispatched via the workings of our Internal Compass or Ethical Fence. Unfortunately, for too many of us, we never reach those structures because our Worldview Window is closed or corroded. We don't see the Other. Therefore, there is no ethical dilemma to resolve. Ethically intelligent managers and leaders never have closed, cloudy, fogged-over or corroded Worldview Windows. There is always an Other in any ethical dilemma. Make sure you can see them. Whenever you examine your Worldview Window and it's a mirror, you have some serious thinking to do.

> Ethically intelligent managers and leaders never have closed, cloudy, fogged-over or corroded Worldview Windows. There is always an Other in any ethical dilemma.

When you enter your Heart Refuge, it's all about you. Your Heart Refuge is your place of personal jurisdiction. As Truman aptly pointed out, you can do whatever you damn well please there. The most important activity that occurs in your Heart Refuge is ethical judging. We are judging all day every day. Not every ethical dilemma requires a heated emotional deliberation like Truman's. It may be the case that *more* ethical dilemma resolutions should be deliberative and thoughtful. But, then again, it's your place. It's your dilemma. It's your ethical judgment. It's your choice, which is precisely my point.

When you're in your Sweatbox, every single character there is you. You are the adjudicator, prosecutor, defense attorney, jury and defendant. You prosecute yourself. You defend yourself. You judge yourself. You wrestle with the facts as you know them, often questioning their validity. You hope the fact supplier(s) are telling the truth. You hope that you're telling yourself the truth. You see the conduit from the limbic brain and rightly recognize it as the fire hose it is, pouring supercharged emotions into your Sweatbox. In the end, you may not like the final judgment, and like Truman, reject it. It's your choice.

Your ethical intelligence and your ethical judging skills, like any other faculty we possess as humans, function best when consistently used. If you are a stranger to your Heart Refuge, you're not going to feel comfortable there. If you've never been in your Sweatbox or engaged in a deliberative ethical judging session, you're going to feel overwhelmed the first time you're forced to go there. If you've never considered the shape, boundaries and size of your DMZ or comfort zone, the first time you must visit will be confusing and uncomfortable. Like playing tennis or any musical instrument, practice is required for proficiency. The same is true for ethical judging.

We have to sweat to become good at it. Simply relying on somebody's rulebook, ethics guide or values statement to guide our ethical judging is not going to cut it. We may use that rulebook, ethics guide or values statement as just another source for informing your Internal Compass, but we cannot become mindless robots in rendering ethical judgments affecting other people. Visit your Heart Refuge often. Nurture and maintain it as a place of solace, peace, and joy. Exercise your ethical judging "muscles." In Part Three of this book, I show you how to become the Michael Jordan of ethical judging!

---◆---

Chapter Highlights

- Our Internal Compass is driven by the core values and principles we've accumulated over a lifetime.

- Your Internal Compass is either infused with knowledge or belief.
- Energized beliefs cause people to strongly resist violating those beliefs.
- Nurture and care for your Internal Compass because it establishes the location of your Ethical Fence or line.
- The Ethical Fence or line structure has roots in antiquity.
- Passionate belief yields not only a bright line or clearly visible fence but also an easily recognizable DMZ well ahead of the fence.
- Stay off the Slippery Slope. No matter how enticing it may be, it never ends well.
- Admit when you're wrong. Your fragile self-esteem can handle it.
- The essence of ethical intelligence is ethical judging.
- When you enter your Heart Refuge, it's all about you.
- Within the Heart Refuge, we find an Internal Compass, Ethical Fence, Slippery Slope, a large capacity cable connected to our Limbic System and the Sweatbox containing the Adjudicator.
- Whether any particular Sweatbox is host to prayer, meditation, learning or healing is a function of the Adjudicator, who is always the Self—the sole owner and occupier of the Heart Refuge.
- It's important to understand how utterly personal and lonely ethical judging is. It's a reflection of you, which includes your worldview. When you're in the Sweatbox, it's only you.
- Ethically intelligent managers and leaders never have closed, cloudy, fogged-over or corroded Worldview Windows. There is always an Other in any ethical dilemma.

Questions for You

- Do you have an Internal Compass?
- What is the source of your Internal Compass?
- Is your Internal Compass full of knowledge or belief?
- Have you ever violated the counsel of your Internal Compass? What was the cost? Was it worth it?

- Do you have an Ethical Fence?
- Do you know where it is?
- How do you know when you're getting too close to the Ethical Fence?
- What does your DMZ or comfort zone look like?
- Have you ever been on the Slippery Slope?
- Have you ever had false hope?
- How often do you admit that you made a mistake?
- Are you and your Heart Refuge estranged? Why?
- Do you spend much time there? Why not?
- Can you describe your Heart Refuge? Do you find peace and tranquility there? If not, have you thought about why?
- Is your Worldview Window crystal clear? Why not?

Endnotes

1. Department of the Navy, USS Augusta Transports President Truman to and from the Potsdam Conference, July - August 1945, in 80-G-603322. 1945, Naval Historical Center: Washington, DC.

2. Samuel W. Rushay, J. Harry Truman and his History Lessons. 2009; Available from: *http://www.archives.gov/publications/prologue/2009/spring/trumanhistory.html.*

3. Hamby, A.L., Man of the People: A Life of Harry S. Truman 1995, New York, NY: Oxford University Press.

4. Truman, H.S., Memoirs by Harry S. Truman. Vol. 1. 1955, Garden City, New York: Doubleday & Company, Inc.

5. Truman, H.S., Memoirs by Harry S. Truman. Vol. 2. 1956, Garden City, New York: Doubleday & Company, Inc.

6. Truman, H.S. Truman's Reflections on the Atomic Bombings. 1953; Available from: *http://www.atomicarchive.com/Docs/Hiroshima/Truman.shtml.*

PART TWO

---◆---

LEADERSHIP: OUR CURRENT PRACTICE AND PROBLEMS

> Kind of like pornography, I just know it when I see it . . . unethical behavior . . . you kind of know when you feel it, when you see it. It makes you uncomfortable. If it does that, I think you should be very aware that you're getting close . . . you're getting close to the line.
>
> *Reflections of a Fortune 300 CEO*

Surprise—leading is not all about you! And I'm going to go out on a limb here—not everyone can and should be a leader unless they're willing to assume its responsibilities. Leading is a privilege and a calling. It's a labor of love. Leading is about serving others. Leaders are gardeners. They are people who are willing to invest in others through teaching, nurturing and coaching. There is no higher calling in this life than lifting people from where they are to where their greatest potential lies, using patient encouragement, detecting light where others see only darkness and freeing them to follow their dreams.

Leaders are dream releasers.

In the chapters and stories that follow, you're going to see good and not-so-good leadership. You'll also see excellent leadership—leaders who willingly pick up the mantle of responsibility for the success of others. Leaders who practice right-thinking-right-acting in the face of stiff resistance. Leaders who, despite great personal and financial danger, act to model right behavior. Leaders who resist the siren song of the Innocuous Imperial Box. Leaders who move people and organizations forward despite an army of hostile Lilliputian entanglements. We begin with R^2 Behavior—right-thinking-right-acting.

CHAPTER 5

---◆---

R^2 BEHAVIOR—MARK OF TRUE LEADERSHIP

And so we took the charge to earnings. The stock took a little hit. But at the end of the day, it was the right decision.

Recollection of a Fortune 1000 CEO

This chapter is a celebration. Within it, we celebrate senior business leaders' instincts to "do the right thing." Without exception, the leaders I interviewed were proud of leading organizations where doing the "right thing" was the highest value. The phrases "we do the right thing here," "doing right," "making it right," "treating people the right way" or some variation were repeated hundreds of times in my interviews. I thought long and hard about the words or phrase I would use to capture what I was hearing as I listened to the stories.

Initially, my Judeo-Christian upbringing led me to hear the word "righteousness" in my interview data. After allowing the heartfelt comments I'd heard to wash over me and soak into my spirit, it became clear that the secular term right-thinking-right-acting, or what I've called R^2 Behavior, best captured the essence of the moments these senior leaders shared with me. As we move through this chapter and beyond, therefore, **R^2 = right-thinking-right-acting.**

Here are some examples of why we're celebrating.

Fortune 500 CEO. "To me it's judgment. It's day in and day out making decisions that are based on the premise that we're going to *do the right thing*. We're not going to be trying to create a spider web or a smokescreen, but we're going to be transparent in what we do. And, that we're going to *do the right thing* as a result of that."

Fortune 500 COO. "So, I think there's no conflict. Every day you decide the size of raises you are going to give. Why don't you give 25% raises instead of 3% raises? The answer would be you would be giving away the shareholders' money, and that really wouldn't be the *right thing to do*."

Fortune 1000 CEO. "Obviously a lot of people wanted to see that [confidential competitor] information. It got out pretty quick that we had it. It was information sent by another customer to us in error. We were able to keep it contained. No copies were made, and it was sent back. Some people might call that stupid, but I called it the *right thing to do*."

Fortune 200 CEO. "People [who do the right thing] think about the impact of their actions on all the different stakeholders that can be impacted, whether it's employees, shareholders or the geographic locations where we do business. People have to be sensitive to those issues. And people demonstrate by their actions that they want to *do the right thing*. It's not just talk. It's demonstrated through their activities. The people that I have respect for are willing to make the hard choices. Sometimes, it may not be the decision that results in the optimal economic result, but it is the *right* ethical result."

Did I mention this was complicated? It's also why we should be hopeful. There's a sincere desire and intention in the hearts and minds of senior business leaders—and most leaders, for that matter—to lead a right-thinking-right-acting organization and personal life. You'll see that desire and intention come alive in this chapter.

We begin with this story from Jodie. She is CEO of a large medical center, an operating unit of one of the country's premier healthcare organizations. Jodie exudes warmth and caring for all the stakeholders of her organization. She is often caught between the rock of regulations, mandates, and financial constraints and the hard place of patients' needs, patient family members' desires and the well-being of caregivers under her leadership. Doing what's right is her guiding principle.

There's a sincere desire and intention in the hearts and minds of senior business leaders—and most leaders, for that matter—to lead a right-thinking-right-acting organization and personal life.

In the following story, the ethical dilemma revolved around an occurrence of seriously adverse outcomes for a patient and her family, potential legal implications for the organization, adverse continuing employment prospects for certain caregivers and the resulting finger-pointing and blame shaming. Jodie described her reaction to the aftermath of this long series of tragic events.

"I think whenever there is a question involving our own (hers and the organization's) ethics...during the experience the only important thing—the way I reflect on the situation—is how do I make things right? I find myself focusing on righting the wrong, if per se there is a wrong to be set right within the dilemma. There is a compass that we each have inside of us, a compass that distinguishes between right and wrong. When circumstances or scenarios get presented to me and I hear all the sometimes gory and disgusting details, I think, my gosh—how is it we got here? And I want to right the wrong.

"There's a feeling that I get inside. At the end of it all, when it's resolved, hopefully in a mutually satisfactory manner, not only is there great relief but, at the end my feeling is, most simply, that indescribable sense that you know you did the right thing. It is like when you find a lost puppy and return it to its owner. You see the face of that owner that says 'Oh my gosh—thank you for returning my puppy.' It's that feeling that validates the compass I have inside of me is always pointing me in the right direction—knowing I did the right thing."

Incidentally, the compass Jodie frequently mentioned as always present in making ethical judgments is the Internal Compass we discussed in Chapter 4. Jodie continued describing how she forms ethical judgments.

"Because we deal with life-and-death issues every day, we get somewhat removed from the emotions of our work. We each, as executives and employees, have to be conscious and conscientious to always consider the patient we're serving. We have to put ourselves into the patient's bed. At the end of the day, it's a human person. For me, the way I approach it is I consider if it were me, if it were my sister, if it were my mom, would I think and feel that this was a fair outcome? If I were laying in the bed or on the gurney, would I think this scenario was right? I think it's really hard for us in healthcare. We work under so many rules and regulations—governmental, health insurers and others—the patient can get lost.

"The rules, regulations and practices we live with ... I think it's like the foreigner who lands in the United States in the Atlanta airport. It's like, 'Whoa, how do I maneuver this?'

That's what I think our patients deal with. So, that's my compass. That's the process I use. I put myself into that person's perspective. At the end of the day, am I going to be proud of whatever decision gets made?"

What Jodie is talking about is a version of the Golden Rule. Many of the senior business leaders I interviewed considered "doing the right thing" as synonymous with the Golden Rule, which leads to the question, which one? There are multiple versions of the Golden Rule, depending on your enculturation and worldview. We'll get to that multiplicity in a moment.

So, what does R^2 Behavior mean? What is its source? We find that the idea of R^2 Behavior is timeless. As we quickly review origins, I ask your indulgence because I am equating R^2 Behavior with the term "righteousness," as used in certain of these ancient texts. As we examine these works, I hope you agree that right-thinking-right-acting is equivalent to the concept of righteousness, as used in antiquity.

A TIMELESS CONCEPT

The concept of R^2 Behavior is at least as old as the pyramid at Giza, perhaps much older. It is a seam of common understanding running through most major ancient civilizations, including Babylon, China, India, Greece and Rome. The idea of R^2 Behavior is found in all major religions, faiths and spiritual traditions. For example, the word "righteousness" (R^2 Behavior) appears at least 500 times in the Bible, as in this abbreviated passage from Psalm 15 (NLT):

Who may enter your presence on your holy hill?
Those who lead blameless lives and do what is right,

speaking the truth from sincere hearts.
Those who refuse to gossip,
or harm their neighbors
or speak evil of their friends.
Those who despise flagrant sinners,
and honor the faithful followers of the Lord,
and keep their promises even when it hurts.
Those who lend money without charging interest,
and who cannot be bribed to lie about the innocent.

The idea of R^2 Behavior is also defined in Islam, as in this passage from the Quran:

Righteousness is not that you turn your faces to the east and west. But righteous is the one who believes in God, the Last Day, the Angels, the Scripture and the Prophets; who give his wealth in spite of love for it to kinsfolk, orphans, the poor, the wayfarer, to those who ask, and to set slaves free. And those who pray, pay alms, honor their agreements and are patient in poverty, ailment and during conflict. Such are the people of truth. And they are God-Fearing.
                    —Al-Quran Surah 2: Verse 177(Al-Baqarah)

Other traditions also teach about R^2 Behavior. Dharma is an Indian spiritual and religious term for R^2 Behavior. Swami Sivananda says Dharma is the principle of R^2 Behavior, holiness and unity. Confucius emphasized R^2 Behavior, which means the "oughtness" of a situation. He called it a categorical imperative.

Dictionaries define righteousness (R^2 Behavior) as "behavior that is morally right or justifiable." The standards for R^2 Behavior typically cited are morality, virtue, justice or uprightness. The

Old English equivalent of righteousness is *rihtwīsnes*, meaning justice. The thesaurus provides us the following synonyms for righteousness (R^2 Behavior): fairness, rectitude, honor, goodness, respectability, justness, uprightness and virtue.

In case you were wondering, I am familiar with that *other* golden rule, "He who has the gold makes the rules." That is not the rule we're talking about here. Incidentally, that cynical rule was never mentioned in any of my interviews.

In our everyday lives, we relate to this yearning for right-thinking-right-acting behavior as responding according to the Golden Rule. For most of us, this means "do unto others as you would have them do unto you." The statement "do the right thing" or its many variations is often a synonym for the Golden Rule. Generically, the Golden Rule is known as the "ethic of reciprocity." It speaks to the essence of the *Primal Relationship*—how we treat the Other and how the Other treats us. The ethic of reciprocity's roots are as ancient as the *Primal Relationship* itself because it flows from that relationship.

So that you can appreciate the age and universality of the Golden Rule and its generic counterpart, the ethic of reciprocity, here are some examples:

- *"That which you hate to be done to you, do not do to another."* —*Ancient Egypt*
- *"Never impose on others what you would not choose for yourself."* —*Confucius*
- *"Avoid doing what you would blame others for doing."* —*Thales*
- *"Expect from others what you did to them."* —*Seneca*
- *"Treat others as you treat yourself."* —*Sanskrit Tradition*
- *"Hurt not others in ways that you yourself would find hurtful."* —*Udanavarga*

- *"That which is hateful to you, do not do to your fellow."*
  —Rabbi Hillel
- *"What we choose is always the better; and nothing can be better for us unless it is better for all." —Jean-Paul Sartre*
- *"Wish for your brother what you wish for yourself."*
  —The Prophet

We express our shared and public understanding of R^2 Behavior as the Golden Rule, but the two concepts are not synonymous. Living the Golden Rule may be one manifestation of our personal R^2 Behavior, but the source of our R^2 Behavior is not the Golden Rule. The source of our R^2 Behavior is our Internal Compass—one of the internal structures of our ethical intelligence, where we judge the rightness or wrongness of our actions. Embedded within our understanding of R^2 behavior is truthfulness.

GROUNDED IN TRUTH

The foundation of R^2 Behavior is truthfulness. In my interviews for this book, truthfulness always accompanied R^2 Behavior. Senior business leaders thought that telling the truth was always the right thing to do. When we use the word "truth," we're not talking about "ultimate" truth or the "truth" of the universe. We'll leave that discussion to the philosophers, theologians and others who tackle such questions, as reflected in that famous question asked by a certain Roman governor—"What is truth?" Addressing this question is where many contemporary discussions of truthfulness get lost in a swamp of theoretical bickering. We're not going there. We're going to be practical in

> Senior business leaders thought that telling the truth was always the right thing to do.

this discussion. And there is one other matter to cover before we get started examining truth.

I want to establish my credentials as someone who knows something about truth-telling and lying. First, I am an auditor. I spent years listening to some of the best liars in the world. I've heard almost every possible deception. Second, I have extensively researched truth, truth-telling and lying. Sisella Bok's two books on lying are the most comprehensive accounts on the subject ever written.[1,2].Third, I am an expert accountant and statistician, and I understand the often seamy underside of the adage, "Figures don't lie, but liars sure can figure!"

Finally, I am a recovering alcoholic. I started drinking at age 16 and quit 12 years ago. Practicing alcoholics are some of the most accomplished liars around. Pursuing the successful business career I was blessed to have required some pretty creative deception—although not so much whilst on Wall Street. When I quit drinking, I promised God and myself that I would never lie again. It's difficult, but it can be done, and it changes your life for the better. (And, no. My wife never asks me if this or that outfit makes her look fat.) My point? I know a lot about this subject.

Our working definition of truth is based on common sense and practical application. It's a definition I've distilled from my interviews, coupled with my decades of experience in business. Here it is: truthfulness is telling or having the intention of telling the truth, which is defined as accurately and sincerely describing reality (including the context of that reality), as known by the person describing that reality.

Truthfulness is telling or having the intention of telling the truth, which is defined as accurately and sincerely describing reality (including the context of that reality), as known by the person describing that reality.

In other words, when you relate your "facts," do you sincerely believe those "facts" are true given the relevant context? Let's demonstrate how this works. Here are some sample questions to which we can apply our definition:

"Were the goods shipped before the close of business on the last day of the quarter?"

"Did the customer sign the order?"

"Is this earnings-per-share number based on operating results?"

These are questions that should be easy to answer. The verity of the answers to the questions should also be easy to ascertain, right? In a perfect world, yes. But, unfortunately we don't live in a perfect world. We live in a world that has become increasingly enamored with laws, regulations and rules. We've become legalistic in our thinking. That type of thinking transforms simple matters like telling the truth into complicated and complex theoretical constructs. Out of those intricately constructed mazes rises a fog of ambiguity, which gives liars the cloaking device necessary to transform deception into apparent "truth." Here is a simple real-life example illustrating this practice.

> We live in a world that has become increasingly enamored with laws, regulations and rules. We've become legalistic in our thinking.

Those who are intent on deception might ask the following qualifying questions:

"How are we defining the word 'shipped?'"

"What do you mean by 'sign' the order?"

"How are we defining 'operating' results?"

These questions may seem absurd, but I have frequently been in situations where qualifying questions like these are routinely posed. Remember, we once had a president who famously answered a question with, "It all depends on what the meaning of the word 'is' is." This is not truth-telling. It's obfuscation. I hope, as a manager or leader, you wouldn't tolerate this kind of behavior. None of the senior business leaders I interviewed would either.

Let's examine the first question, "Were the goods shipped before the close of business on the last day of the quarter?" This is an actual case from my days as an auditor. The shipping manager verified that the goods were loaded on a truck, and the truck left the premises en route to the customer on the last day of the quarter. She had the documentation showing the "facts."

We later learned, however, that the truck returned nine days later with the goods. The goods were unloaded and returned to stock. So were the goods shipped before the close of business on the last day of the quarter? What do you think? Is the shipping manager telling the truth when she says yes?

If we narrowly define the word "shipped" as physically loading goods on a truck that leaves the premises before the close of business on the last day of the quarter, then, yes. The goods were shipped. This, however, is an inadequate analysis because we have to look at the broader context of the question—were the goods sold? Delivering a good or performing a service is an essential consideration in recording a sale on the books of an enterprise. And the date of the delivery determines in which accounting period the sale is recorded—in this case, the current quarter. So we ask a question and expect a response appropriate to the broader context of the question.

As the CEO asking this question, I'd say the shipping manager is lying. Why? I would expect the shipping manager to understand the context of my question. Additionally, I would expect the shipping manager to know about the return of the goods. Clearly, the goods were returned and not sold. In this case, there was never an intent to deliver the goods to the customer because the customer hadn't placed an order. The truck carrying the goods was deliberately parked a few miles away from the plant in an abandoned warehouse. It was returned nine days later. The only purpose of the charade was to increase sales within the current quarter.

As a manager and a leader, you shouldn't have to carefully craft your questions to get a truthful answer. If the person from whom you are expecting an answer parses every word of your question, you need to carefully examine your organization's culture and that person's future in that culture. Organizational cultures based on transparency, trust and truth-telling contain people who understand the context of questions and respond accordingly. (Note: We'll discuss organizational culture in Chapter 7.)

Here are two stories illustrating lying, including parsing the words of not only actual questions but also implied questions.

Jack is the CEO of a Fortune 1000 industrial products company operating in a market segment where the products are commoditized, prices are extremely competitive and sales and service often are the deciding factors in customer relationships. Jack's company had recently hired Brad, one of the top three salespeople in the industry. In order to recruit Brad, Jack's company created a special compensation plan for him and even made him a nominal vice president. Jack related an incident involving Brad that was amusing—until it wasn't.

"I'd just returned from lunch when a call came in from a friend of mine who happens to belong to one of the same industry groups that I do. After exchanging a few pleasantries,

Tom said, 'I ran into your new president and chief operating officer today. I didn't know that Russ had left you.'

"I was really taken aback with what Tom had just told me because I'd just walked by Russ's office, and he was on a conference call. Not knowing what in the world was going on, I kind of played along with the conversation. I asked Tom, 'Well what did you think of him?'

"Tom said, 'He's no Russ, but he seemed like a really energetic nice young guy, and he presents himself well. He does seem a little too young to be your new COO, though.'

"I just couldn't play along with the drama any longer, and I was starting to get really angry that somebody was presenting himself as our COO at an important industry association meeting. So, I told Tom, 'We don't have a new COO, and Russ is just down the hall from me in his office talking on the telephone. So who in the hell is the person you're talking about?'

"Tom quietly said, 'Well I have his business card here, and it says his name is Brad Chalmers.'

"I told him, 'You say you have the business card? Does it look authentic? Does it have our logo?'

"Tom said, 'It sure looks authentic to me. What's going on, Jack?'

"I said, 'I'll get back to you on that one.'

"I nearly dropped the phone. Brad Chalmers was our new sales guy. This really pissed me off. Who the hell does this motherf***er think he is? So, I called Margaret, my admin, and asked her to get him into my office pronto.

"A couple of hours later, Brad came strolling into my office beaming ear-to-ear. He said, 'Boss, I made some really great high-level contacts today. And I guarantee I'll bring in some really large and new customers very soon.'

"I said, 'That's great, Brad. Let me see how your new business cards turned out.' He handed me one of his business cards, and it was our standard issue showing his name and his correct title. I said, 'These look nice, but I'd like to see the business cards you were handing out at the industry association meeting today.' Without missing a beat, Brad reached into his other coat pocket, pulled out a business card and gave it to me.

"As he did, he said, 'Now, these cards are just for show. They're designed to just get me into the door, kind of like additional marketing materials.'

"I asked him, 'Where did you get these?'

"Brad said, 'I have a friend who has a print shop. He made them for me. They look pretty good, don't they?'

"I just blew up on him. I said, 'You see nothing wrong with this? You're not our president and chief operating officer. This is a lie. You're misrepresenting yourself. You're misrepresenting the company. And you're making me look like a f***king jackass!'"

"Brad said, 'But it's just marketing materials. Having that kind of title gets me in the door. No one wants to talk to just another sales guy.'

"I said, 'But, it's a f***king lie! What part of *It's a lie* don't you get? How can I ever trust you again? If you'll lie about this, what else have you said that's a lie?'

"I fired him on the spot and threw his ass out of my office."

As Jack was relating this story, he got angry all over again. You could nearly see the steam coming out of his ears. I ask you, did Brad think he was lying? Do *you* think Brad was lying? What would you have done in this situation?

Here are my answers: It doesn't matter what Brad thought. He was lying. Even though the people in this story considered Brad a young guy, he was in his early forties—old enough to know what he was doing. He knew the "facts" he was relating were false. Like Jack, I would have fired him on the spot.

Let's take a look at another story.

I've been teaching MBA students now for more than 12 years. Most of the students in my classroom have been in their careers for a few years, and they're typically in their late thirties or early forties. As you might expect, I include an ethics component in all of my courses. We work on case studies based on my real-world experiences. I've talked about some of those cases in this book already.

About five years ago, I was teaching a corporate finance class. We were approaching the end of the course. One evening one of the students stopped by to talk to me after class. Brenda was working as a financial analyst for an operating division of a large multinational corporation. As she walked up, Brenda had a big smile on her face.

"I resigned from my job today," she said.

"Wow," I said. "That must have been a hard decision."

She said, "No, after being in this class, it wasn't."

I was intrigued. "What do you mean?" I asked.

"These ethics cases we've been working on in class have really opened my eyes," she said. "Until this class, I had no idea that what we were doing in my office was unethical."

Even more intrigued, I said, "What do you mean?"

Brenda went on, "Every month we do a budget comparison. We compare our budget to the actual results. Except, we don't report that information. We do the comparison, and then we adjust the numbers to what our controller and divi-sion vice president say corporate wants to see. When I asked about it, my manager told me that it was just the way we operate and not to worry about it. Until this class, I didn't think anything about what we were doing. Now I know what we've been doing all this time is lying to corporate. I don't want to be involved in lying anymore. So I quit."

No, this is not fiction. I've had doz-ens of similar experiences over the past 12 years, especially in my MBA courses. There's so much lying in our culture, peo-ple are accustomed to it, and they unfor-tunately expect and tolerate it. When they see it, they think it's no big deal. Lying is one of the primary reasons that so many leaders are no longer trusted. It's incum-bent upon ethically intelligent managers and leaders to change this. It's simpler than you think. Stop lying! When you do, the people who follow you will stop lying. It starts with you and me.

> Lying is one of the primary reasons that so many leaders are no longer trusted. It's in-cumbent upon ethically intelligent managers and leaders to change this. It's simpler than you think. Stop lying!

R^2 Behavior is founded upon truth-telling, and its practice is guided by discernment.

GUIDED BY DISCERNMENT

Like R^2 Behavior, discernment is another powerfully descriptive word that has fallen out of favor in our postmodern society. It's often associated with religious or philosophical discussions, ac-quiring a patina of inaccessibility as an unwelcomed result. Al-though the word "discernment" was not often overtly used in the stories I heard from senior business leaders, like truthfulness, its meaning always accompanied the idea of R^2 behavior because discernment is how we choose.

Discernment is often defined as "choosing wisely." This is a limited definition, and it greatly diminishes a complex, beautiful and necessary human ability. Discernment is essential, however, to the concept of R^2 Behavior or "doing the right thing." I give you a thought from both Aristotle and Augustine and a story from a Fortune 500 CFO.

Aristotle and Augustine believed an ethically intelligent person possessed a finely tuned discernment that not only distinguished parts from wholes but also comprehended that the beauty of the whole is often more than the sum of its parts.

When I interviewed an executive named Stan, his experience demonstrated this balancing act.

"Our CEO gave me the responsibility of finding $400 million in financing for a promising but high-risk project. The problem was he didn't want to be involved in any of the details. He said, 'Just get it done.' I got the loan closed, which was the primary mission. It had covenants that were kind of normal, usual and necessary. What I failed to do was get the CEO to understand the ramifications of those covenants. I later found out that he didn't want to be involved in the details so that he could disavow any foreknowledge of the transaction's details if it didn't work out in the end. He wanted someone to blame when the board demanded answers as to why the company was in violation of the loan's covenants.

"Was that an ethical issue? I don't know. I don't know if that was an ethical issue or not. But in that case, I knew what was right for the company and all of its stakeholders and did it. At the end of the day, the CEO didn't like what I did. He wanted free rein to use the funds however he decided. The covenants said otherwise.

"Sometimes, if you do your job, you're not going to keep it. And, frankly, I lost a couple of jobs like that. As a CPA, you know the ethical constraints we've got. You've got to uphold the rules, and part of the rules are, you have to tell people the truth. And sometimes people don't want to hear the truth. Is it the right thing to do or not? Frankly, I think it was the right thing to do. I try to make sure my fellow C-Suite members, especially the CEO and the board, understand that they're paying me to tell them the truth. Sometimes you lose your job by doing it."

Unfortunately, Stan's experience as a licensed professional is not unique. For example, Rick is the Chief Compliance Officer for a Fortune 500 natural resources company. Rick is also a lawyer with deep experience as a federal regulator, which included the Securities Exchange Commission and several other agencies. You'll hear some of his stories later in the book. As an introduction to our discussion of integrity, however, I want to give you one of Rick's comments that echoes Stan's discernment dilemmas.

"This is my dream job. Every morning I walk into this beautifully appointed sixtieth-floor office with this gorgeous view of the city, and I pinch myself. I've been here four years, and the exhilaration is always with me. This job is an opportunity of a lifetime. It's given me the ability to provide for my family beyond anything I could have ever imagined. Yet I walk into this office every morning and sit at this custom-made teak wood desk knowing this may be the day—the day that I have to walk away because I've been asked to do something or agree to something that I know isn't right. It's always on my mind. This is a very competitive business. We have an aggressive leadership team here. They like to push the envelope. When that day comes, I pray I have the courage to do the right thing and leave it all behind."

Courage has consequences. It's at the heart of integrity. As in the case of truthfulness and discernment, every discussion of R^2 Behavior during my interviews included the virtue of integrity. As it turns out, R^2 Behavior has three components—truthfulness, discernment and integrity. We'll now complete the third leg of the three-legged stool that is R^2 Behavior with a look at the meaning of integrity.

> Courage has consequences. It's at the heart of integrity.

Sustained With Integrity

The definition of integrity is a bit like beauty—it's in the eye of the beholder. It's a word loaded with ambiguous meaning, which is a bit surprising, because everyone knows what having integrity means. Right? Maybe not. When I've asked a group of 10 executives or 10 business students for their definition of integrity, I've gotten widely differing opinions. It seems we all talk about integrity, but we're not exactly sure what it is.

Here are some examples I've heard:

"Doing the right thing when no one is looking."
"Doing what you say you're going to do."
"Being who you are (the same person) in all situations."
"Knowing what's right and doing it every time."

The common thread running through these definitions is that they're all action oriented, containing the verbs "doing" and "being." So let's take a look at some formal definitions and see if we can add clarity.

The Merriam-Webster dictionary gives us three potential meanings:

1. Firm adherence to a code of especially moral or artistic values.
2. An unimpaired condition.
3. The quality or state of being complete or undivided.

These definitions are a start, but they're incomplete and need further enhancement. Wikipedia provides us with some additional clues: "Integrity is the quality of being honest and having strong moral principles; moral uprightness."

Vocabulary.com adds some additional depth: "Having integrity means doing the right thing in a reliable way. It's a personality trait that we admire, since it means a person has a moral compass that doesn't waver."

Finally, the thesaurus provides these synonyms: honesty, purity, sincerity, goodness, forthrightness, candor, rectitude and honorableness.

I don't know about you, but this still seems ambiguous. Let's try building something meaningful ourselves. The word integrity is derived from the Latin word integer, which means whole or complete. Being whole or complete implies internal consistency. But consistency with what? For that answer we look at the first selection Merriam-Webster provided, a code of values. Everyone has a code of values that governs their behavior. I may not like your code of values, but I must acknowledge its existence.

We combine internal consistency with a code of values, and we can say that integrity is consistently acting in harmony with a code of values. We could shorten this definition by saying that **integrity is having the courage of your convictions**.

Integrity is having the courage of your convictions.

Yes, I can see you frowning. You're thinking, *This definition could allow a criminal the claim of integrity.* Yes, you would be correct. Using this definition, a criminal could assert that he or she has integrity. However, our satisfaction with such an assertion revolves around the appropriateness of the code of values, which is reflected in the operation of our Internal Compass.

Most of us are uncomfortable with the amorphous condition we've just discussed. So, as a response, we complicate the idea of integrity to alleviate our discomfort, which has resulted in our wide range of opinions about the meaning of the word. Clearly, understanding not only the meaning of integrity but also letting it govern our lives is an essential mark of an ethically intelligent person.

James is a Senior Vice President of Operations for a Fortune 500 electronics manufacturer. He summarized his understanding of integrity as follows.

"Integrity is a rock solid agreement between words and actions. We say what we're going to do, and then we do it. In this organization, it's one of our core values. We hire and fire to it. You won't be here very long if you don't have integrity, and that includes your whole life. It's the way you deal with your marriage. It's the way you deal with your children. It's the way you deal with your friends. These are people who don't cheat on the golf course, which is a game of honor.

"I think it's important to go beyond the letter of the law. I think that people should feel great about how the company conducts itself, not because it hasn't had any infractions, but because employees really feel inspired by what they perceive to be higher order leadership, which I think is strongly based in integrity. So, on that basis and since I think that integrity is more than telling the truth and being fair, I think it's something that can be a cornerstone of a great culture."

---◆---

Chapter Highlights

- R^2 Behavior is timeless.

- R^2 Behavior has three components— truthfulness, discernment and integrity.

R^2 Behavior is timeless, and it has three parts— truthfulness, discernment and integrity.

- The Golden Rule is the same as R^2 Behavior to many people.

- We are hardwired to engage in R^2 Behavior. We have an instinctual desire to receive it, render it and live it.

- Truthfulness is telling or having the intention of telling the truth, which is defined as accurately and sincerely describing reality (including the context of that reality), as known by the person describing that reality.

- Lying steals someone's freedom.

- Aristotle and Augustine believed an ethically intelligent person possessed a finely tuned discernment that not only distinguished parts from wholes but also comprehended that the beauty of the whole is often more than the sum of its parts.

- Integrity is having the courage of your convictions.

- Courage has consequences. It's at the heart of integrity.

Questions for You

- Must leaders tell the truth? Why? Why not?

- Is telling "white" lies wrong?
- Is padding your budget lying? Why? Why not?
- Can you be right-thinking-right-acting and tell lies?
- Can a drug dealer have integrity?
- Can you not have integrity and engage in R^2 Behavior?

Endnotes

1. Bok, S., Lying: Moral Choice in Public and Private Life. 2nd ed. 1999, New York, NY: Vintage Books.
2. Bok, S., Secrets: On the Ethics of Concealment and Revelation. 1989, New York, NY: Vintage Books.

CHAPTER 6

◆

LEADING BY EXAMPLE— GREAT LEADERS ARE GREAT ACTORS

> I told him, I just cannot tolerate it [a senior executive hired a family member and allowed that family member privileges others were denied]. My chief of staff said, he's married, he's got three kids. I said I couldn't tolerate it. You wouldn't tolerate it from a third-party. . . There is no difference here. In fact, actually, if we don't act, we'll lose the respect of the people in our organization.
>
> *Fortune 100 CEO*

It's 8:20 in the evening. Frank just walked through the door, laid his briefcase on the bar and hung up his coat. It was a long, exhausting day at the office. His wife Millie was attending a church dinner. Just as he finished pouring himself a scotch, the front doorbell started ringing. Frank ran to the door, looked out and saw his oldest son standing on the front porch crying. Quickly opening the door, he asked,

"Chip! What's wrong? Why are you crying?"

"Jenny's left me," Chip said. "She emptied the house, and my kids are gone! She left me this note."

Frank grabbed the note from Chip and read it out loud,

"I've had enough! You can find someone else to intimidate, berate and ridicule. I'm not going to be your verbal punching bag anymore! And I hope that slut I saw you with gives you an incurable disease. You'll be hearing from my lawyer. And don't try to contact me because I'll get a restraining order!"

Frank gently said,

"Come on inside. Let me pour you a drink. Let's sit down and talk about this. Your Mom is not here, so you can tell me what happened."

"It's all your fault!" Chip yelled at his father.

Shocked, Frank asked, "What do you mean it's all my fault?"

Chip yelled again, but louder. "I did exactly what you taught me! Now my life is ruined."

Dumbfounded, Frank asked, "What do you mean 'I taught you?' We've never even talked about your marriage. I've never interfered in your life."

Chip yelled again, but this time in a more threatening way. "I treated Jenny just like I saw you treating Mom all these years. And don't think I didn't know about those affairs you had. I used to sneak out and follow you around just to see why you weren't at home at night. Now, because of you, my Jenny's gone forever."

Chip jumped off the couch, headed toward his dad and, with clenched fists, seemed ready to attack his father. At the last second, he headed for the door and said, "I don't ever want to see you again. Don't worry. Your secret affairs are safe with me. I wouldn't want to hurt Mom by letting her know what a miserable human being you are!"

As he stormed out of the house, Chip slammed the door, shattering one of its windows. Frank sat in stunned silence, overcome by guilt and despair. All he had ever wanted for his family was the best he could provide. Although he knew he had hurt Millie's feelings over the years, she never complained. So he never thought much about it.

Yes, he had strayed from his marriage during the early years. But that was a long time ago, and he had forgotten about it. Yet Chip claimed that Frank had taught him the behaviors that had destroyed his family. Frank couldn't remember a single time he ever spoke to his son about these matters. It was almost as if his life had been a movie with his son as a spectator. It was then that Frank realized he had been on stage his entire life.

My pastor says "more is caught than taught," meaning we emulate behavior. We are all teachers, but we don't use words. We teach with our actions. Psychologists tell us that children study our actions and don't miss a thing.

> We are all teachers, but we don't use words. We teach with our actions.

When my children were young, my oldest son would frequently come up to me and ask why I was doing one thing or another. Most of the time, I wasn't consciously aware of the action he was observing because it had become a habit to me. But it became clear to me that, as far as my children were concerned, I was always on stage. If you manage or lead, you are, too.

> If you manage or lead, you are always on stage.

Being on stage means people are watching your every move. Is what you're doing consistent with what you say? Are you kind and considerate in the checkout line? Do you lose your cool when the barista gets your order wrong? Are you checking your email on your smart phone during a staff meeting? If you're champion-ing a green initiative at your office, do you recycle at home?

You may think these are trivial questions and beside the point, but I could introduce you to C-Suite colleagues who have been embarrassed by these kinds of questions. Incidentally, that list would include me!

My pastor tells a story illustrating this principle. One of our church's teachings is honoring God by living a life of excellence. One cold, rainy and windy day, he'd just finished shopping at a lo-cal supermarket. As he left his cart at the cart corral, a large piece of paper trash blew out of the cart. As he tried to pick up the piece of paper, the wind kept blowing it further and further from his car. He said he thought for a moment, *I don't want to chase this piece of trash all over this parking lot. It's cold. It's raining. And this parking lot is practically empty. I'll just let it go. No one's watching anyway!*

But then, he said, *I heard this soft inner voice telling me you're a pastor of a church that teaches excellence. You have to be an ex-ample of excellence!* So, he continued chasing the piece of trash until he finally caught up with it, picked it up and headed for the trash can. Just then, he heard a voice from a nearby parked car.

> "Hi pastor! My wife and I have been sitting here watching you chase that piece of trash, and we were wondering whether you were going to pick it up."

As a manager or leader, you're always on stage. So let's see if you're ready.

Our "always on stage" discussion has four parts:

1. Leading by Example
2. Tone at the Top

3. Role Model Fatigue
4. We're All Leaders

Before we get started, let me give you a heads up. There are some stories in this chapter that you might consider self-serving or maybe even a bit "whiny." All I ask is that you try putting yourself into the shoes of these senior executives. Leadership is not easy, and leading by example is both challenging and misunderstood.

LEADING BY EXAMPLE

There's a commercial for an auto insurance company in which one person says, "You can save money on your auto insurance in just 15 minutes." In response, the other person says, "Everyone knows *that*!"

I often get the same result when I mention leading by example: "Everyone knows *that*."

When I hear that comment, I ask, "But do you really know what it means?" Here are some common responses.

"Do as I do, not as I say."

"Model the behavior you expect from others."

"Do what you expect us to do."

"Walk the talk."

"Follow the rules and don't deviate."

And, my favorite: "Don't ask us to do something you won't do."

As we found with the word "integrity," there's not a common understanding of this concept. It's such a trite phrase, we utter it almost as blithely as asking the question, "How are you today?"

Here are a couple of definitions from our executives.

Gwen said, "You've got to do the right thing. You have to embrace the culture of the company, which, for us, our values and vision are at the top. You have to always stay true to that. And you have to be able to lead by example."

Fred said, "I think everybody learns by example, a lot. A lot of time in business I've thought *What would this guy do,* or *What would that guy do*? For example, senior guys that I have seen in the past. What would that guy do here?"

Gwen's response is along the lines of, "How are you today?" She sprinkles it into the conversation as something that's expected. Fred, however, is onto something.

Leading by example has a package of meaning. All the answers in the previous paragraphs contain elements from that package. But, there's more to it. Leading by example means you're a philosopher, teacher and actor. We start with philosopher.

Philosopher. When I use the term "philosopher," I'm not talking about philosophers like Aristotle, Hume or Kierkegaard. I'm talking about having a philosophy of leadership, which is different from a leadership style. You must have a philosophy of leadership if you intend to lead by example.

My leadership philosophy is simple. People want to be led *somewhere*. Create a vision that is a place, a destination. Make sure everyone understands the destination by painting a clear picture of it, much like a travel brochure shows us a vacation spot. After everyone understands the destination, make sure they see themselves in that place and would be comfortable being there. Then, ask those who would be comfortable in the new destination to follow you there. Those who cannot see themselves or are not comfortable with the destination won't follow you there. They will self-select out of your organization, which is better sooner than later.

For instance, we had a client that had too many warehouses

across the country. We studied the situation and recommended significant changes to the configuration of warehouses. The recommendations included closing some warehouses and expanding others. The total number of people employed in the warehousing operation wouldn't change, but their locations would. Through his management team, the CEO used the leadership philosophy I just explained.

At each location slated for closure, the senior leader created a picture of the warehouse configuration after all the changes were made. They told everyone at each of those locations they would have the opportunity of relocating—at company expense—to the location of their choosing that required their skillset. No one was to be laid off. In many cases, the client flew the employee and their spouse to the new location so that they could check it out.

Over a period of time, those who couldn't see themselves in any of the reconfigured locations found new jobs and voluntarily left the organization. As it turned out, it was a win-win for everybody. The reconfiguration was successful, and no one was involuntarily terminated. Everyone was offered the possibility of following the leadership where they were taking the company.

Just as people want you to lead them somewhere, they also want you to *teach* them.

> People want you to lead them somewhere. They also want you to teach them.

Teacher. As we saw earlier, we teach not just with our words, but with our actions. In doing so, teachers add value. If I am a math teacher, I'm teaching you math skills. It's adding to your overall skillset. If I am an accounting teacher, I'm teaching you accounting skills. It's adding to your overall skillset. If I am your leader or manager, and I arrive for work every day on time and dressed appropriately, I'm teaching you about work ethic and dressing for success. All of this teaching is adding value to you not only as a professional but also as an individual.

As a manager or leader, you teach from the strength of your core values, which, hopefully, correspond with your organizational values. If what you do flows naturally from your core values, people will see you as authentic and genuine. This perception of authenticity and genuineness adds value to those you manage or lead because you are teaching them to do the same.

Authenticity and genuineness in a manager or leader are essential for earning trust and respect. This teaching is a two-way street. In order to earn trust and respect, we must give trust and respect. If you give people what they need, they'll reciprocate. Let me show you this idea in action.

I once taught an undergraduate course in personal finance. It was the third or fourth course new students took as part of the introductory curriculum. The students in my classroom were a mix of working adults, many of whom had not graduated from high school but held GEDs. Most of them came from distressed social economic backgrounds and families where education was not particularly valued—in some cases, it was scorned. In one of those classes I met Clara. I'll never forget her. She had stunning long red hair, which was unkempt the first time I met her.

At the beginning of the course, she sat in the very back of the classroom, slouching in her chair. When she walked, she was hunched over. She looked like life had beaten her up and down. Despite her appearance, Clara was bright. She studied, knew the material and actively participated in the class. When we had a group project, she always became the group leader. In every class, I would encourage her to continue doing well and told her I believed in her. In one of our conversations, she told me how hard it was for her because her family thought she was wasting her time. They told her that their family had never been college material, and she was just kidding herself thinking she was different.

As time went by, I could see her slowly changing. She started wearing better clothes. She began styling her hair and wearing makeup. She moved up to a seat in the middle of the classroom. She stopped slouching in her chair. And when she walked, you could see a difference in her personal carriage. I continued talking to her after class, encouraging her to stay the course, pursuing excellence at all times. As respectfully as possible, I urged her to disregard the negative comments from her family because I could see college success written all over her. Clara continued to excel, and she finished the class with an A grade.

On the last night of class, Clara came up to me and said, "I want to thank you for all you taught me in this class. And I'm just not just talking about the book stuff. That was good, but the other was better. Every night you came in here dressed like a businessman should, in a nice pressed suit, clean white shirt and a nice tie, and those shiny shoes. I still can't get over the fact that someone keeps their shoes looking that good. You inspired me to see myself as a businesswoman. I can't afford the kinds of clothes you wear yet, but I will someday. Because of this class, I know I can do this."

About six months later, I ran into Clara before classes started. I almost didn't recognize her. She looked professional. She walked up to me with a big smile on her face and said, "I've got a new entry-level professional job, a new car and I moved out of my parents' house. They're still telling me that I'm wasting my time, but I don't believe them anymore. Again, thank you so much for what you gave me."

Adding value to every person you manage or lead is what a leader does. You do that through living your core values. Live your values passionately, and you're teaching them to others and simultaneously adding value to them.

Actor. As managers and leaders, we're always on stage. An actor rarely appears on stage without the appropriate costume and makeup. Regardless of what's going on in other parts of your life, you act the leadership role you're blessed to have. If you're young and inexperienced, you just have to fake it until you make it. Dr. Martin Luther King, Jr., learned this truth early in his career, when he was just 27 years of age.

> Regardless of what's going on in other parts of your life, you act the leadership role you're blessed to have.

When he completed his doctorate, King and his wife Coretta debated about moving back to the South. He had grown up in a privileged and protected environment. His parents had shielded him from rampant racism and had provided him with an excellent education. In the end, he and his family were living in Montgomery, Alabama, in early 1956, coincident with Rosa Parks' refusal to give up her seat on a Montgomery bus. Shortly after Parks' bus moment, black residents of Montgomery formed the Montgomery Improvement Association (MIA) and launched the famous bus boycott.

Although King wanted no part of leadership, he was thrust into becoming leader of the MIA. He resigned his leadership post several times, and each time his resignation letter was unanimously rejected. With the notoriety of being the face of the boycott came increasingly hostile acts towards King and his young family, including drive-by shootings at his house on numerous occasions and constant death threats. Despite his confident public persona, King was scared, afraid for his family and ready to run.

One night he came home late from an MIA meeting. His wife and children had already gone to bed. He quietly undressed and got into bed but couldn't sleep. He got up and made a pot of coffee. He thought about how much easier his life would be somewhere else. The phone rang, and he quickly answered it so that it wouldn't wake his sleeping family. It was around midnight. The caller said, "Nigger, we are tired of you and your mess now. And if you aren't out of this town in three days, we're going to blow your brains out, and blow up your house."[1]

This call came just three days after King found bullet holes in his daughter's bedroom window. As he sat there staring into that black cup of coffee, King didn't think he could continue putting his family in that kind of danger. His youngest daughter was just a baby. He was scared of being shot or lynched. He hadn't sought this and didn't want it. King didn't think it was his fight, and he just wanted to run away to somewhere safe where the air wasn't filled with hatred and hostility.

After he had decided to give up, King said he heard a soft voice urging him not to, and assuring him that he would have Divine protection. King said he felt comforted, a strange calm descended upon him, and he went to bed. The boycott lasted another several months, and it ended in success. During the entire period, no one suspected the depth of the turmoil embroiling his life behind the scenes. King continued leading and giving impassioned public speeches and exhortations to those participating in the sit-ins and the boycotts. King masterfully acted the leadership role into which he had been thrust. Great leaders are great actors.

> Leading by example is a package of skillsets, including philosopher, teacher and actor.

Leading by example is a package of skillsets, including philosopher, teacher and actor. The people you manage or lead want to be led *somewhere*. They want you to *add value* to them by teaching them. Every day, every manager and every leader must effectively *play the role* they've assumed even though, internally, they may not feel fit to lead.

We now turn our attention to a different form of acting—modeling tone at the top.

TONE AT THE TOP

Tone at the top is a recent entry into the leadership lexicon. Leading by example focuses attention on the individual manager or leader. But tone at the top focuses attention on an organization's entire senior leadership team. Specifically, we say that tone at the top encompasses the behavior of the entire C-Suite, including members of the board of directors.

We expect this group to set the behavioral standards for the entire organization. Setting the proper tone is much more difficult to achieve and control because this group often includes dozens of individuals, many of whom are not employees and have their own separate public persona.

So what is tone? We've all heard someone mention an individual's "tone of voice," as in, "Her tone of voice was very soothing to her patients." Or, "The CEO entered the room and spoke to the board in a threatening tone of voice." Or, "Standard Poodles are very sensitive to your tone of voice." It's all about the content of the personality of something—in this case, an organization.

Here's what some of our senior business leaders had to say about tone at the top.

> "I think we set the tone at the top by asking the questions, 'Is our core culture working? Are we really meeting our core values every day?' And if not, what are we going to do about it?"

"Leading by example is much more effective than promulgating ethics codes and rulebooks. If the leadership team doesn't set the right tone by living an ethical life in accord with personal and organizational values, followers won't either."

"I think some people, when they are in charge, they kind of believe they're not on stage every day, and they're not accountable. I think you're more accountable. Because everything you do is reviewable. It's seeable. It sets the tone of the company."

There is another word for tone. That word is culture. It, too, is established at the top of the organization. Here's a story illustrating how Bill, a Fortune 500 COO, works to establish the tone at the top of his organization.

"My son works from a home office. So, when I'm out for business lunches or dinners that I am going to expense on my expense account, I'll often text him and ask if he wants me to bring food home. It doesn't make any difference who I'm with, I always tell the waiter or waitress, I want a separate bill for his food. It would be very easy for me to put it on the same receipt with a business lunch or dinner. But I never do that. I don't do it for a couple of reasons. Number one, I'm with somebody who is observing me—and probably most of the time they wouldn't even care—but it matters to me. Its leading by example. The second one is, I've got to get up every morning and look in the mirror and feel good about what I see."

The tone at the top of an organization is set by the leadership team, including the Board of Directors. It isn't accomplished by grand proclamations, ethics codes and policies and procedures. It's accomplished every hour and every day by the actions of every manager and leader in the organization beginning with the chairman of the board.

Managers and leaders are always on stage. For many, it becomes a significant burden, knowing that everything you do and every word you say is potentially influencing someone, is subject to misinterpretation and always reflects on your organization. And you don't want to be the manager or leader who creates the wrong impression for someone who considers you a role model.

ROLE MODEL FATIGUE

Most organizations take role modeling very seriously, especially when it involves senior managers and leaders. Early in my career, I had the opportunity to join the elite corporate finance staff of the Ford Motor Company at World Headquarters in Dearborn, Michigan. Working in the "glasshouse" was considered a great honor and achievement. Even though I was three or four levels down on the organizational chart, I was invited to the CFO's office on my first day for an introduction and a chat—a kind of high-level orientation.

It was a rather heady experience walking past the office of Henry Ford, II, who was CEO at the time, on my way to the CFO's office. I walked into the CFO's office, and I couldn't believe how large and sumptuous it was. It was so well outfitted—including a full bath with a shower—you could have comfortably lived there. After exchanging some pleasantries, the CFO laid out expectations for someone at my level in the organization. Prior to that meeting, I didn't realize how "high" in the organization I was.

First, it was important where I lived and in what type of structure. Apartments were definitely out, but well-appointed houses were in, especially one with central air conditioning (central air conditioning in Detroit at that time was unusual). Fortunately for me, I was living in a modest brick bungalow situated in an acceptable neighborhood on the east side of Detroit, not far from where the CFO lived. Except he lived in a luxurious gated community.

Second, we were expected to drive a late model Ford automobile. That was a problem because I was driving a 600 horsepower hemi Chrysler product. Those were the heady days of Mopar. (Gee, I hated to get rid of that car!) Third, we were expected to wear well-tailored business suits with white shirts and ties. In our off hours (which turned out to be fewer than anticipated) we were expected to be well groomed and dressed at all times. We were expected to enhance the Ford image.

When we worked on summer Sundays—a fairly frequent event—our families came, and we had a picnic on the front lawn. Although the company provided lunch and it was quite enjoyable, I always believed it was an opportunity for senior leadership to inspect our families. Oh, I forgot to mention, your family was expected to be well-dressed and behaved.

No, this is not fiction. And I can tell you without reservation that, although the overt promulgation and enforcement of this kind of personal behavior code may no longer exist, it's still expected.

Yes, I know about Google, Facebook, and other high-tech firms and how their employees and even senior members of management dress and look. Don't let outer appearances fool you. Every one of those organizations has expectations for personal behavior, especially among senior management and leadership. Don't believe me? Let's look at a couple recent examples.

In April 2015, Mozilla's CEO Brendan Eich voluntarily resigned because he'd made a 2008 contribution to a group promoting traditional marriage in California. Although Mozilla's board issued a public statement insisting they had nothing to do with Eich's resignation, I believe otherwise. Supporting traditional marriage, especially in California and within the high-tech community, is a politically incorrect position. Eich took a publicly contrary position and paid for it with his job. This may not be as quaint a standard as the type of car you drive or how well behaved your children are, but it's an expectation. Remember, a rose by any other name is still...

During the late summer of 2010, Hewlett-Packard's CEO Mark Hurd resigned due to alleged sexual misconduct with a subordinate, a resignation that wouldn't have happened 30 years ago. Hewlett-Packard later said he was fired. Although the allegations were never proven, Hurd was nonetheless stigmatized. He was uninvited from several speaking engagements and conference appearances, and some of the CEOs I interviewed during that period inferred that Hurd wouldn't be welcomed at any of their corporate functions.

Then we have other less publicized examples. All during his career, the Reverend Billy Graham had a reported personal conduct rule that said he would never allow himself to be alone with a woman who was not his wife. I, and many of my C-Suite colleagues, maintain a similar standard. Why? We don't want to give even the appearance of impropriety. Why invite trouble? Even the most innocent and innocuous scenario can lead to misperceptions that can place you in the precarious position of having to prove yourself "not guilty." We are role models, and we must act the part.

The point is that managers and leaders are still held to behavioral standards in their professional *and* personal lives. Even though a recent president tried to establish a dichotomy, there is no difference between your professional and personal life—there is only your life. Today's

The point is that managers and leaders are still held to behavioral standards in their professional *and* personal lives.

standards may be entirely different, but they still exist. And you must adhere to them or be prepared for the consequences, which is especially true today with cameras everywhere feeding ubiquitous social media sites. Senior managers and leaders are always on stage. It's inescapable. But, over time, most of us become weary.

Until I did the research for this book, I thought my personal experiences were unique. I got tired of always being on guard, always looking over my shoulder, hoping that I wasn't setting a bad example. After conducting the interviews for this book, I realized I wasn't alone. Role Model Fatigue is real. It comes with the job. But it can exact a serious toll on your health and relationships, especially family.

Some people may think, "*Cry me a river! With the kind of money you guys make, just get over it.*" Remember, we're not judging here. We're reporting the way it is. But it doesn't apply to just the C-Suite.

I once worked for a very capable woman executive who was not a member of the C-Suite at the time. She occasionally complained about always being in the spotlight. She said she would never leave her house without fixing her hair, applying makeup and donning the appropriate apparel, even if she was just running errands.

Early in my career, when I was still drinking adult beverages, I attended a professional football game with some colleagues. We enjoyed the game and imbibed far too many of those beverages. As we were leaving the stadium, still having a great time and walking with an unsteady gait, I ran into one of my direct reports. I felt embarrassed when he said, "Wow, boss! I would never have expected you to get it on like this!" Ouch!

Here are a couple more revealing stories.

Ross was a former CEO of a Fortune 300 organization. He reported the following:

> "I used to feel great pressure. We worshiped at a church that was fairly casual and fundamental, and as I would participate in the church service, I was always mindful I was CEO of the company and there were probably 20 other people in the congregation that worked at the company and were looking at me. Within that environment, you always have this kind of stiff upper lip of invulnerability, if you will. That is tremendous pressure. You feel like everyone that sees you needs to see that you are all work and no play. Everybody needs to see that you are always willing to do the extra thing. Everybody needs to see that you're in control, you're confident in everything else, and that facade takes its toll. It was absolutely terrible."

Here is another story from Ray, the COO of a Fortune 1000 organization. He was in charge of procurement for the entire organization. This story also shows how role modeling standards have changed, but are still the same.

> "It was on my 50th birthday. When I was in New York, seven vendors of mine knew I was a huge Giants fan. They wanted to pay for a trip to the training camp for the Giants. I thought that

was ... wow! They all showed up with a cake, and they read the card that said 'We're sending you to Giants' Camp.' Talk about one of the nicest days in your life. You've got people who want to do that for you. And, then I realized—wait a minute! These are vendors of mine, and they're sending me somewhere.

"It's kind of a joke about the little devil on your shoulder. And on the other shoulder is the angel. You can't tell me they're not talking to you ... 'If you do this, I think you're crossing a line.' And the other one is going, 'Oh, don't worry about it, no, no, no.' I believe it happens to everybody. Some just don't listen to the angel telling them, 'I wouldn't do that.'

"It was a pretty miserable situation. So I went to see my CEO. I explained the situation, and his comment was, 'Thanks for telling me. I appreciate you coming to me. I think you're pretty tough on these guys. I know these suppliers are very good. They've been loyal to the company. They've been around with us for a long time. I know you're tough on them even though they've been with us for a while. So I don't see anything wrong with this.' I've got to tell you I don't think I would do that now. So, here it is 20 years later, and I probably would say, 'I can't go.'"

Managers and leaders are always on stage. So, the question is, if you don't like the heat, should you go into the kitchen?"

We're All Leaders

For some of us, managing or leading were not conscious choices. Like Martin Luther King, Jr., we were thrust into management or leadership by circumstances. At one time, business organizations in the United States were structured so that if you wanted to advance your career, it inevitably meant moving into management and/or leadership. That has changed in many organizations where there are now technical or competency ladders of success in addition to management and leadership ladders of success. We now have a choice. Or, do we?

Almost all aspects of daily life require leadership skills from us. First, you're the leader of you, your life. You're the author of its content, commitment and consequence. That is an important task requiring leadership skills.

Second, you're the leader of your family or household. Those who depend on you look to you for leadership.

Third, in your business or profession, you're a leader. You may be a project leader, department leader or subject matter expert leader. Everyone leads something or someone. The question is, are you willing to make the commitment?

Do you have a philosophy of management or leadership? Can you teach from the strength of your core values and add value to others' lives. Can you act? Or, perhaps the question should be, are you willing to learn how to act? I'm not going to ask if you're willing to be on stage, because, if you're leading, that's a given.

Leading is more than adopting a popular leadership style. I'm more interested in your leadership substance, and so are your followers. We'll spend a lot more time on this subject in Section Three as we create our Roadmap to leading an ethically intelligent organization and personal life.

———————◆———————

Chapter Highlights

- Managers and leaders are always on stage.
- Great managers and leaders are great actors.
- People want you to lead them somewhere.

- Managers and leaders are teachers.
- You lead and teach others by adding value to them.
- As a manager or leader, you teach from the strength of your core values.
- Encouragement is the Rosetta Stone of adding value.
- Tone at the top is another way of describing culture.
- Most organizations take role modeling very seriously. You should too.
- Your leadership style is of lesser importance than your leadership substance.

Questions for You

- Can you separate your personal from your professional life?
- Have you ever been caught doing something you shouldn't have? How did you feel about letting down those who were learning from you?
- Would you follow a leader not knowing where the leader was taking you?
- Does your manager or leader add value to you?
- Do you add value to your spouse and children?
- Do you ever tire of being a role model?
- Are you more influenced by your peers or your manager/leader?
- Make a list of the important lessons you've learned from your managers or leaders. Did you learn these lessons by observing actions or listening to dialogue?

Endnotes

1. Garrow, D.J., Martin Luther King, Jr. and the Cross of Leadership. Peace & Change, 1987. 12(1/2).

CHAPTER 7

CULTURE—A FORCE FIERCE AS FIRE

You control ethical behavior with culture.
Culture is everything.

Fortune 1000 CEO

It's early on a summer morning, and a semi-retired chief executive is sitting on his back deck enjoying a freshly made cup of Kenyan coffee. His yard guy is manicuring a wondrous garden-like back yard. The birds are singing, and the mountain peaks in the distance are lit up by the sun. Sam, who holds a doctorate in engineering, is talking about the importance of organizational culture in controlling ethical behavior. He's finally put down his iPhone, to which he's been glued. And to illustrate his point, he relates a story of a young straight-arrow West Point graduate, hired to work a trading desk.

The story unfolded when, earlier in his career, Sam was running a high-pressure, high-stakes financial instrument hedge fund. Sam was a quantitative guy, a "quant," competing in a cutthroat take-no-prisoners industry where a trading desk could make or lose millions in a matter of hours. So whatever "edge" a trader could establish translated into extraordinarily high returns. Everyone pursued any "edge" available. Sam worked hard to keep his firm legal and ethical within that high-pressure milieu, but the anything-goes industry culture made it a constant challenge. He began his story:

"We hired a 38-year old guy as a trader for our bond desk. We always told people when we hired them, don't bring your Rolodex. We don't want you to bring any information. If there is any doubt, don't use any knowledge that might be proprietary to your former job. Secondly, we encouraged people when they joined us to make sure they had done whatever they had to do—including we'd give them time off to go back—to close out tasks and projects so that they had left their previous employer on a good note wherever possible.

"After [the new trading guy] had been there a couple of weeks, he stopped in my office one Friday afternoon and told me he was not going to be in on Monday because he had to take care of some business for his previous employer. I said, 'Okay. When will you be back?' He said, 'I'm not sure. I'm being indicted by the grand jury on Monday.' So I said, 'Well, maybe we ought to talk about this.'"

At this point, I asked Sam what he was thinking as this young man's story was unfolding. Taking a sip of coffee, Sam thought for a moment. Then he said, "My heart was greatly saddened. The industry and that band of crooks he worked for ruined his life." With a more solemn face, Sam continued his story.

"So my CFO and I sat and talked to this young man. The CFO asked him what happened. The young man said, 'We never gave kickbacks. What would happen is we would bid on a deal, and if we won the bid, we would return a small portion of our profits as a thank you to the guy on the other side of the deal for doing business with us. Because, in that business, it was all word of mouth and there was no advertising, we would just share the advertising dollars we would have otherwise spent. It was never quid pro quo. It was never you give us the deal, and we give you the dollars. It was just—if we were awarded the deal, a small portion of our profits on that deal would go back to the other counterparty rep.'

"So our CFO, being more astute about this than I was, asked, 'How big were these numbers? What kind of dollars are we talking about?' This 38-year-old young man said, 'It would never be over *$200,000 a month*.' Now, remember, this was a Boy Scout, a graduate of West Point, a commander, a strong Christian with a strong ethical foundation—but he was sitting in an organizational culture where the company had created these myths and its rationale for doing things.

"He had been immersed in it, and he had just sort of bought into the party line and never really thought about it. He was sincere in our meeting. He was just as sincere as it is possible for a human being to be—he believed that there was nothing wrong with this, even though a typical counterparty rep would have earned about $400,000 per year. He was convinced it was not a quid pro quo."

HIDDEN HAND OF CULTURE

The young trader in Sam's story had lost his connection to the realities of the outside world because of the toxic cultural pool in which he swam every day. I imagine that young trader walked through the door of his former employer with his West Point values intact—honor, integrity, truthfulness and service. But unbeknownst to him, his subconscious mind was absorbing the hidden corrupting particles of the organization's culture. He was like a fish swimming in polluted water.

The philosopher and economist Adam Smith gave us the idea of the "invisible hand" of economics: pursuing your own self-interest serves the greater good of the economy and society. In the case of the hidden hand of culture, the greater good is served when there is a healthy and righteous culture. The opposite case is also possible, as we see in the story of the young trader. He marinated every day in an organizational cultural stew in which an obvious case of bribery became something virtuous and "just the way we do things around here." Culture will change you or you can change it, and you'd better know the difference.

> Culture will change you or you can change it, and you'd better know the difference.

Knowing the difference, however, is not easy. We can objectively evaluate the young trader's story, mystified at how he missed it, because we have perspective. We have objective benchmarks that inform our judgment. But when you're sitting in a distorted environment day after day, that setting steals your perspective. You begin to see the world not as those outside the situation would see it, but only from the distorted point of view from within. We often want to believe that what we feel in our gut is not real. We want something so badly we override the flashing red lights, the alarm bells and the knot in our gut. This is exactly what happened in our next story.

The CEO who related this story began his career in finance. Tom earned his MBA from a prestigious school and passed the CPA exam right after graduating. He was on the fast track to success, moving up rapidly in his career. Tom became CFO of a publicly traded company before the age of 30. He prided himself on his ability to read people and situations, but he succumbed to the kind of cultural seduction that happens to all of us.

"Early in my career, there was an international organization that I really wanted to work for. It had a stellar reputation and hired only the best and brightest. The recruiting process was very selective, arduous and included a daylong assessment with a psychiatrist. The company was growing rapidly, and landing a job there often meant receiving valuable stock options.

"I was thrilled to get an offer and to begin working there. After a couple of months on the job, however, I realized, from the inside, the company looked more like a criminal cartel than a business. We lied to everyone—and

> "From the inside, the company looked more like a criminal cartel than a business. We lied to everyone—and we were proud of it."

we were proud of it. There were highly valued stories of how we had fooled the auditors time and time again. I remember one story in particular that still stands out in my mind. We'd signed a deal to construct a factory in a foreign country. Unfortunately, the ship containing all of the equipment for the factory sank in a bad storm. Instead of writing off the investment, we kept it on the books and lied to the auditors whenever they questioned the investment's value.

"There was a legendary story of how we flew a team of auditors to the site of the factory in a helicopter. Of course, the site was overgrown with the tall grass and vegetation of the kind you would expect in a jungle. Our team had given the auditors waist-high boots and machetes, suggesting that we could land in a clearing and let them hike to the factory that was nestled in some trees, which is why it couldn't be seen from the air. Our team mentioned to the auditors that the place was infested with poisonous snakes and several other types of threatening wildlife. After thinking it over, the auditors decided that a close-up look was unnecessary."

This story seemed so incredible to me, I interrupted Tom with a question. I asked him how in the world a Big Eight (now Big Four) CPA firm could be so easily duped. He said, "They wanted our business. We were an up-and-coming client, and in the grand scheme of things, that one transaction wasn't a big deal."

Tom continued, "There were many other 'stories' that were a part of this company's culture. All of these stories were touted as highly successful episodes of deceit, and these very smart and highly accomplished professionals saw nothing unusual about this. One day, I went home and my wife mentioned to me how working for this company was changing me. She said, 'When you first started telling me these stories from work, they made you uncomfortable. Now you seem unconcerned and accepting even though what the company is doing hasn't changed. I don't like the changes I'm seeing in you.'

> One day, I went home and my wife mentioned to me how working for this company was changing me.

"That's when I knew I had to leave. It was a hard decision to make because I had only been there six months, and that's not something you want on your resume, especially with the excellent reputation this company had. It took a while, but I found a better job. Within a year, my previous employer had filed bankruptcy and was in the midst of an SEC investigation. Eventually, several of the executives went to prison, and the people who still worked there had their personal and professional reputations tarnished forever."

Like our young trader, this CEO had allowed the culture to seep into his subconscious without noticing it. He had slowly acclimated to an organizational culture that at first seemed incompatible with what he knew was right. This can happen to anyone. We enter into a situation thinking we know what is right, but over time, we are swayed by peer influence, especially if we believe those peers are smart, well-educated, know more than we do and are on the fast track to success.

This also is especially true if it's something we really want. Our emotions subtly kick in, and we rationalize. We make excuses. We override our instincts. Over time, our denial dulls our instincts, and what we once knew was unacceptable slowly becomes just the way things are. Fortunately for Tom, he had someone from outside the organization's culture—his wife—holding him accountable to an external reality.

If organizational culture has such hidden, seductive and effective powers, how do we define it?

CULTURAL GESTALT

The power and influence of organizational culture on behavior can't be overstated. Organizational culture is a force as fierce as fire. A controlled fire is a force of creation. It can conquer, calm and create. An uncontrolled fire is a force of destruction. It can damage, disrupt and destroy. Organizational culture is an all-consuming force. When controlled, it will create an environment within which ethical conduct and R^2 Behavior flourish. When neglected and uncontrolled, it will create an environment within which the survival of the fittest devours all within its path, including the C-Suite and board of directors.

I use the term cultural gestalt because culture is more than

simply the sum of its parts. Organizational culture is multiplication, not addition.
It's a set of values, stated and otherwise.
It's a collection of myths. Organizational
culture is a mystique created by a founder, a set of traditions people hold dear. It's
a dress code one dare not violate, it reflects the CEO's behavior,
it's a force that gets into our collective unconscious. Organizational culture controls you without you even noticing.

> Culture is more than simply the sum of its parts. Culture is multi-plication, not addition.

Many years ago, I was privileged to be part of the Price Waterhouse accounting and consulting organization, now PricewaterhouseCoopers (PwC). At the time I was there, PwC had a company
dress code that was strictly enforced. Men wore dark suits, white
shirts and subdued ties. Women wore dresses or professional pantsuits, a modicum of makeup and very little jewelry. Even
though that was decades ago, that dress code has stuck with me.

Recently I attended a business meeting
wearing my dark suit, white shirt and
subdued tie. Other attendees, who were
dressed more casually, chided me for "ru-
ining" the dress code. My retort was, "I
can't help it. I was raised at PwC."

> The men at Price Wa-terhouse wore starched underwear, but the men at Lybrand Coopers wore no underwear at all.

Organizational culture controls you
without you noticing, even decades later. When Price Waterhouse
and Lybrand Coopers were merging, there was much talk about
the clashing cultures. The standing joke at that time was that the
men at Price Waterhouse wore starched underwear, but the men
at Lybrand Coopers wore no underwear at all.

Because the CEOs of both firms understood the hidden hand
of culture, they spent years successfully merging the two dissimilar cultures. These two CEOs instinctively knew that organiza-

tional cultural gestalt was more than the sum of its parts. They also knew you have to pay attention to the parts because they can either help or hinder your drive to create the organizational culture you want. So let's examine four of the most commonly cited elements of culture: values, myths, artifacts and tradition.

Values. Values are ephemeral things. They have no physical being, but we see their manifestation in the things people and organizations do. I discuss values and principles throughout this book because they loomed large in the stories I heard from C-Suite executives. In this instance, we are talking about organizational values as opposed to personal values. And make no mistake, these two sets of values are different and not always aligned.

Many organizational cultures have split personalities between their stated values and the values that actually prevail within the culture. This creates a condition I call *cultural hypocrisy*. It's a lot more prevalent than most C-Suite executives might care to acknowledge. We've all seen organizational values statements prominently featured on posters, computer screensavers and internal corporate bling such as coffee mugs. Typically, such statements might say:

- *We value integrity.*
- *We value fair dealing.*
- *We value truthfulness.*
- *We value respect.*
- *We value accountability.*
- *We value hard work.*

When these values statements are aligned with actions taken by all members of an organization, we say the culture is healthy and R^2. A COO of a Fortune 300 company described it this way:

"In this company, if you're not highly ethical—and I would add to a great extent moral—you're not going to move up in the company. One of the things we say is, 'We hire and fire to our core values.' I can think of several situations where we let people go who were good performers, very strong performers, because they missed it from an ethical standpoint. You can't work here if you don't live by our number one core value—doing the right thing every single time regardless of what you believe are the consequences."

The question is, can personal values be at variance with organizational values? Does it matter how one of your team members treats their spouse or children? Is it important that your CFO cheats a little bit every time she plays golf? In Chapter 11, we'll talk about this issue in greater depth, and I will introduce a tool—Heart-Mind Maps—to disclose personal and organizational value misalignments. This next story emphasizes the importance of that misalignment.

I was gratified to be sitting in Gwen's expansive 40th-floor office overlooking the skyline of one of the world's largest cities. She earned an engineering degree when most women didn't pursue such an education. Gwen began her career on the bottom rung of the ladder wearing a hard hat, boots and coveralls. She had more than a passing familiarity with dirt, debris and danger. Gwen fought her way to success in a world once solely dominated by men. Now she is a Fortune 400 Chief Administrative Officer. Given her educational background and practical mindset, there's little gray in her understanding of values and the difference between right and wrong. She described the importance of values in her organization, as follows.

"You've got to do the right thing. You have to lead by example. You have to embrace the culture of the company, which for us, our values and vision are at the top. You have to always stay true to that. And if you don't have it from the top... so you see that poster over there [points to a poster containing company values]...I've been in different leadership situations through my whole career when sometimes it was a poster. And sometimes it was really, really pushed as being a foundation. And not that the people that had it more as a poster didn't believe it, they may have. But you can't just put it on a poster.

"A guide that we use is, if you are thinking about a decision and you question that decision, think about it in perspective of if it would be on the front page of the Wall Street Journal...and you were reading about the decision you made, how would you feel seeing that? How would you feel with your family reading about that decision that you made? And, if you are the least bit uncomfortable, you are probably making the wrong decision. So, that's how we continue to reinforce it [pointing to the poster on the wall]."

Gwen went on to describe something unique within their organizational culture:

"I think every once in a while, you have people making bad decisions because they are worried about what might happen if they made a mistake and they're trying to cover it up. But, again, lying, cheating...it's not the right thing to do. Hopefully, we have a nice balance. Like for us, we use mistakes, if there wasn't any bad intent, as a learning opportunity. That's part of our culture. I think it all works, but

I think leaders need to be mindful of the fact that they can't pressure people to not make mistakes. And encourage them to learn from it because if people are worried about losing their livelihood because they made a mistake...maybe they'll lie or try to cover something up."

If we closely examine Gwen's last paragraph, we see a value that's not listed on the organization's values statement. Her organization allows people to learn from their mistakes. Although this value doesn't appear on any "official" organizational literature, it's well understood within the culture. The important takeaway here is that values statements are good, but values behavior—R^2 Behaviors—are better and have a much more profound effect on organizational culture. Why?

> Values statements are good, but values behaviors—R^2 Behaviors—are better and have a much more profound effect on organizational culture.

The answer is simple—actions speak louder than words. Living your values is more important and effective than listing and talking about them. And more important still, we get more of what we reward. If we want our organizational culture to reflect our values, we must reward values behaviors that are consistent with our values statements. When we don't, we get cultural hypocrisy.

Myths. Organizational mythology is another element of organizational culture, and often it's the product of values behavior as opposed to values posters.

The dictionary tells us that a myth is a traditional or legendary story—with or without basis in fact—usually of a heroic or notable deed. All organizational cultures have myths. Some are true, some are true but highly embellished, others are completely false but conveniently fit into a preferred narrative.

Whether true or not, myths are a powerful foundation upon which organizational cultures are built. The young bond trader we met in Sam's story acted upon his organization's cultural myth: We don't advertise. Therefore, we share a "small" portion of our profits with those individuals who give us business—and it's never been considered a bribe!

Here are two real examples of "myth" creation.

This first story was related to me by Gordon, an up-and-coming youngish CEO running a Fortune 500 international pharmaceutical company. Confidential and proprietary information in that industry is the lifeblood of competitors' market positions. This is especially true of new drug development pipelines. One day, a treasure trove of competitive information about a major competitor made its way into Gordon's organization. What he did is the sort of thing from which myths are born.

"We recently received an email containing some very highly confidential information by mistake. When it came to light, I made sure few people saw it, other than those who had already seen it. Then we sent it back. Organizationally ... it shocked a lot of people. Many of our research folks really wanted to see that information. It got out pretty quick that we had it. It was information about a competitor, and we were able to keep it contained. No copies were made, and it was sent back with the appropriate level of disclaimer. Some people might call that stupid, but I called it the right thing to do.

"So, I just think it's hard to pinpoint ... that golden moment when you have to make a critical decision ... like the confidential information. It would have been nice to be able to read through that stuff, but the reality was, if the employees saw me doing that, then how could I ever argue that it wasn't the right thing to do? If I would've done the wrong thing, I'm sure the next time something similar happened, I wouldn't have seen it. It made me feel like we have the right values as an organization."

This organization has thousands of employees. The story will be remembered and repeated. Over time, the details of the story will change, be embellished and take on a much more heroic tone. But the essential message of the myth—that we do the right thing here even when the wrong thing would have been to our advantage—will remain intact.

The second story, related to me by Randy, a Fortune 500 COO, may also be a heroic tale, but it has a different ending. It also created a myth with very different overtones—well, I'll let you decide. This story took place early in Randy's career, when he and several other members of the company's leadership team accompanied the CEO on a trip to Africa in an effort to close an elusive but crucial deal with a particular tribal chief.

"Early in my career ... I was probably in my early thirties and just married... our entire leadership team and our CEO went to Africa to close the largest and most important deal our company had ever proposed. We were trying to get exclusive mineral rights and a contract to build a major refinery. We had been negotiating with this particular tribal chief or warlord, with sketchy results. Our people on the ground told our CEO the only way we could close the deal is if he personally came and dealt directly with this chief.

"The CEO insisted that all of us accompany him—must've been eight or nine of us—as a show of respect and honor. We got there and spent four days in hard negotiations and finally agreed on a contract. As a sign of his gratitude, the chief threw this sumptuous party and celebration the last night we were there. It was quite an event. The chief pulled out all the stops. The event was held on the shores of this beautiful lake with flowing white sand. We had big bonfires, all kinds of food, unlimited adult beverages and native dancing girls.

"After everyone had eaten, carried on and participated in many toasts, some of the chief's men erected a tent a ways down the beach. The chief brought out a—shall we say 'attractive,' if you know what I mean—young woman and introduced her to our CEO as one of his most prized wives. The chief stopped the music and very publicly presented the woman to our CEO as a show of friendship and great respect for our new venture together. The chief explained that it was a tradition with his people on such occasions for chiefs to exchange valuable gifts, at which time he sent the young woman off to the tent to spend the night with our CEO."

At this point in the story, we were both laughing so hard, we took a short breather. I asked Randy if this "gift" was unexpected, or if anyone had even thought about the local culture before the celebration. He said he didn't know, but for the rest of his career, he made sure someone did! He continued.

"Our CEO began feverishly explaining to the chief that he was unable to partake of such a wonderful gift for 'manly' reasons related to a 'war' injury. But he did offer one of us in his stead. Suddenly, we're looking at each another like deer in the headlights. We were speechless. It was kind of like watching your career pass before your eyes in slow motion. We knew someone was going to have to step forward. There were only two guys on our team who weren't married—Jerry and Nelson. After what seemed like an eternity, Nelson stepped forward and said he would be delighted to honor the chief's 'gift.'"

As you can imagine, Nelson's willingness to do what it took for the team's success became legendary. His level of "sacrifice" eventually became a litmus test within the organization. It became "the way we do things here," and Nelson marked the path to the top. Eventually, Nelson became CEO, and he is now regarded as a senior statesman in the industry. As I said at the beginning of the story, I'll let you decide about this particular myth, whose origins were grounded in a true story.

As time passes, myths like these accumulate and solidify into an organizational cultural mythology that forms a strand of the DNA of an organization's cultural gestalt. One myth was about always doing the right thing. The other myth was about doing whatever is necessary for the team's success.

Artifacts. An artifact is a monument or a remembrance. It is a physical manifestation of an important event or myth. Artifacts are important because they remind those who weren't there of the significance of whatever the artifact symbolizes. The Washington Monument in our nation's capital is a reminder of the greatness of our first president. It symbolizes his dedication to the values underlying our nation's founding. Artifacts serve the same purpose within organizational cultures.

For example, it's common for an underwriter to provide the CEO of an IPO client a Deal Lucite containing a replica of the cover of the firm's S-1 Registration Statement. I was once privileged to have the inventor of voicemail serving on one of my Boards of Directors (yes, he was frequently chided for the "monster" he had invented). His company maintained a framed copy of the original voicemail patent as a cultural artifact.

Sometimes an artifact is a major public and decisive act, as related by the following CEO. Tom is a burly take-charge kind of a guy—some might say he's impulsive. He doesn't suffer fools well, and he doesn't like hearing excuses.

"I jumped on a plane and went to New York along with a couple of my key direct reports. We did an on-site investigation with our internal audit staff for about three or four hours. We did some interviewing, and we fired the entire department. It was difficult to do. It was the right thing to do. The employees had decided that if they couldn't get signatures on contracts, they would be in trouble. So they decided to forge customers' signatures. We started getting calls from customers who wanted to know why their service was continuing. In a concerted effort to get ahead of this, we immediately began contacting customers. We alerted them about the forged contracts. At the end of the day, we were successful in retaining a lot of the business because we acted."

> We did an on-site investigation. We did some interviewing, and we fired the entire department. It was difficult to do. It was the right thing to do.

In that organization, this act is memorialized as the "massacre in New York." It has informed and affected the organization's culture to this very day because of its suddenness and finality. The "massacre" enshrined the CEO's passion for taking action— as in "we don't talk; we act." The "massacre" also set the standard for doing the right thing even when it hurts.

A final element of the organizational culture gestalt is tradition.

Tradition. Merriam-Webster's dictionary defines tradition as "an inherited, established or customary pattern of thought, action or behavior." Most of us understand traditions and the power they can have on behavior. For example, Thanksgiving is not only a holiday but also a long-standing tradition in the United States, and the Thanksgiving turkey is the entrée of choice.

Several years ago, my wife and I went to an extended family member's home for the holiday. After arriving, we sensed there was an unusual level of consternation because the host was serving ham instead of turkey. Traditions have a powerful effect on our behavior, and in most cultures, deviations from traditions are not welcomed.

> Traditions have a powerful effect on our behavior, and in most cultures, deviations from traditions are not welcomed.

Organizational cultural traditions are very similar. For example, part of the Avon organizational culture is the annual Avon Walk for Cancer held in cities across the United States. This is a cultural tradition that raises millions of dollars for cancer research, and it exhibits the three important elements of any tradition: shared identity, unique ritual and a remembrance of past triumphs. This organizational cultural tradition is a win-win for all participants. It adds value to the Avon brand, and it brings together cancer survivors and their family members as they generate valuable research funding.

An organizational cultural tradition can also be a long-term loser. Earlier in my career, I worked for a major auto manufacturer that we'll call Acme Motor Company. Acme's founder was a firm believer in the company's "self-sufficiency"—some called it paranoia. Over the years this belief morphed into the tradition that if something didn't originate at Acme, it wasn't important enough to consider adopting. This tradition was called "the Acme way," and it stifled innovation and enshrined obsolete practices within the organization's culture. In the long run, "the Acme way" nearly bankrupted the company.

CULTURE DYSFUNCTIONS

We've all heard the term "dysfunction" as applied to social groups, families, teams and bureaucracies, just to name a few. Webster's dictionary defines dysfunction as "a consequence of a social practice or behavior pattern that undermines the stability of a social system." In other words, something is not working correctly or is simply malfunctioning. From my research, I've identified six organizational culture dysfunctions, which I call the Sick Six:

> Organizational culture dysfunctions are like termites, silently eating away at the foundations and structures of organizations.

- *Organizational hypocrisy*
- *Wet work*
- *Omerta*
- *Arrogance, hubris and entitlement*
- *Pressure to perform*
- *Shoot the messenger*

These dysfunctions are like termites, silently eating away at the foundations and structures of organizations. Left unchecked, these destructive pests will reduce even the largest and most powerful organizations to skeletal shells, unable to withstand even the slightest breeze of adversity. When the Sick Six are silently at work in your organization, you have jumped the shark without repellant or Kevlar wetsuit. It will be bloody. Just hope the blood's not yours.

Hypocrisy. Organizational hypocrisy is defined as establishing desired standards of behavior but then rewarding behavior that deviates from those standards. Hypocrisy is one of the most destructive and toxic dysfunctions. Like a weak acid, it slowly erodes shared values.

Jack grew his career under such conditions. He is a former COO of a Fortune 100 firm. Jack has lived and worked in some of the toughest and most undesirable places on earth. His language often runs to the "salty," and he had this to say about organizational hypocrisy:

"Companies have stated missions, visions and ways of doing business. But in actual operations and in the running of the business, those are not rewarded. People are smart. If the company says you ought to do this, this and this—ethically and for safety reasons—but the guys who get promoted are those who just get things done no matter what, they break all the ethical rules. Then the culture fails. It generates an undercurrent and an underculture. And that underculture becomes a wink-and-nod of how to get ahead no matter what's said.

"When you look down [the ladder], people are smiling at you. And when you look up, you're seeing a different view. The point, is the only way up the ladder is to be an asshole."

"The bad thing is that, over decades, those people get to be CEOs. And those CEOs got there by looking up the ladder and smiling and doing what's expected—not what's written. Of course, when you look up the ladder, there is a queue, and when you look down the ladder there is a queue. When you look down, people are smiling at you. And when you look up, you're seeing a different view. The point is, the only way up the ladder is to be an asshole. Once you have that in place, culturally, deviant behavior takes decades to change out."

The condition that Jack is describing is every manager and leader's worst nightmare. Unfortunately, all too many managers and leaders are clueless about how quickly even a little organizational hypocrisy spreads. Or they're fearful about the short-term effects on operating results if they take a principled stand.

I once consulted with a business services organization where Lamont was the star sales performer. Lamont sold ten times as much business as anyone else. Because of that, he was not only allowed to break whatever rules he liked but was handsomely rewarded for it. Senior leadership looked the other way because they were afraid of losing the business Lamont was generating. It was widely known throughout the organization that Lamont was "bulletproof," or that "no one screws with Lamont." Slowly but surely, Lamont's bad behavior metastasized throughout the sales organization. Organizational hypocrisy is a lot like cancer—you can't tolerate or contain just a little of it.

Then, one day, the organization received a subpoena from the U.S. attorney's office. The U.S. attorney was investigating allegations of bribery and other illegal activities involving certain members of the sales staff's dealings with federal contracting officers. You might be surprised to learn that Lamont was not involved. Lamont's transgressions ran more toward sexually harassing female colleagues. He was very good at selling, so bribery was unnecessary. But many of Lamont's colleagues needed an extra edge because they weren't endowed with Lamont's selling prowess.

As a result, some of Lamont's colleagues engaged in questionable activities they *thought* were countenanced by senior leadership. Lamont's colleagues believed the only thing that mattered was the end result. After all, Lamont had been sexually harassing female colleagues for years, and it was always "handled." This is frequently the result of a wink-and-nod culture. You can't have one set of stated values but reward a different set of values behavior. If you do, it invariably leads to what I've called organizational wet work.

Wet Work. Organizational wet work is doing what *you believe is expected*—not what's written in the company's code of conduct—and then *not mentioning it to anyone*. I have adopted this term from the world of spies and espionage. In that world, "wet work" is a euphemism for assassination. But the term has the added connotation of giving plausible deniability to your superior. This means you understand the hidden content of a superior's message even if that content is unspoken or unwritten. So, if you're caught, your superior can deny having had any foreknowledge of your activities.

> You understand the hidden content of a superior's message even if that content is unspoken or unwritten.

In some cases, this can be a benign aspect of an organization's culture, but in most cases it's not. Life is messy. It serves up dilemmas that don't conveniently fit into a formula or get resolved using a rulebook.

Here is a case related by Derek, a senior executive whose career included stints as a country manager and drillship captain, discussing some of his work overseas. You judge whether this case is benign or something more serious.

"We have to realize that, over a couple hundred years in the United States, our ethics and jurisprudence have evolved to a point where we don't tolerate baksheesh payments or lagniappe considerations. In other parts of the world, this is not only tolerated but part of the culture. And, in fact, recompense is based upon this understanding.

"The question becomes then, what does the country manager do when he has a motor in customs, and it's going to take a couple hundred dollars U.S. to get it out today? And if that doesn't happen, it's going to stay in there for another week, and the company's going to lose a half million dollars. But that's okay. I can handle it with my expense account. I can say it's just the cost of doing business. And when you think about that as a concept, and it just takes a couple hundred dollars, you can hide that amount in your expense account, and nobody says a word. Or you don't even report it on your expense account. You just think of it as the cost of doing business, and you're getting plenty of money for doing it.

"But what happens if the customs guy says, 'I need $300,000?' And if the country manager pays it, he still saves the company a million dollars in shutdown time for a week. What does he do? What does the company do? Our lawyer would say, 'Look, if you're faced with this $300,000 question, you've got to call the legal department.' And then the country manager says, 'Well, we've got a local contractor that can take care of this for us, and no one will ever be the wiser.' Then the lawyer says, 'You can't tell me that!'"

> The country manager says, "Well, we've got a local contractor that can take care of this ... [$300K 'gratuity']." Then the lawyer says, "You can't tell me that!"

This is a typical and straightforward case of organizational wet work. The official company policy is, "We don't pay bribes of any size and for any reason." But the work still needs to be done at the lowest possible cost. So the company may decide that paying a $300,000 gratuity to save $1 million is a logical trade-off if it can be done quietly and under the radar.

Using a third-party local vendor, in this case, would be a convenient way of accomplishing that objective. The local vendor makes the payment, which is most likely not illegal in that country, and increases his invoice to the company by the $300,000. Except for a small group of individuals who all have something to gain by remaining silent, no one ever knows the difference. If the payment is ever discovered, senior management can rightly claim they had no knowledge and certainly didn't approve of the payment. Everyone wins! Or not—I'll let you decide.

Here is a much more subtle case of organizational wet work as related by Mark, the CEO of a Fortune 1000 multinational distribution company. Mark described himself as someone who "lives his life pretty straight ahead." He attended parochial schools and had a fond memory of Sister Mary, who "kept everybody on the straight and narrow." He described a wet work situation where the company had recently missed its numbers and was punished by Wall Street with a sharp stock price decline.

> If someone's got to be held accountable, and if it's *you*, you've got to step up to it.

"Situations surface all the time. If certain things come down that are not good, people will try to pass the buck. I think someone's got to be held accountable, and if it's you, you've got to step up to it. That's the ethical thing to do.

"Recently, we had a situation where we missed our numbers, and everybody was blaming everyone else. I said, first of all, I am the CEO. I am responsible. So I could've been pointing my fingers, and I certainly had plenty of places to point. I expect people to be accountable.

"There's tremendous pressure [to hit Wall Street expectations], and I think there was a desire on my people's part to come up with a forecast that they thought was acceptable to me. I do think, looking back on it, I may have been a little bit too aggressive with my expectations, and maybe people weren't as objective as they might otherwise have been in preparing the forecast. So we took an unnecessary hit."

Mark's story is a more refined case of organizational wet work because there was no illegal or unethical activity involved. Mark had been aggressive in describing his intention to reach a certain quarterly "number." He didn't overtly tell his staff to overstate the forecast. Such a statement wasn't needed. His staff "understood" what was necessary, and they obliged. Then Mark had to deal with the aftermath.

Having spent a large portion of my professional career in accounting and finance, I am all too familiar with this organizational cultural dysfunction. In one organization, every quarter we'd get the "number" we had to hit. Upon receipt of the "number," we'd work our accounting magic, figuring out a way to reach it without going to jail, and everyone would be happy. We all knew what was expected, and it was *never the subject of conversation*, which leads to our next cultural dysfunction, organizational omerta.

In many organizations, speaking the unspeakable, no matter how true, is a career ending event.

Organizational Omerta. Organizational omerta is a code of silence, an organizational silence that often accompanies organizational wet work. I have borrowed this term from the world of organized crime, in which violating the code of silence is often a death sentence. This may seem like a harsh characterization, but in many organizations, speaking the unspeakable, no matter how true, is a career ending event, as this senior leader clearly articulated.

> "[A code of silence] is an inherent belief that has been supported over a culture inside the organization for years. If an employee stands up and says, 'This is unethical, I'm not going to do it,' they are viewed as someone who doesn't understand the corporate goals and what should be considered a gray area. Hence, they're not fit for their position. They [the employee] have taken a position that will be difficult for the corporation to explain, and they should have chosen not to bring the subject up. It should have been resolved *without anyone knowing about it.*"

Recent allegations about the Veterans Administration (VA) serve as an example of organizational omerta. A senior medical director of the VA informed senior VA leadership about a serious backlog of veterans awaiting treatment. Instead of recognizing the problem and working on a solution, senior VA officials drummed the concerned medical director out of the organization and found other "team players" who subsequently engaged in a multiyear cover-up, which allegedly caused the deaths of numerous sick veterans.

Here are short comments that provide further examples. The first is from a Fortune 1000 COO describing his initial experience as an operating executive.

> "The first time, I ran a P&L. And after my first year, I was having a conversation with my vice president, and I said, 'I've

learned three lessons from my first year here.' And she said, 'What are they?'

"I said 'One, pad your budget by 20% because it's going to get cut. Two, spend as much capital money as I can regardless of my budget until you tell me to stop because that's what everybody else does. And three, don't raise my prices so I can grow my business until you start screaming at me for margins.' She laughed and said, 'You're a piece of work!'
"Now, I never did those things. But those literally were undertones in that business that were the unspoken truths."

We also have this CEO's recollection of working in a foreign environment where executive kidnapping was a common occurrence:

"I worked for a major company where we had one of our executives kidnapped in a foreign country. No one ever talked about it. But one of the guys out of our internal security group, who once worked for the FBI, showed up with a briefcase. The briefcase changed hands, and the executive was freed. And nobody talked about it."

At this point, you might be asking yourself what's the big deal with these situations? It makes sense that you'd pay a ransom for a valuable executive and hope that no one heard about it. And padding your budget is something everybody does.

But a cow can't be a little pregnant. She's either pregnant or not. An organization either has a code of silence or it doesn't. Organizational members either engage in activities they can discuss freely, or they don't engage in those activities. The VA enforced a code of silence, and we now understand the aftermath.

An organizational code of silence is often accompanied and enabled by the toxic triangle of arrogance, hubris and entitlement.

Toxic Triangle: Arrogance, Hubris and Entitlement. Most organizations have some level of arrogance, hubris and entitlement. Market leaders, especially, may expect to earn the highest margins because they have the "best" in their industry segment. This triangle of egotistical attitudes becomes toxic when it so infects an organization's culture that everyone within the culture actually believes what they say about themselves and the organization. This is one of the poisons that killed Enron.

The following Fortune 100 CEO was keenly aware of this toxic triangle as he described an incident within his organization.

Hal is one of the most senior executives I interviewed. He's led some very large organizations with far-flung operations. In this story, one of his direct reports, Bill, the COO, had hired his son to run a significant part of the company's business. Because Bill's son didn't report directly to Bill, the company's anti-nepotism policy was waived. Hal had learned, via an "unofficial" company grapevine he nurtured, that Bill's married son was having an affair with a married woman who worked in his organization. The affair wasn't completely "undercover" and was causing problems because certain staffers were getting "favors" and "special treatment." Arrogance and hubris in action aren't pretty. Here's what Hal had to say.

> "People think that because they're in the C-Suite, things should be swept under the doormat."

"People think that because they're in the C-Suite, as in this case, things should be swept under the doormat. Or they believe matters can be treated differently than if you're handling somebody several rungs down the ladder. I've seen it before. I've even had people that know me think that these things [ethical problems] can be just managed away. They'll propose, 'Let's relocate the individual. Let's put them into a different department.'

"Usually those things don't work anyway. The reality is I think they [lower level employees] lose respect for the organization. And I think it causes a loss of trust in the leadership of the organization. I think it tends to bring a number of other things into question, especially if it's prevalent in the company."

In the end, Hal saw to it that Bill's son realized his career aspirations would be more successfully fulfilled in a different organization, and he left the company.

Remember Sam, whose story about the young bond trader opened this chapter? He offered these incisive comments about the toxic triangle.

"As you move up in an organization, as you get increasingly more responsibility, the temptations toward hubris get bigger, and they frequently get more subtle. As the chairman and CEO, it's easy for me to justify an action because I do have an obligation to the shareholders. Any guy who's smart enough to be a CEO is smart enough to figure out a way to rationalize anything he wants to do. You tell me whatever you want to do, and I can rationalize why that's good for the shareholders."

I'll let Terri, one of the few women I was privileged to interview for this book, end our discussion of the toxic triangle. This subject was of particular interest to her because she had never considered herself arrogant, full of hubris or entitled to anything. She had to fight her way through the glass ceiling to reach the C-Suite of her health care organization. Nothing had ever been just handed to her. But in the end—well, I'll let her explain.

> "Your driver picks you up at your front door. When you arrive at your office, everyone is attentive to you. Anything you want is quickly provided. Staff even begins to anticipate what you'll need or want, and it appears magically on your desk or conference room table. When the company jet is not available, you always fly business first class, with all arrangements made to the smallest detail. Once the plane is off the ground, you find your staff has already ordered your drinks, selected your wine and ordered your favorite meal. After years of this kind of treatment, you're tempted to think of yourself as royalty.
>
> "Once that kind of thinking creeps in, you're really in trouble because royalty can do anything they want without adverse consequences. They simply decree it, and it happens. If you're able to do that, and you do, you lose your ethical moorings. Your moral compass becomes unhinged from reality. And, because you're surrounded by people whose job it is to please you, you rarely get pushback from clearly unethical acts."

These moral lapses often manifest as an unhealthy organizational pressure to perform, regardless of the costs.

Pressure to Perform. We all feel a pressure to perform at our best, and for most of us, this pressure comes from within. Pressure to perform in this context, however, refers to the overwhelming and relentless 24/7/365 pressure to meet short-term organizational goals that often override the stated organizational core values or the code of conduct. For example, meeting Wall Street's expectation for this quarter's earnings or not missing periodic creditor-imposed debt covenants. One CEO described his constant struggle with the unrelenting pressure this way:

> "Well, I think it's just the short-term nature of the demands for results *every* quarter. Quarterly earnings, and now we have Wall Street analysts forecasting our earnings to the *penny* ... a one-penny shortfall and your stock price tanks five to ten percent, and it's not even our forecast. So I think the endless short-term quarterly demand for results. Sometimes I think, 'Man, if I do [the right thing] it will trash the quarter.'
>
> "The right answer isn't always obvious when you're under pressure. A lot of money is involved, you're personally financially at risk, you're strung out financially and you're trying to make some stock option number. Or other pressures are weighing on the situation, like keeping your job. Your thinking can get really cloudy."

"A lot of money is involved, you are personally financially at risk, you're strung out financially and you're trying to make some stock option number."

As you're reading this, I know your heart really bleeds for this guy. He's making well into seven figures, lives in a beautiful home with a well-manicured lawn, has access to a chauffeured limousine and flies on the company jet. That may all be true. But do you really want someone who's running a company in which you have invested your money living in constant fear? Remember, in Chapter 1 we showed how fear of loss is one of the most powerful of all human motivators. This type of fear almost always leads to irrational judgments. Ethically intelligent organizations don't motivate people this way.

Stan was one of the most experienced and well-seasoned CFOs I interviewed for this book. He is a CPA and has an MBA from one of the top business schools in the country. In his three-decade career, Stan has seen just about everything. He and I have much in common, especially when it comes to the unbearable pressure to "make a number." He talked about a scary experience he had early in his career.

"About 25 years ago, I was working for a private equity fund. The fund had borrowed about $250 million from a 'Mideast oil sheik,' if you know what I mean. It was for a big marina real estate project on the West Coast. The project was maybe 85% done, but out of money. And we had to ask the 'Mideast oil sheik' for more money to finish the project. I was sent in to help get the funding and save the project.

"So the project CEO said, 'Let's put together a sales forecast showing how we'll sell off the condos and the boat slips. That will cover everything

"My CEO said, 'Just increase the sales price.' And, 'I said I can't do that. I'm out here every day, and we can't even sell them at the current price.'"

and make everybody happy.' I did that, and I discovered we were short $30 to $40 million from where we currently were, much less the additional money we needed to fund the project. The project CEO said, 'That's easy, just increase the sales price to a level that will close the funding gap.' And, I said 'I can't do that. I'm out here every day, and we can't even sell the condos at the current price, much less a fictitious higher price just to hit a number.' I didn't know what to do.

"I knew a guy who was the chief executive officer of a similar management firm. This was a guy who really knew how to run the business. I went to him. He was kind of a mentor, and he said, 'Don't ever cross that line.' He said 'Once you cross it, it gets easier to cross it again.' So he said, 'The first thing is be upfront about it. If you hide it, then you hide the second thing, and the third thing and the fourth thing.'

"So, I learned early in my career just to be upfront about it. Let the chips fall where they may. You'll never regret it, and you won't have to keep looking over your shoulder. So, now that's the model I always follow. I went back to the project CEO, and I gave him a letter that said 'I will not present these numbers, and if you force me, I'll resign. I won't do it. I can't do it. And here's why. We're asking people for more money based on false projections, and it's just not the right thing to do. Let's just tell them the truth. The project may be screwed, but it will be a hell of a lot more screwed if we don't get the money. Or, we get the money under false pretenses, which is even worse.'"

> "I will not present these numbers, and if you force me, I will resign. I won't do it. I can't do it."

We all live with stress. As managers and leaders, we're expected to live with it and produce results. If we can't, perhaps we're in the wrong line of work. Unfortunately, this is the prevailing attitude in many organizations today. I'm asking us to think differently. We can produce the same or better results with a better approach. In today's world, too many organizations use fear as the chief motivator: fear of loss, fear of shame or fear of failure. It doesn't have to be this way. In Chapter 11, we'll pick up this subject again, and I'll lay out a better way.

Once organizational culture is infected with the pressure-to-perform toxin, it invariably leads to our final cultural dysfunction: shoot the messenger.

Shoot the Messenger. The shoot the messenger dysfunction is an organizational practice that outwardly encourages truthfulness and "whistle blowing" but, in practice, secretly punishes such behavior. This cultural perversion forms a barrier to truthful information flow—something managers and leaders desperately need—and indirectly encourages unethical behavior. Stan, our senior CFO, offered this observation about shooting the messenger and the resulting fear injected into the organizational culture.

"What I see is a lot people who are—especially in the financial world—just scared. They're scared of getting yelled at. They're afraid they might get punished. I run into financial people who would rather hide under their desk—they would rather cover things up—then tell somebody that they made a mistake when they prepared their budget, or that the operating results are actually that bad. Instead, [some will say] 'I'll cook the books. Hope things get better and cover it up.' Or, instead, 'I'll move these numbers around a little bit, and, hopefully in a month or two, things will get better, and I'll be able to fix it.' Then, the problem instead of reversing itself gets bigger. So, to disclose the bigger problem, they would have had to disclose how they covered up the smaller problem. So they bury themselves deeper and deeper."

I hope you're beginning to see a pattern in the stories. These organizational cultural dysfunctions—organizational termites—

create an undercurrent of fear. People who are motivated by fear often make deadly judgment calls. Think back to the airline crash we discussed in Chapter 1. Almost 600 people lost their lives because of one person's fear-based judgment. Ethically intelligent organizations don't function this way.

Gerald is another CEO who started his career in accounting and finance. In addition to his "day" job, Gerald mentors up-and-coming leaders not only in his organization but also through various charitable outreach initiatives. We talked in his office, which was somewhat cramped due to overflowing floor-to-ceiling bookcases. Gerald's story is unique because it demonstrates how a fear-based culture can jump from a single organization into an entire industry.

"Earlier in my career, I was CFO of a Fortune 500 organization. One of our subsidiaries was a military contractor that had been underperforming for several years. Our board decided it was time to change out the subsidiary's leadership team. My CEO and I arrived at the subsidiary's offices early one Tuesday morning. Our plan was that my CEO would interview and discharge the subsidiary's president, and I would interview and discharge the subsidiary's controller and CFO. After informing the controller that he was being terminated, he asked me how we had found out about their secret overbilling scheme. I was shocked to hear his spontaneous admission of perpetrating a fraud [double billing on several military contracts]. As the controller talked, I recorded several pages of notes detailing the overbilling fraud.

"Later on during lunch, I relayed the story to my CEO, a retired army general. The CEO advised me that [the controller's allegations] were probably just the ranting of a disgruntled employee and to forget the entire matter. He further advised me to 'shred' my notes and to proceed as if nothing had happened in my meeting with the controller.

> "[The CEO] further advised me to 'shred' my notes and to proceed as if nothing had happened in my meeting with the controller."

"Later that day as we were flying home, I began to worry about the bind I was in. Following the CEO's order was unethical and illegal. If I followed his order, I'd violate my professional ethics and open myself up to prosecution for covering up a crime and obstructing justice. But on the other hand, if I didn't follow the CEO's direct order, I would be fired. He didn't tolerate any hint of insubordination.

"After much anguish, I turned the information over to our outside legal counsel. Our outside legal counsel forwarded the information to the appropriate governmental officials, and eventually both the subsidiary's president and controller were sentenced to prison. Ironically, my CEO and our organization received a 'good citizen award' from the military for turning ourselves in. Within a year of the convictions, however, I was dismissed. My CEO, who was quite influential in our industry, made sure the word got out that I was not 'team player.' I never worked in that industry again."

> "My CEO, who was quite influential in our industry, made sure the word got out that I was not a 'team player.' I never worked in that industry again."

Destroying someone's ability to make a living working in a particular industry sends a powerful signal. It's a pernicious strategy for enforcing not only an organizational code of silence but also industry-wide omerta. It enables organizational and industry wet work, which is how we get deadly mine explosions and chemical spills. This is how seemingly rock solid organizations like Enron collapse in a single day. It's how a financial stalwart like Bear Stearns threatened the entire financial system. Organizational termites are deadly.

Most of these cultural dysfunctions are not singular occurrences. They occur as pairs or even triangles. The effects are synergistic. Organizational wet work rarely happens by itself. It requires organizational omerta to succeed. Organizational omerta is enforced with shoot the messenger. We know that arrogance, hubris and entitlement occur as a toxic triangle. The effects of these dysfunctions are multiplication, not addition, which is why I've called this the cultural gestalt. Once these dysfunctions are embedded, they're extremely difficult—but not impossible—to change.

A SUCCESS STORY

Can toxic cultures be rescued? Yes, but once the fire of a toxic culture is out of control and consuming everything in its path, stopping its advance takes strong actions. Tough measures are required to turn around an out-of-control organizational culture. Illustrating that difficulty, a COO related the following experience.

> "The only force to change unethical behavior is leadership that doesn't promote those who are ethically questionable. Fire a few people. Leadership has to make examples. People have to make it known that this is not just bullshit we're talking

"The only force to change unethical behavior is leadership that does not promote those who are ethically questionable. Fire a few people."

because we have to please Wall Street. The tough thing about that is now and again you're going to have to fire somebody who has delivered really good business results. I went through some of this back in the early 1990s. I delivered tremendously good business results. But the company said, 'You're broken; we're going to fix you.' It was a big investment by the company. The company also said, 'You're going to have individual coaching. We're going to coach you for 24 months. But if you don't pass this program, you're fired.'"

This executive was "fixed," but the personal cost was high. He had to unlearn much of what had led to his prior success. The industry in which his company competed had succumbed to organizational termites. His company was cleaning out its termites, but the industry was yet unchanged, and he was required to produce the same operating results without resorting to well-known "shortcuts" that his competitors still used. During his two-year reeducation program, he and his organization paid a heavy price. But in the end, they emerged more respected and one of the preferred providers in their market space.

In my research, I heard several success stories in which CEOs made gut-wrenching decisions and restored ethically intelligent organizational cultures. Here is one of those stories. As with all the stories I've presented in this book, I have changed many details to ensure the anonymity of the storytellers. In this case, the company competed in an industry with odious marketing practices. I have selected the electronics industry as a stand-in for the real industry. If you work in the electronics industry, please don't be offended.

The CEO in this case has a reputation as a standup guy, and for good reason. He is well known, and many of his colleagues were surprised when he accepted the challenge of turning this organization around, particularly given its industry. But turn it around he did. And in so doing, he showed the way forward. He demonstrated the possibility of cultural redemption and changed the way an industry operated.

From Strip Clubs and Ladies of the Evening to Family Outings.

"One of the toughest issues I faced is when I became CEO of an electronics components business. This was a tough business, and the people who were in it—and the rules of the game—were such that a large part of the business was done in men's strip clubs and sometimes involved procuring prostitutes—and in some extreme instances exchanging things like cocaine or other illegal substances. It was the existing culture. We had products that we had to market, so we needed to do what was necessary to compete.

"The rules of the game were such that a large part of the business was done in men's strip clubs and sometimes involved procuring prostitutes."

"The ethical dilemma was obvious. So we made a policy decision, and it was implemented though our culture, which was: We don't entertain customers in men's clubs. And we don't engage in or fund immoral behavior. But we recognized the rules in this business were very loose. When we would hire a new marketing rep that was coming from one of our competitors that did [strip club marketing], we would sit down before we hired them and explain that we don't do this. We explained that we wouldn't pay expense reports from places like Vera's Cabaret, Lucy's Love Palace or similar establishments. First of all, that practice self-selects. You begin hiring people who don't really believe in Vera's Cabaret or Lucy's Love Palace. But you have to provide an alternative that works.

"So we struggled with this for a couple of years. We got together what I called an Advisor's Council. And to be on the Council you had to be active in your church. And it involved hourly workers in the warehouse. It involved the support staff members who were active in their church. We took people from all levels of the company. It wasn't just the management. I would present these issues to the Council. It was a group that varied from about 8 to 12 members over the years. I presented this particular problem to them.

"The alternative the Advisor's Council came up with was that instead of doing business in men's clubs, we're going to do business with the customer's family in a family-friendly way. So instead of spending $400 at Vera's or Lucy's to take Mr. Smith to the men's club, the alternative was we're going to send an airline ticket to Mr. Smith's wife and invite her to visit with him. So the rule was you send the ticket to Mr. Smith's wife, and you and your wife or girlfriend can take Mr. and Mrs. Smith to anywhere *Mrs. Smith wants to go*. If she wants to go to the men's strip club, you can go there, and we'll reimburse you. If she wants to go to the opera, you'd better learn to like opera.

"If she wants to go to the men's strip club, you can go there, and we'll reimburse you. If she wants to go to the opera, you'd better learn to like opera."

"So that's the solution—you can't just say no. You can't just say we're not going to do business in men's clubs. You have to replace it with a different philosophy. In this case, it was we're going to be the smartest and hardest working guys, and we're going to have an alternative social venue that we control—our culture will reflect our core values."

This strategy was extremely successful. Customers' wives eventually heard about what this CEO's company was doing and demanded their husbands begin buying from them. The CEO ended up changing industry practices. But don't think it was easy. This transformation took many years and a lot of hard decisions. For a period, the organization experienced a high turnover rate. And many in the industry thought this CEO was fighting a losing battle and would eventually fail. Changing a dysfunctional organizational culture is heavy lifting. Creating and nurturing an ethically intelligent organization is easier and smarter.

One of the most senior CEOs who participated in the research for this book had these well-chosen words of wisdom about organizational culture:

> "I will tell you without any reservations ... there are very few things I am absolutely certain about ...very few. But one of the things I am absolutely certain about is that you control ethics/morality in any organization with culture. The culture is about who you are and how you do business. And you don't do it with statements ... those silly little things you hang on the wall ... those motivational posters. You do it every single day by conscious example and parables."

This chapter about cultural fire is one of the longest in this book, and for good reason. Organizational culture is the foundation upon which ethically intelligent organizations are built. Unless you've created a solid foundation, everything else, while important, is secondary. It's like building a house on a weak, unsteady and shaky foundation. The walls, the roof, the interior fixtures, can be of impeccable quality. But if the foundation isn't right, all of the other quality is wasted.

It's hard to execute an exquisite strategy when the windows won't open and the doors won't close.

I end this chapter with a quote about organizational culture from Peter Drucker: "Culture eats strategy for breakfast." Culture is like a fierce fire. It can create or consume. As a leader or manager, you have no choice but to pay attention to culture. Ignore it at your peril because it will burn you every time.

> You have no choice but to pay attention to culture. Ignore it at your peril because it will burn you every time.

———————◆———————

Chapter Highlights

- Organizational culture is a gestalt. It's a set of values, stated and otherwise, a collection of myths, mystique created by a founder, a set of traditions people hold dear, a reflection of the CEO's behavior, a force that gets into our collective unconscious.

- Culture will change you, or you can change it, and you'd better know the difference.

- Organizational culture is multiplication, not addition.

- Organizational culture is the foundation upon which ethically intelligent organizations are built.

- Culture is like a fierce fire. It can create or consume.

- It's much easier to heat a room with a controlled fire in a fireplace than to extinguish a blaze that's destroying the building.

- Values statements are good, but values behaviors are better and have a much more profound effect on organizational culture.

- Organizational cultures are destroyed by dysfunctions (termites), which are the Sick Six—hypocrisy, wet work, omerta, toxic triangle, pressure to perform and shoot the messenger.

- Exercise constant vigilance and, if you see termites, call the exterminator.

Questions for You

- Are you okay with your CFO cheating on the golf course on Sunday and signing your SEC filings on Monday?
- Who or what outside of your organization holds you accountable?
- Can you list some of the key traditions in your organizational culture?
- Do you have any organizational termites? How do you know?
- Are there any unspoken truths in your organization? Do you know what they are? How do you find out?
- Can you describe your organizational culture in a single sentence?
- When was the last time you had a cultural audit?
- Do your team members engage in wet work? Do you know? How do you find out? If they do, would you like to know what they're doing?

CHAPTER 8

◆

LEADER SOLITARY CONFINEMENT— THE ROAD TO RUIN

> Sometimes I feel like I am locked inside
> a cocoon with no lifelines.
>
> *Fortune 200 CEO*

It was a snowy Saturday morning in Philadelphia. Members were arriving at the Crowne Faith Church and being ushered into a large room in the basement. The room was bare but comfortable. The aroma of brewing coffee and cooking bacon filled the air. There was a large circular table with 30 executive-style chairs. Although people were finding seats at the table, serving themselves breakfast from a buffet and making final preparations for the session to begin, the room was strangely quiet because small talk was discouraged.

This was an informal but highly secured, secret and invitation-only executive forum. Security was robust but only occasionally visible, as when all electronic devices were confiscated at the door. Van, the moderator, took his seat at the table. He invited everyone to take their seats. After everyone was seated and the doors closed and secured, Van began the session.

"Welcome, everyone! As usual, no electronics are permitted in this room. It has been swept for listening devices, and no one is allowed to take notes. Whatever happens here stays here. Although some of you know one another, we only use first names, and our organizations are never identified.

"We have a new member, Mark. And Mark is going to start us off."

"Good morning. My name is Mark, and I'm suffering from executive confinement syndrome. In other words, I don't know what the hell to do next!"

The entire room chuckled and said, "Hello, Mark. Welcome to our group."

"I'm so grateful to be here this morning," Mark said. "I have a problem that's been tearing at my gut for weeks. And I have no one I can talk to about it."

In unison, the entire room responded, "We know. That's why we're all here."

Mark went on, "About four months ago I went to a certain Latin American country to negotiate a significant contract with that country's state-owned natural resources company. We took a small team of about seven people because we wanted to stay under the radar until we could publicly announce the deal. You know how some of these hedge fund guys behave. They have private spies follow you around monitoring your every move, hoping to get an edge on trading your stock.

"We were there six days. We made a great deal. It was a win-win all around. Afterward, we had a small, discreet celebratory private dinner at the hotel the night before we were leaving. During the meal, we had several toasts—probably a few too many. The group broke up around 11:30, and I went up to my room to go straight to bed because we had wheels up early in the morning. I had just gotten into my bathrobe and stretched out on the bed when I heard a knock at the door.

"I looked through the peephole. There was this gorgeous young woman wearing a maid's uniform holding a tray with food and drink. Thinking she had the wrong room, I opened the door. Before I could say a word, she walked into my room and put the tray down on the coffee table. Dumbfounded, I just stood there not saying a word. She walked over to me. Effortlessly, slipped out of her uniform. Put her arms around me and started kissing me.

"She said, 'My name is Luisa, and I'm a gift from Señor Diego. He told me to make your last night in our city a most memorable occasion!'

"Before I could protest—not that I really wanted to that much—she threw off my robe, pushed me onto the bed and jumped right on top of me. By that point, I was so out of it, I just couldn't resist. That's how I spent my last night in that country. When I woke up the next morning, she was gone and had left me a note with her phone number. For months, I hadn't heard a word from anyone. I was beginning to think maybe it was just going to blow over. Then, last Wednesday, I received a cryptic text message on my personal cell phone. I don't know how the sender got my private number.

"The message said, 'I hope you enjoyed your last night in our great city. Luisa sure did! She would like to see you again next time you're in the city. Señor Diego requires some high-level international banking assistance, separate and apart from our main deal.'

"The message didn't come from Diego but from someone claiming to represent him. The sender said he would be back in touch with further instructions. I'm really worried about what's coming next. I haven't told anyone about this, especially my wife. If anyone finds out, I'll be in big trouble."

Mark looked around the table, and said, "Okay! I can see it in your faces. You're thinking what a dumbshit I am, and how I should learn to keep my junk in my pants."

At that, an older, more experienced participant said, "Mark, we're not here to judge you. We're here to help. Hell, when I was a new CEO, I had a similar experience. I didn't, as you say, keep my junk in my pants, either!"

At this point, the entire room broke into laughter.

> "Mark, we're not here to judge you. We're here to help. Hell, when I was a new CEO, I had a similar experience. I didn't, as you say, keep my junk in my pants, either!"

Van concluded the meeting, but not before Mark received priceless advice and counsel from this assembly of experienced peers—colleagues who could give objective nonjudgmental observations based on their own personal experiences. Mark left the meeting with a vision for creating an action plan because he received candid non-legalistic and non-agenda-driven counseling unavailable from any other source.

This story is based on a first-hand account of someone who was there. If I had attended that meeting, I would have advised Mark to tell the truth. I would have said something like this: "You made a mistake. You can't hide from it. And it isn't going away. You have to make it right." I would have counseled Mark to have an immediate and confidential personal meeting with his firm's senior outside legal coun-

> ... tell the truth! You made a mistake. You can't hide from it. And it isn't going away. You have to make it right.

sel. "Come clean. Lay the whole thing out. And then go home and talk to your wife and ask for forgiveness."

The ethically intelligent leader runs toward problems, not away from them. Problems like this never go away. They just get bigger. Remember the wise adage, "The cover-up is always worse than the original problem!"

I've heard about these secured and secret meeting forums in my discussions with other senior business leaders. As in the movie *Fight Club*, one of the first rules of these groups is that you don't talk about Fight Club. Why? Because what happens in these meetings is most-

As in the movie, *Fight Club*, one of the first rules of these groups is that you don't talk about Fight Club. Why? Because what happens in these meetings is mostly illegal.

ly illegal, made so by Regulation Full Disclosure or Regulation FD, imposed by the Securities Exchange Commission in August, 2000. We'll discuss Regulation FD in more detail in just a moment. But, this is only one dimension of executive isolation. There are others.

In this chapter, you'll see just how isolated senior business leaders have become. Access to them is controlled by any number and description of gatekeepers. The internal advice they receive is often skewed to serve only the advisor's or firm's agenda. Most internal advice is not objective because it emanates from the organization's culture, which the senior leadership team has created. As a result, senior leaders have no meaningful outside lifelines.

Welcome to the Captivity Cloister, a well-intended "soft" solitary confinement. Senior business leaders are smothered in good intentions that eventually result in corrupted ethical judging.

CAPTIVITY CLOISTER

In my research for this book, I reached out to 300 of the Fortune 1000 companies. Of those 300, 77 were impenetrable. In many cases, voicemail systems were designed to yield dead ends, meaning you could never reach a human person. In other cases, hundreds of emails directed toward specifically designated email addresses (listed as such on the company website) went unanswered. In most cases, multiple dozens of voicemails were neither acknowledged nor answered. Those organizations had created impervious inbound communication channels, which might be expected from private or secret organizations or societies. But these are publicly held corporations holding their senior leadership teams within cloisters—some might say hostage.

My first encounter with the Captivity Cloister was the unpleasant telephone conversation with Jeff Woodson that I mentioned previously. As you may recall, Woodson made it quite clear that communication with their CEO—or any other member of the senior leadership team—was tightly controlled.

The dictionary definition of a cloister refers to it as a place of seclusion, often surrounded by high walls. Cloisterization in the C-Suite is a gradual and well-meaning practice of shepherding senior leaders into a type of unforced seclusion surrounded by metaphorical walls of assistants and gatekeepers. Those assistants and gatekeepers screen and monitor phone calls, e-mails and other forms of communications. In many cases, the organization's communications department determines when and where these leaders appear in public, ensuring such activities are not only congruent with the company's "brand" but also well-vetted and approved by the legal department.

One CEO described his experience this way.

"Slowly, the organization and the culture will build a 'bubble' around you so that you're not really experiencing anything outside that bubble. The higher you get, the more there is a tendency for you to be in a bubble, and the more impenetrable the walls of that bubble become. Then you wake up one morning and realize just how isolated you've become. This level of isolation is not healthy and often leads to regrettable results."

Personally, I've seen this isolation multiple times. One of the reasons boards of directors and C-Suite executives hire outside consultants is to get an unbiased view of their organization from professionals whose opinion is not skewed by being a member of that organization. I've seen C-Suite executives routinely show displeasure to team members who bring them news they consider "undesirable." After a time, such executives receive only information their team members think is "acceptable." Other information never makes it up the pipeline, which is a recipe for unwanted nasty surprises.

Here's a real world example, ripped right from the headlines of the *Wall Street Journal*.

Volkswagen has admitted to falsifying emissions data on all of its diesel automobiles sold in the United States, impacting almost 11 million vehicles. It has been reported that this deception had been ongoing for several years. From the evidence collected so far, it appears this has been a *deliberate* deception. After a few days, the CEO of Volkswagen resigned. He maintained that he knew nothing about the scheme. Many think the CEO is lying, and that he had full knowledge of the arrangement. I wouldn't rush to that conclusion. There is an equal probability that the CEO was totally clueless about what was taking place in his organization. Being held captive within the cloister often yields these results.

Here's another example from my professional experience.

I once reported to a CEO, Colonel Muir, who never left his office except to attend various social functions where he represented the organization. His breakfast, lunch and dinner were catered into his office suite. He spent his days poring over reports, talking to board members and reaching out to his selectively placed cronies throughout the organization. Colonel Muir's personal needs were met by several staff members who served at his pleasure.

Colonel Muir had a driver and a company car. He traveled exclusively using either the company helicopter or jet. Colonel Muir's schedule was tightly controlled and rigidly enforced by his chief of staff, who was a very nice lady, and whose background included a stint as an MP in the Army. No one gained access to Colonel Muir unless granted by Phyllis. Scheduling such access usually required several days, often weeks. This was my first encounter with the Innocuous Imperial Box.

INNOCUOUS IMPERIAL BOX

Although my experience with Colonel Muir was many years ago, in my interviews with senior business leaders, I found the Innocuous Imperial Box (Box) alive and well. I've defined it as a metaphorical box in which many senior business executives find themselves trapped. The Box is called Imperial because it has the accoutrements of royalty, including power, prestige and prerogatives. It's called innocuous because it was usually well-intentioned, allowing the executive's time to be spent efficiently and productively on behalf of the organization.

In the next several paragraphs, you're going to hear directly from senior business leaders who have been in the Box. Most of them didn't find it very innocuous. Instead, it was suffocating. Others could see clear and present dangers from being in the Box. Most of them would tell you that being in the Box was a life-changing experience, and not necessarily for the good. Here's how Roger, a former Fortune 200 CEO, summarized his five-year experience in the Box.

> "I was trapped in this metaphorical box created by a slew of well-meaning gatekeepers. So that's kind of what I did. The box floated around—right? It was in the air. It was moving around. It was in my office. Or it was in the Caribbean with customers or whatever. But it was still a box where I wasn't doing anything that I really wanted to do. I wasn't doing anything with my family. I was doing what I needed to do to be president and CEO.
>
> "I look back and I can't believe that for all those years, I just gave up my life. If someone said to me, 'I will give you $5 million a year for five years to go sit in this box and at the end I will give you $25 million—of course, you're going to have to pay tax and everything else,' I would say you're nuts. I would never do that.
>
> "But that's exactly what I did. You don't fully recognize that you made the choice until you walk away from it. So I don't say any of this in judgment toward the folks that are in those roles. I say it almost in sympathy. I couldn't see it until I stepped away from it. Fortunately, I was younger when I did. Because that's the other thing you see. You see the CEOs

who are in their 60s and 70s that have nothing. Sure, they have a lot of money and a couple of board seats but nothing else because everybody else in their life has written them off. And if you talk to their kids and their wife, they all say the same thing—we got tired of waiting."

Jake, a retired Fortune 500 CEO—now an active hedge fund investor—talked about the results of living in the Innocuous Imperial Box.

"CEOs occupy a unique position in the organization. They are generously compensated and are often allocated perquisites of substantial content. They wield nearly uncontrolled power within the organization, and they create the organization's culture. Because of those factors, the CEO and the CEO's time are considered highly valuable. The organization, working through its members, is determined to optimize the use of that resource. In a well-meaning but potentially dangerous practice, the CEO is secluded behind various barriers and becomes captive to the organization and its culture. And, to a lesser extent, so are other members of the C-Suite."

I just know some of you are dabbing at the tiny tears appearing at the corner of your eyes because you have such great empathy and sympathy for those who have suffered along the road of kingship.

Okay, probably not.

As you read these stories, though, I ask you to keep in mind that senior business leaders control multiple hundreds of billions of dollars in assets—assets that are probably in your 401(k) retirement account. This is a serious issue. Putting anyone into solitary confinement almost always has a downside. Placing our senior business leaders in solitary confinement, soft or otherwise, almost always produces negative results.

Here's a description from Fred, a Fortune 1000 CEO with a long tenure in the box.

Placing our senior business leaders in solitary confinement, soft or otherwise, almost always produces negative results.

"It begins and is a slow gradual path to self-delusion. I had my own company plane and helicopter. And I was driven everywhere in a chauffeured limousine. Everybody begins telling you how smart and good-looking you are. Everybody, when you have an idea, says they love it. Now, who knows what they say behind your back. But the further along you go, you get paid more money, everybody says that you're smartest guy in the room.

"Your time is incredibly valuable. So everybody accommodates your schedule, your every whim. If somebody wants to meet with you, they need to meet when you want and where you want. And in all of these roles, they're like mini-presidents of the United States where there is tremendous infrastructural support that is designed to treat you like a king. Ultimately, the company gets every possible minute out of your day.

You begin to believe that it is about *you* and who *you* are and that *you* are truly special.

"It's very seductive. After a while, you begin to believe that it is about *you* and who *you* are and that you are truly special. At first, you could possibly believe you're smarter than anybody else. Then you believe you work harder than anybody else. Because of that, you grant yourself indulgences that others wouldn't have. And, I think some people eventually lose all perspective about not only what is right and wrong but also believing in their own impunity.

"I think that after ten or more years of everybody around you accommodating you, including looking the other way when you do things that are borderline, you can have moral lapses. Your judgment is cloudy and muddy. Eventually, you ask the rhetorical question, how can I possibly be wrong when everyone agrees with me?

Denied access to alternative perspectives because of the Box, particularly in matters of ethical judging, CEOs become restricted to seeing the world only through their organization's prism. This explains how Dennis Kozlowski, former CEO of Tyco, saw little problem with spending corporate funds on a *$15,000 shower curtain* for his private office.

Being captive behind the cloister walls and living within the Box leads to a certain kind of leader loneliness I've called Lonely Unease.

LONELY UNEASE

Lonely Unease is an emotionally stressful state experienced by C-suite executives, especially CEOs of publicly held companies subject to Regulation FD, who are unable to reach outside the company's culture for advice and counsel on matters subject to ethical judgments, except within legally defined privileged conversations. Lonely Unease is not confined to CEOs of public companies. If you've ever been a manager or leader, you understand your position can be a lonely one. Because you are the manager or leader, you are unable to socialize with your direct reports.

Those of us who have tried it understand the unwanted and un-intended consequences that can often develop.

It's easier if you're not the only manager or leader at your level in the organization. If you aren't, you have peers with whom you can associate and to whom you can reach out for advice and commiseration. Even in that situation, however, the politics of the group may preclude any close associations, especially if everyone is gunning for the boss's job. Many of the C-Suite members I interviewed thought they could not appear weak, indecisive or solicitous of emotional support. One CEO commented said this:

> "You cannot nor should you go drinking with the 'guys' or fraternize with your direct reports. The relationship should be one of mutual respect. We're in a unique position. It's inappropriate to reach down, and it's potentially embarrassing, politically unwise and potentially unsettling to the board to reach up. You're out there all by yourself."

Another CEO prefaced his comment with the proviso that he wasn't seeking sympathy. Instead, he was trying to explain something few understand.

> "Although no one forces us to become CEOs, it can be a lonely job. We're supposed to have all the answers and model the right behavior, especially when ethics are involved. Yes, I can get counsel and advice from my management team, and I do. But the counsel and advice that comes from within the culture—if I'm doing my job right—I helped create. Therefore, I am probably not going to get opinions contrary to what I may already believe. Going outside the company for advice

is problematic because of Regulation FD. Sometimes I feel like I am locked inside a cocoon with no lifelines."

Here's another CEOs' description of Lonely Unease.

"As you get higher, it becomes harder and trickier to have outside lifelines. But you've got to have those outside lifelines. Maybe it's a spouse, a pastor, a lawyer or a psychologist. It needs to be somebody that you can have some privileged communication with. Because in order to get other perspectives, you have to share things that are sensitive. In some cases it's just flat illegal unless they are privileged communications. But you've got to have that lifeline."

Finally, here's an observation from a vice president of a public company that has experienced some negative press from the CEO's office. The question he's answering is "What are your thoughts about seemingly irrational behavior from senior leadership?"

"... I think they think they're just above everything because they're so isolated. They've been taken care of for so long, they've lost touch with reality. They just think whatever they do is fine because no one ever disagrees with them. And because they're wealthy, they can do whatever they want and get away with it. I think people are just stupid the way they do some things. Just because you might have had a couple drinks and some beautiful girl, whatever the circumstances are ... and you think no one will ever know. And then when you wake up in the morning—it's like holy shit!"

The solitary confinement of senior leaders, coupled with Lonely Unease, is a combustible mixture. Even for those of us who have a finely tuned Internal Compass, a strong commitment to acting righteously and a crystal clear Worldview Window, isolation and Lonely Unease can seriously compromise ethical judging. All of us must be held accountable for our behavior by someone. For some of us, a spouse provides that accountability and is a legally permissible party. Absent a legally cleared confidante (spouse, clergy, attorney or doctor) most of us are on our own and alone. Let's examine one of the major sources of this problem.

ENFORCED EXECUTIVE SILENCE

On Wall Street, information is the most valuable commodity—much more than money. Real-time widely disseminated information is the fuel that powers open and fair financial market operations. Anyone who possesses actionable information unknown to other market participants holds a supremely competitive edge, which is why trading on such information is illegal.

Trading in so-called "inside" information has long been the bane of financial markets and regulators. Since its founding more than eight decades ago, the Securities Exchange Commission has pursued increasingly draconian remedies to this problem, mostly to no avail.

Controlling the flow of information, especially now when the entire world has access to the Internet, is like trying to hold water in your hand. It's nearly impossible. The task was marginally easier prior to the

Internet, but still difficult. In addition, the problems of inside information and insider trading have worsened in the last several years because the *definition* of inside information and insider trading has become a moving target. United States attorneys and other prosecutors have been expanding the definitional envelope in seeking indictments and convictions for insider trading.

Recently, the United States attorney in Manhattan had a number of insider trading convictions overturned on appeal. These voided convictions added further confusion and muddied the waters surrounding all areas of inside information and insider trading. What are the practical and real-world consequences of this current state of affairs? Corporate counsels and securities lawyers in general have become hypersensitive and, in most cases, substantially overprotective of clients. This is one of the unintended and unwelcome consequences of ethics based on laws, regulations, rules and court cases.

The primary regulation of interest to us in this context is Regulation Full Disclosure, or Regulation FD. As with most rules or regulations, the intentions and objectives of any particular rule or regulation are noteworthy. In this case, the intent and objective of Regulation FD were to ensure that any new important information about a company or security was released to all market participants at the same time.

Previous to the promulgation of Regulation FD in August 2000, Wall Street analysts and many large institutional investors had early access to company information. The unintended consequence of this well-intentioned regulation, however, was the silencing of business leaders at all levels of the organization. Here's an early enforcement example of this regulation in action:

In 2002, the CEO of Siebel Systems was fined $50,000 for telling an assembled group of Wall Street analysts and institutional

investors that he was "optimistic" about Siebel's business returning to normal. Just three weeks earlier, Siebel's management had
publicly issued guidance that was "pessimistic" about the company's near-term prospects. Whether you agree that this was a just
fine or not, the real-world practical lesson most senior business
leaders and their corporate counsels took was "Keep your mouth
shut. The best policy is silence." Or, "Say less with more accompanying legalese. "

We have unintentionally muzzled our senior business leaders. This matters because, as we experienced with Truman's
ethical sweat, ethical judging is an utterly solitary activity. If I
am the CEO and I'm wrestling with a potentially harmful ethical
dilemma, it would be very helpful if I could reach out to trusted
advisors—ones who don't fit the safe harbor provisions of Regulation FD—for perspectives that are totally outside the purview of my organization. As an example, let's use Mark's ethical
dilemma from the story that opened this chapter—the one in
which Mark was put in a compromising position by a "gift" from
Señor Diego.

Mark is CEO of a public company. He's had an experience that
is personally embarrassing, unethical and harmful to his family.
Moreover, he's had an experience that has potentially devastating legal and economic consequences for him and his company.
The information about this problem is undoubtedly covered by
Regulation FD. So he has few advisory options outside of his
organization to which he can reach for advice and perspective.
Where does he go for objective advice? Inside his organization,
the advice is most likely going to skew in the direction of the
company's best interests. Unfortunately, his spouse is probably
not an objective source, either.

So, what does he do? Unfortunately, the most common reaction is to lie, cover up the problem and run away from it, hoping it gets better. Running away from problems never works. The problems only get worse.

Mark could ease into a long-term relationship with Luisa and pay her money to keep quiet. He could also do Señor Diego's bidding, hoping the potentially illegal "favors" go undiscovered.

In both cases, can you detect an obliterated Ethical Fence and a joyride down the Slippery Slope? Neither ever works out well. Add to all of this the crushing stress resulting from Mark's never-ending fear of discovery, and you have a significantly compromised chief executive officer.

I believe we must free leaders from enforced solitary confinement. No one disputes the need for appropriate organizational security, especially cyber security. But the metaphorical moat and razor wire behind which many organizations have retreated is unhealthy for not only organizational culture but also its leadership team. Leaders becoming captive to the cloister is not a condition that contributes to appropriate ethical judging. The Innocuous Imperial Box is a well-intended but potentially harmful transition to the Slippery Slope.

Finally, silencing senior leaders who control trillions of dollars of national and personal wealth isn't the way to preserve and grow that wealth. Public openness and transparency are worthy goals, but sometimes that openness and transparency need to occur behind appropriately closed doors, outside the reach of law enforcement. Solitary confinement may be appropriate for incarcerated felons, but it's poison to leaders as they make ethical judgments. So, in the words of one of our former presidents, "Tear down these walls ..." We'll discuss some potential remedies in Part 3 of this book.

———————◆———————

Chapter Highlights

- The ethically intelligent leader runs toward problems, not away from them.
- Regulation FD had the unintended consequence of muzzling business executives in unexpected and undesirable ways.
- Senior business leaders are smothered in good intentions that eventually result in corrupted ethical judging.
- The Innocuous Imperial Box is a metaphorical container in which many senior business executives find themselves.
- The Box is called Imperial because it has the trappings of royalty: power, prestige and prerogatives.
- It's called Innocuous because it's usually well-intentioned, allowing an executive's time to be spent efficiently and productively on behalf of the organization.
- Placing our senior business leaders in solitary confinement, soft or otherwise, almost always produces negative results.
- Lonely Unease is an emotionally stressful state experienced by C-suite executives—especially CEOs of publicly held companies subject to Regulation FD—who are unable to reach outside the company's culture for advice and counsel on matters subject to ethical judgments, except within legally defined privileged conversations.

Questions for You

- Are you captive to a cloister? How do you know?
- Are all of your incoming communications screened?
- Has anyone ever told you how hard it is to reach you?
- Who sets your schedule and agenda?
- Do you write external communications? Or do you just approve what someone else has written?

PART THREE

———————◆———————

ETHICALLY INTELLIGENT LEADERSHIP: OUR SOLUTION

> If you don't know where you're going, you'll end up someplace else.
>
> *Yogi Berra*

I began this book with a bold statement: "Ethically intelligent leaders are the solution." In Part Three, I lay out a roadmap that shows the way to that solution.

Ethical intelligence is your birthright. It's a shining birthstone living in your consciousness, awaiting your call to awaken it from slumber. I have embraced my ethical intelligence. I've trod the path of discovery for more than 12 years. Because it was unknown territory, my journey took many unnecessary detours, and I encountered many needless roadblocks, but I now know my way. It's my honor and privilege to share my way with you in the following chapters.

Become a Warrior of Hope!

PART THREE

ETHICALLY INTELLIGENT LEADERSHIP OUR SOLUTIONS

CHAPTER 9

---◆---

YOU MAY BE ETHICALLY
INTELLIGENT IF...

You know in your gut what the right answer is . . .
you feel it, okay?

Fortune 500 CEO

This chapter is about recognizing ethically intelligent lives and learning from them. It's the first and an integral part of our Roadmap for awakening and nurturing an ethically intelligent life.

I want you to be able to know ethical intelligence when you see it. Then you can recognize it in yourself. You need to be able to see it in yourself. I want you to look in the mirror every morning and boldly declare:

"Wow! My ethical intelligence looks awesome today!"

In this chapter, we'll recall ancient wisdom about the look and feel of an ethically intelligent life. We'll comparing that to what the senior business leaders I interviewed said about the ethically intelligent people they've encountered. Along the way, we'll examine some exemplary ethically intelligent lives and discover what those lives can teach us.

As we proceed, remember that your ethical intelligence lives in your consciousness but shows itself in the world within relationships. Like beauty, ethical intelligence is something we recognize when we see it—*always within relationships*.

We begin with our first story of an ethically intelligent life—Adolf Busch.

Adolf Georg Wilhelm Busch was welcomed into this world on August 8, 1891, in Siegen, Germany. Busch, a musical child prodigy, was born into a musical family. He studied violin at the Cologne Conservatory and was mentored and tutored by Hugo Grüters, whose daughter Busch later married. At the age of 21, Busch founded the Vienna Konzertverein Quartet. After World War I, he founded the Busch Quartet, which debuted during the 1920-21 musical season. The Quartet played together with varying membership until 1951.

Although Busch was not Jewish, he had many friends and acquaintances who were, including members of his quartet. Rudolf Serkin, another child prodigy, joined the musical company when he was 18 years old. A renowned pianist, Serkin, who was Jewish, later married Busch's daughter Irene. The Busch Quartet and Serkin teamed up to form the Busch Chamber Players. Busch and his musical company flourished, playing in venues all over Europe. Busch was hailed as one of the greatest violinists of the twentieth century. In Italy, Busch was the Taylor Swift of his day. His musical career was soaring. Then, along came the Third Reich.

With the rise of Hitler and the Nazi party in Germany, Busch was one of the few renowned German musicians to publicly denounce Hitler. In 1927, he left his beloved Germany and moved to Switzerland. Hitler was well aware that Busch was a cherished national treasure and an important testament to his "master race" narrative. But despite receiving multiple personal pleas and written assurances from Hitler, Busch refused to return to Germany. In fact, he said, "I will return with joy on the day that Hitler, Goebbels und Göring are publicly hanged!"

As the Nazi persecution of Jews intensified and Mussolini rose to power in Italy, Busch also stopped performing in Italy because Mussolini began the same persecution of Jews in Italy. Because Germany and Italy were the two largest markets for Busch and his musicians, Busch's income plummeted. Out of deeply held principles, Busch had walked away from his musical career at its zenith, forsaking certain fame and fortune.

> Out of deeply held principles, Busch had walked away from his musical career at its zenith, forsaking certain fame and fortune.

At the outbreak of World War II, Busch left Europe and emigrated to the United States. He and Serkin cofounded the Marlboro School of Music in Vermont. Although Busch and his musical company continued to record music and play venues in the United States, his brand of chamber music was never appreciated as it had been in Europe. Busch's income never again approached its European zenith, but he continued teaching and recording music. Some of his more renowned students were Stefi Geyer, Erica Morini and Yehudi Menuhin. Arturo Toscanini reportedly called Busch a saint.

At great personal cost, Adolf Georg Wilhelm Busch lived an ethically intelligent life.[1]

WE KNOW WHAT IT LOOKS LIKE!

One of the most important ways we learn is through emulation. We watch others perform a task or display a skill. Then we try to duplicate what we've seen. This is one of the ways we awaken our own ethical intelligence and begin living its principles in our own lives.

One of the challenges with this approach, however, is that not all of us see the same characteristics in the same scenario.

We attach meaning to the reality our senses provide us by passing that reality through our worldview prism. So, teaching someone to recognize ethical intelligence is like teaching someone to recognize beauty. It is always seen through the prism of the beholder's worldview. That being the case, we're going to have a look at different perspectives, hoping that one or more of those perspectives resonates with you.

> ... teaching someone to recognize ethical intelligence is like teaching someone to recognize beauty.

Aristotle believed that everyone possessed an inherent ability to recognize the beauty of a correct ethical judgment. Following Aristotle's lead, Schiller said those who were aesthetically gifted would most easily recognize the beauty of a just ethical judgment. Yet we have cases where a substantial majority of people fail to recognize or acknowledge questionable ethical behavior. For example, how could Abraham Lincoln recognize and say that, "If slavery is not wrong, nothing is wrong," when the majority of those around him were blind to that truth? We're going to answer that question with examples and stories.

Ancient Wisdom. For the purposes of this discussion, I'm going to use Confucius as a model of ancient wisdom. The following passages from the *Analects* represent the same concepts and ideas about ethical intelligence available from many other ancient sources. Some of us, for instance, might recognize the similarity of meaning contained within the following passage and Psalm 15.

> The Master said, don't worry about whether other people understand you.
> Worry about whether you understand other people.

The Master said, virtue is not alone. It invariably has neighbors.

The Master said, the humane person wants standing, so he helps others to gain standing. He wants achievement, and so he helps others to achieve.

If when he spies gain, he remembers what is right.

When he spies danger, is ready to risk his life.

When faced with old promises, does not forget his past words.

Then he can be termed a humane, complete person.

Fan Chi asked about humaneness. The Master said, Love others.

Humaneness has been translated as *Ren*, a word used more than 100 times in the *Analects*. Over the millennia, using contextual analytic methods, scholars have interpreted *Ren* to include the following:

- *Altruism*
- *Benevolence*
- *Compassion*
- *Empathy*
- *Faithfulness*
- *Kindness*
- *Love*
- *Righteousness (R^2 Behavior)*
- *Trustworthiness*
- *Truthfulness*
- *Wisdom*

Some of the words on this list implicitly include other characteristics. For example, we know that R^2 Behavior includes dis-

cernment, integrity and truthfulness. Also, this list is in alpha-
betical order because the ancients attached no particular weight
or importance to these characteristics, although Augustine did
mention that ethical intelligence was necessary for understanding and living other virtues. So what does this mean?

These are character traits of ethically intelligent people. Using the redneck joke construct made famous by Jeff Foxworthy, I
offer the following statements:

- *You may be ethically intelligent ... if you're kind and always tell the truth.*
- *You may be ethically intelligent ... if you keep your promises, even if it costs a lot more than you anticipated.*
- *You may be ethically intelligent ... if you give your trash haulers a cold drink on a scorching summer day.*
- *You may be ethically intelligent ... if you anonymously pay a single mom's check as she treats her three kids to a meal in a nice restaurant.*
- *You may be ethically intelligent ... if you encourage someone every day.*
- *You may be ethically intelligent ... if you pick up a piece of trash in the parking lot even if it's not your trash.*
- *You may be ethically intelligent ... if you take full responsibility for a missed delivery date even though the late delivery result-ed from one of your team member's mistakes.*
- *You may be ethically intelligent ... if you never say, "It's not my fault!"*

These are the personal characteristics the ancients say we
should consider in recognizing ethical intelligence. Something
to keep in mind, however, is that ethical intelligence is a holism.

Simple seeing some of these character traits in action doesn't necessarily mean the person is ethically intelligent, but it can indicate that they're on the path.

Let's look at what our senior business leaders had to say about this same subject.

Senior Business Leaders. The senior business leaders I interviewed had some very specific ideas about this subject. You may be surprised to see how their list of character behaviors of ethically intelligent people lines up with the ancients' list.

Here is the business leaders' list, ranked in order of importance. In eliciting these responses, I asked, among other questions, the following: "Tell me about a person you highly admire for the way they live their lives, run their businesses and exhibit ethical behavior. Please describe that person to me." The results were consistent from leader to leader. Here is that list.

- R^2 *Behavior*
- *Discernment*
- *Leads by example*
- *Truthfulness*
- *Integrity*
- *Courageousness*
- *Transparency*
- *Wisdom*
- *Directness*
- *Honesty*
- *Trustworthiness*
- *Respects insignificance*

Allowing for the ancient language differences, the two lists are closely aligned, affirming how timeless and unchanging these truths are. We've already talked about most of the items that are on this list, some meriting complete chapters in this book. Out of the hundreds of different responses to these questions, here is a small sample of what senior the business leaders had to say.

R² Behavior. "I'll give you a composite example. People who think deeply about the impact of their actions on all the stakeholders, whether it's employees, shareholders or the geographic locations where they do business. And people who demonstrate by their actions that they want to do the right thing. It's not just talk. It's demonstrated through action. Those are the people that I have respect for. They're willing to make the hard decisions. Sometimes it may not be the decision that results in the optimal economic result, but it's the right ethical result."

Discernment. "I think being straightforward, transparent, realistic and having good judgment. You don't want to find the opposite, which is finding somebody who is doing something that really turns out to be unethical, and they don't even know it. They don't even realize that they're crossing the line. Ignorance or lack of knowing is a more dangerous problem."

Leads by Example. "He [a new CEO] does not just say what he would like. He holds people accountable for their behavior. And he's just beginning to do that. That's going to be a good thing. It's going to turn the company around. If you take that example and generalize it, I look for someone who not only describes with clarity mores of ethical conduct but also lives by and exhibits them."

Truthfulness. "Although not a living business peer, I have the highest regard for George Washington and his ethics. Washington placed the welfare of others before himself. He was a man who always told the truth and valued his honor and integrity. He was nearly obsessed with living his life in accord with his personal values and honor. He valued his good name more than fortune and fame."

Integrity. "Most of the individuals I admire have a high degree of integrity in their own personal life as well as their business life. Most of these people are good people, and they make good decisions. They do what they say they're going to do. So, high integrity both in their personal and business lives is what I look for."

Courageousness. "He is principled, a self-thinker or a critical thinker. He puts others before himself. The people that I have looked to in my career, like this guy, have done the longer-term things. People I've admired have been willing to stand on the island by themselves when that's what it takes. They know how to walk away."

Transparency. "She has the ability to separate herself from the situation. She walks the talk and has a level of truthfulness that shines through consistently. She consistently approaches things in a transparent way, no smoke and mirrors. And, openness. So, I think it's those kind of qualities: openness, transparency, consistency. For her, the implications of the decision don't outweigh the ethics."

Wisdom. "I hate to say this, but wisdom usually comes with a few gray hairs. During my career, the people I thought were wise had those gray hairs. Wisdom comes from long experience. You don't get it from reading books. You get it from living. You get it from being knocked around and picking yourself back up. Wisdom is knowing what battles are important. Wisdom is carefully considering all alternatives.

Wisdom isn't fast, but it's worth waiting for."

Directness. "If you want to move things in this world, you need to be straight with people. People need to be able to trust what you say and not have to go through a whole analysis of what they think you mean because then nothing ever gets done."

Honesty. "She's very honest. She makes the right decision every time. She recognizes her mistakes. She admits if she could have done something better. I just mean she's very candid. She's an open book, and her honesty is always on display, but not in a preachy or condescending way. When she tells you something, you can take it to the bank!"

Trustworthiness. "He's trustworthy. I believe that, over time, the ethical behavior and the ethical history of an individual builds. In most cases, trust, respect, and admiration grow over time with consistent ethical behavior. And I think that gives him much more permission to lead when people see consistent ethical behavior."

Respects Insignificance. "It's letting everyone know they're important. It's not about just making them feel important. It's making sure you have an organization where there are important things to get done, and the people who are taking care of them are important, and they know it."

A Composite Profile. Now that we have the two lists, let's meld them together and create a composite profile. Approximately half of the words on each list are directly correlated—the other half not so much. Most of the difference is due to the vocabularies used by each group. Business leaders talk like business leaders. Philosophers and theologians use an entirely different word set. For example, we don't normally see business leaders using words like love, benevolence, and altruism. These are not business terms, but their meaning can be inferred from their context, which I have done. Here is the composite set of character traits or behaviors for ethically intelligent people.

- ***R^2 Behavior***
  - *Truthfulness*
  - *Discernment*
  - *Integrity*
  - *Courageousness*
- ***Cares for the Other***
  - *Altruism*
  - *Benevolence*
  - *Compassion*
  - *Empathy*
  - *Kindness*
  - *Love*
- ***Trustworthy***
  - *Faithfulness*
- ***Leads by Example***
  - *Transparency*
  - *Honesty*
  - *Directness*
- ***Respects Insignificance***
- ***Wisdom***

Some of these are families of characteristics. R^2 Behavior and Leads by Example are two of those families. Since we've devoted chapters in this book to them, we won't consider them further here. But we'll discuss the other four in more detail.

Before we begin, I want to emphasize again that these are

outward signs or clues about someone's ethical intelligence. Ethical intelligence is a holism that's greater than the sum of its parts. Regard these outward characteristics as evidentiary clues, but remember that it takes the whole package. Now, let's briefly explore each of these in reverse order.

> Ethical intelligence is a holism that's greater than the sum of its parts.

Wisdom. Wisdom is a mosaic consisting of knowledge, long experience and patient tolerance of uncertainty, ambiguity and complexity. Although not directly related to the age of its possessor, wisdom implies a long melding of the mosaic's components. An appropriate metaphor for the acquisition of wisdom is the aging of single malt scotch whiskey. Typically, the older the scotch, the better the scotch. Wisdom is a lot like beauty—you know it when you see it.

Throughout the ages, wisdom has been known as a person. Depending on the civilization, religion or belief system, wisdom has been known as Isis, Athena, Achamoth, Black Virgin, Sister Wisdom, Mary, Prudence, Minerva, Spenta Armatii, and the Eternal Feminine. Socrates significantly enlarged the definition of wisdom and showed how it's an all-inclusive term for ethical intelligence. Whatever your personal understanding of wisdom, it's an essential cornerstone of ethical intelligence.

Respect Insignificance. Respecting insignificance is a direct reflection of the condition of our Worldview Window. We respect everyone and everything we can clearly see through that window, even if that someone or something appears to be of little importance or value. Insignificance may imply someone who can neither hurt nor help you. Insignificance may imply the state of wellness of the local bird or honeybee population. The ethically intelligent person respects all the degrees of insignificance.

Trustworthy. Trustworthy is an adjective describing someone or something we can trust. Trust is a belief in someone or something that's true. Synonyms for trust include faith, hope, confidence and expectation. When we trust in someone or something, we're confident that our expectations will be fulfilled. The content of our expectations is based on our relationship with the object of our trust. For example, we trust that our money will have continuing value. The implied expectation is that our money will not become worthless.

Trust is one of the most important elements of the *Primal Relationship*. It's the cornerstone of the connection between Self and Other. You can't have a successful relationship without trust because your ethical intelligence lives in your consciousness, but it manifests within relationships. Trust is an irreplaceable element of ethical intelligence, and it's an essential element of leadership. You can't lead anyone anywhere without first creating a mutual trusting relationship.

Cares for the Other. Caring for others is intrinsic to our nature as humans. We're hardwired to care for others. We see this in young children. They have instant compassion and empathy for one another. As we grow older, and for reasons we've already discussed, we lose this innocence. But, it still lives within us encased within a hardened shell of Violative Paranoia, Hostile Otherness, selfishness and ambivalence. Despite that hardened shell, however, we see it frequently spring openly to life.

For example, Americans privately gave over $1.3 billion to the Haiti earthquake victims. On a per capita basis, the people of the United States historically have been the most generous givers in the world. I'm talking here about private giving, not government assistance. Don't get me wrong, this is not a self-serving gratuitous statement about the goodness of the American people, although I think we are good. I'm citing this as evidence that it isn't too late to awaken the gift of ethical intelligence that lives within all of us. It's from that gift that caring for others flows.

So, how does this work? Even if our Worldview Window is completely closed and resembles a mirror, our connected world has a way of showering us with images of the Other in distress and need. We see compelling images on our televisions, smart phones, computers and other connected devices that penetrate that hardened shell and immediately stir our gift of ethical intelligence, if only for a brief moment. Our hearts are moved by images of people and animals in dire need of assistance. So we give of our time, talents and treasure.

I'll freely admit that many of the charities I support began with me seeing an image of someone or something in great need. For example, I began supporting the Humane Society of the United States and ASPCA after seeing images of abandoned and disheveled puppies. My support for St. Jude's Children's Hospital also began after reviewing a series of pictures of young children battling cancer. No matter how hardened our internal shells have become, they can be pierced because our submerged ethical intelligence cries out for action. For some of us, this remains a mystery. So let's have a deeper examination.

Cares for the Other is a large family of separate but interrelated components—altruism, benevolence, compassion, empathy, kindness and love—woven into an integrated whole. Altruism and benevolence are terms not used very often in everyday discourse. But they give important meaning to the idea of caring for others.

Dictionaries tell us that altruism is unbiased and selfless concern for the well-being of others, and benevolence is a desire to be charitable to others. Both of these definitions are Other-centric. Within these two definitions we see the implicit operation of the Worldview Window.

We must first see the Other in order to be altruistic and benevolent, which means our Worldview Window must be open, void of prejudice and free of the possibility of personal gain. Charity without strings attached is true charity. Giving substance to someone who can never repay you is true benevolence.

I hope you see the idea of respecting insignificance implicated in this discussion because even though we're isolating these terms and discussing them individually, all of these ideas are interrelated and part of an inseparable whole.

Compassion and empathy are more easily understood.

The literal meaning of compassion is "suffering together." Empathy is vicariously experiencing the feelings, thoughts and attitudes of another. Empathy is being able to walk in another person's shoes.

If we look at the nearby photo, most of us instantly recognize its meaning. A mother is mourning the loss of a child. Parents who have lost a child immediately identify with the mother in the picture. Even those of us who haven't experienced that type of loss identify with the mother in the picture. That's empathy.

The feelings we experience when empathizing with the mother constitute compassion. We suffer with her. We feel her pain.

We experience her tears. We know the emptiness in her heart. We feel her grief. We feel the void in her life. We're built for such a moment as this. It's intrinsic to our human nature. Compassion is akin to an autonomic bodily response, like breathing. Unless we've closed our Worldview Window or we've allowed our *Primal Relationship* to thoroughly corrode and become a toxic waste dump, it happens simply because we're human.

Kindness and love are the last two members of the Cares for the Other family of ethically intelligent characteristics. These two words can evoke widely varying meanings for all of us. The English language also presents certain challenges with respect to both of these words, especially love. Here are some of the various dictionary definitions of kindness: "The quality of being friendly, generous, and considerate." "The act of going out of your way to be nice to someone or show a person you care." "A sincere desire for the happiness of others."

These are all good and effective. My personal favorite is the last definition because it's in harmony with an open and crystal-clear Worldview Window. We must first "see" people to be kind to them.

Here are some of the various dictionary definitions of love: "A strong affection for another arising out of kinship or personal ties." "Attraction based on sexual desire." "Affection based on admiration, benevolence or common interests." "The most spectacular, indescribable, deep euphoric feeling for someone." Or, love is (courtesy of the Urban Dictionary) "nature's way of tricking people into reproducing." I'll let you pick your favorite.

...love is (courtesy of the Urban Dictionary) "nature's way of tricking people into reproducing."

My definition of love within this context is that special intimate bond of affection for the Other arising from the original pristine environment of the *Primal Relationship*. I believe this is what Jesus meant when he said the second greatest commandment was to love your neighbor as yourself. When asked to define ethical intelligence, Confucius echoed this imperative. He said, "Love others." The entire "Cares for the Other" family of ethically intelligent traits can be summed up in one word—love. We'll see this in action as we celebrate the lives of two exemplars.

CELEBRATING EXEMPLARS

I began this chapter with the story of Adolph Busch, a lesser known but compelling exemplar. There are thousands of lives I could have chosen to showcase, but I've selected George Washington and Abraham Lincoln because they're well known, much has been written about them and they aren't as controversial as some other possible candidates. Besides, I admire both of them immensely. Their lives exemplified ethically intelligent humans, which is the meaning of exemplar.

As you read these life stories, please keep in mind these weren't perfect humans. They had flaws like all of us. But, despite those flaws, they rose to meet the incredible challenges of their time. Each of them led a purposeful life dedicated to serving something larger than themselves. Lincoln courageously relinquished his life in the service of the Other. Both of these men made enormous sacrifices unrelated to personal gain. They showed us how ethical intelligence looks. We begin with George Washington.

George Washington. George Washington was a third-generation Washington. He'd hoped to receive an education in England, as had his two older brothers, but his father's premature death ended his formal education after only five years in school.

The remainder of his education was acquired from mentoring by older and wiser men, reading the classics in the libraries of influential family friends and through experience. Although Washington considered his life's experiences the most valuable portion of his education, he lived his entire life feeling inferior to his contemporaries due to his lack of a formal college education.

Washington's family was not of the nobility, but he desired to emulate the noble lifestyle of culture, manners, erudition and honor. That desire became one of the major influences in Washington's life—to become an honorable gentleman as defined during his time. One of his first acts in pursuit of that desire was to transcribe, at age 16, all 110 rules contained in the *Rules of Civility and Decent Behavior in Company and Conversation* (Rules) created by the French Jesuits in 1595.[2]

Washington lived by the Rules his entire life. The Rules spoke to all aspects of life, addressing manners, social graces and even personal hygiene. The Rules reflected the essence of Aristotle's definition of ethical intelligence. Aristotle defined wisdom as existing on two levels, the theoretical and the practical. The Rules were practical and designed to encourage living an ethically intelligent life. Many of the Rules were pithy restatements of sage advice given by other ethically intelligent exemplars—Confucius, Socrates and Jesus. Washington memorized and internalized the ancient advice contained in the Rules and lived his life accordingly.

Washington also studied Holy Scripture; *Seneca's Morals*; Addison's play, *Cato, a Tragedy;* and the life of Lucian Quintus Cincinnatus. *Seneca's Morals* was written by Lucius Annaeus Seneca, a Roman scholar, philosopher and moralist who lived during the first century of the new era. Seneca served at the court of Nero, engaged in Roman political intrigue and suffered the same life-ending fate as Cicero a century earlier. Seneca's work was similar to Cicero's in that he provided guidance for living a moral and ethical life. Throughout his life, especially those years when engaged in politics, Washington endeavored to be the "good man" Seneca described throughout his book on moral behavior.

Over the course of his life, Washington was dedicated to the ideal of republicanism, which explained his affection for the play, *Cato, a Tragedy*. Addison's play was set in the Roman North African province of Utica, which in current times is known as Libya. Cato was a Roman senator who was opposed to Caesar's quest to become emperor and absolute dictator. Caesar and his army had already vanquished most of the other North African provinces. As he marched on Utica, Caesar offered Cato a chance to not only enrich himself but also become a key player in the new Roman Empire. At that moment in history, Rome had been a functioning republic for more than three centuries. In the play, Cato stayed true to the ideal of republicanism, refused Caesar's offer and committed suicide rather than live in slavery under Caesar.[3,4]

Early in his life, Washington had also been influenced by the story of Lucius Quintus Cincinnatus, a Roman military hero who, during the 5th century B.C.E., not only gained the respect of his fellow Romans but also became a legend for declining the opportunity to become emperor after winning a decisive victory against the invading Celts. Instead, Cincinnatus retired from the military and returned to his farm. Because of Cincinnatus's virtuous act, Rome remained a republic. That lesson was not lost on Washington.

After the peace treaty that ended the Revolutionary War was signed in 1783, the people wanted to make Washington king of the new confederation of states. He was both honored and appalled, and he made the case for a strong republican form of government instead. To emphasize his recommendation, Washington declined the offer, resigned his military command and returned to his farm. Following Washington's example, several of his senior commanders also resigned military commissions and returned to civilian life.

As happened in the ancient Roman case, Washington's actions not only earned him the highest admiration and respect from his fellow citizens but raised his public stature far above all other public figures of the time. Years later, when it became apparent the original Articles of Confederation were inadequate for governing the new republic, Washington was asked to add his advice, counsel and stature to the efforts of crafting a new constitution underway in Philadelphia. Washington's influence and presence were instrumental in the creation and ratification of the Constitution. In the end, it was Washington's integrity and character that carried the day.

After the Constitution was ratified, Washington hoped to return home and resume his civilian life. At that moment in the history of the new republic, people were highly distrustful of politicians. Sound familiar? The divisions and disputes that created the need for a new Constitution developed into a groundswell of support for Washington to become the first President. It appeared that no one but Washington could both garner majority support and hold the fragile union together.

Washington reluctantly agreed to serve one term and was sworn in as President of the United States of America on April 30, 1789. In his inaugural address,

> Washington reluctantly agreed to serve one term and was sworn in as President of the United States of America on April 30, 1789.

Washington talked about Aristotle's ancient link between living the life of the "good man" of *Seneca's Morals* and happiness.

> There is no truth more thoroughly established than that there exists in the economy and course of nature, an indissoluble union between virtue and happiness; between duty and advantage, between the genuine maxims of an honest and magnanimous policy, and the solid rewards of public prosperity and felicity.

Washington went on to serve a second term because of the fragility of the union and the meddling in America's internal affairs by both the British and the French. In his farewell address, Washington thanked the American people for having honored him with election as its first president. In his eight years as president, Washington was fastidious in his conduct because he knew he was establishing a model for those who would follow him.

Washington was not without his faults, but the way in which he handled those faults was also reflective of an ethically intelligent person. Two examples illustrate this point. When still in his formative years, Washington spent considerable time studying in the library of the Fairfax family. The elder Lord Fairfax served as a mentor to Washington for many years. During the years of his contact with the Fairfax family, Washington fell in love with the reportedly flirtatious Sally Fairfax, the wife of William Fairfax. When Washington was injured in the French and Indian War, Sally was his attending nurse.

Their mutual love lasted for a lifetime. The two corresponded in writing throughout the remainder of their lives, even after Sally permanently moved to England. Despite the ready acceptance of womanizing and the institution of the mistress in Washington's time, the couple never consummated the relationship. Knowledge of the love affair remained hidden until after Washington, Sally and their respective spouses had died. It had remained a secret love affair of the heart. Washington understood self-discipline and the importance of virtue, even the *appearance* of virtue.

> Washington understood self-discipline and the importance of virtue, even the *appearance* of virtue.

As with most of the founders, Washington and his wife Martha owned slaves. Washington was criticized for that lapse in morality. His response to the criticism was that holding the union together was a higher priority. He believed that as the economy and country grew stronger and more diverse, slavery would no longer be an economic advantage, and the practice would fade away. In his will, Washington freed all of his slaves and provided them with handsome property allotments. He was the only founder to take that action.

Abraham Lincoln was cut from the same ethically intelligent cloth.

Abraham Lincoln. Abraham Lincoln, the 16th president of the United States, personified ethical intelligence, and his life served as a living model of Aristotle's vision of such a life. On the occasion of the Centennial celebration in Philadelphia, Charles Fowler eulogized Lincoln. The portion of Fowler's eulogy presented here is an eloquent summary of Lincoln's ethically intelligent life.

> Abraham Lincoln was the representative character of his age. He incarnated the ideal Republic. No other man ever so fully embodied the purposes, the affections and the power of his people. He came up among us. He was one of us. His

birth, his education, his habits, his motives, his feelings and his ambitions were all our own. Had he been born among hereditary aristocrats, he would not have been our President. But born in the cabin, and reared in the fields and in the forest, he became the Great Commoner. The classics of the schools might have polished him, but they would have separated him from us. But trained in the common-school of adversity, his calloused palms never slipped from the poor man's hand. A child of the people, he was as accessible in the White House as he had been in the cabin. His ethical intelligence made him the wonder of all lands.[5]

Abraham Lincoln exhibited the character features of ethical intelligence. The three examples from his life I've included illustrate humility, a holistic understanding of circumstances and an ability to exercise judgment in compromise. At one of his first Cabinet meetings in March of 1861, Lincoln was assessing and getting to know many of its members, most of whom were either former governors or senators. His cabinet members were also assessing the new president. In a biography published after Lincoln's death, his personal secretaries Nicolay and Hay published the following comments, taken from the notes of that meeting.

Lincoln came from humble circumstances. He never lost touch with his roots, and he retained that humility during his entire life.

The recognition and establishment of intellectual rank is difficult and slow. Perhaps the first real question of the Lincoln Cabinet was, "Who is the greatest man!" It is pretty safe to assert that no one—not even he himself—believed it was Abraham Lincoln.[6]

ETHICAL INTELLIGENCE: THE FOUNDATION OF LEADERSHIP

Lincoln came from humble circumstances. He never lost touch with his roots, and he retained that humility during his entire life.

The capacity for holistic thinking enables the assessment of the contextual elements surrounding an ethical dilemma, leading to a fully informed ethical judgment. Historian Harry Jaffa offered this assessment of Lincoln's approach to ending slavery: Lincoln "[knew] what is good or right, [knew] how much of that good is attainable, and [acted] to secure that much good [without abandoning] ... the attainable good by grasping for more."[7]

Although he was opposed to slavery, ending slavery was not Lincoln's first priority when he was elected. Preventing the looming civil war and keeping the Union together was. Nonetheless, Lincoln was under unrelenting pressure from the abolitionists to take action, despite the potential unconstitutionality, and the potential for disturbing an already inflamed populace. Historian Jaffa evaluated Lincoln's approach to mediating those opposing demands.

"No one was, in general, more prone than Lincoln to follow the dictates of ethical intelligence by which one attempts always to remove evils without shocking the prejudices that support them— allowing time and circumstances to wear down the prejudice."[7]

Crafting compromises between groups holding mutually exclusive beliefs required patience, respect, empathy, compassion and a clear vision, all of which Lincoln demonstrated.

Another incident relating to the slavery issue also shows Lincoln's ethical intelligence. An abolitionist from Illinois asked Lincoln to commit to writing some understandings he had reached with the governor of Illinois and one of its senators. Following is the salient portion of Lincoln's reply, conveyed in a letter dated April 4, 1864.

My dear sir, you asked me to put in writing the substance of what I verbally said the other day, in your presence, to Governor Bramlett and Senator Dixon. It was about as follows: I am naturally anti-slavery. If slavery is not wrong, nothing is wrong. I cannot remember when I did not so think and feel, and yet I have never understood that the Presidency conferred upon me unrestricted right to act officially upon this judgment and feeling. It was in the oath I took that I would to the best of my ability preserve, protect, and defend the Constitution of the United States. I could not take the office without taking the oath. Nor was it my view that I might take an oath to get power, and break the oath in using the power.[8]

> "If slavery is not wrong, nothing is wrong. I cannot remember when I did not so think and feel ..."

Lincoln's reply reflected both the anguish he felt about slavery and the solemn inviolate commitment he had made in his oath to preserve, protect and defend the Constitution.

In those circumstances, Lincoln faced a classic ethical dilemma. He knew slavery was wrong, but he had also sworn an oath to obey the Constitution, which didn't grant him the authority to end slavery. During his first term, Lincoln issued the Emancipation Proclamation, knowing the authority for such an act was not vested in him by the Constitution. Some regarded Lincoln's action as a cynical attempt at reelection. Lincoln believed it an act of conscience and eventually successfully amended the Constitution, officially ending slavery in the United States, an act that confirmed forever the ethical intelligence of the 16th president.[9]

On April 14, 1865, Abraham Lincoln paid the ultimate price for honoring his ethical principles. He was shot from behind while watching a play at Ford's Theater in Washington D.C., and died early the next morning. Lincoln achieved all of his objectives. He held the Union together, won the war and ended slavery. His ethical intelligence enabled him to thread the ethical needle to victo-

Lincoln fulfilled Aristotle's vision of the ethically intelligent person.

ry. Lincoln followed his head, heart, instincts, intuitions and common sense in carefully selecting courses of action while in the grip of intractable ethical dilemmas. Lincoln fulfilled Aristotle's vision of the ethically intelligent person. He'd pursued the mean.

In a letter to his brothers, the poet John Keats spoke of the quality he believed formed the character of a person such as Abraham Lincoln: "I mean [the quality is] *Negative Capability*, that is, when a man is capable of being in uncertainties, mysteries, doubts, without any irritable reaching after fact and reason."[10] It is that capacity for holistic thinking and judging that defined Aristotle's conception of ethical intelligence.

So, what can we learn from these two ordinary men who lived extraordinary ethically intelligent lives?

WHAT DO THEY TEACH US?

I see shining examples of righteousness (R^2 Behavior), wisdom, and trustworthiness in the lives of both of these men. Both men led by example in all aspects of their lives. Lincoln demonstrated his respect for insignificance, his open and crystal-clear Worldview Window and his care for others in his fight to end slavery.

During the Revolutionary War, Washington showcased empathy and compassion as he cared for the lives and living conditions of the men under his command. In his affair of the heart with Sally Fairfax, Washington showed us how to stay away from the Ethical Fence and off of the Slippery Slope.

Here are some additional takeaways from my study of both of these men's lives. We'll talk about many of these in more detail in the next chapter.

- *Reflecting the deep-seated cynicism we now find in our postmodern society, some historians and scholars contend that the written accounts of these men's lives were deliberately distorted in order to make both men appear better than they were. Some historians and scholars have gone so far as to claim that George Washington was a myth. In their view, he never lived. My sincere belief and desire is that we can rise above this dark thinking.*

- *Each of these men led a purposeful life dedicated to serving something larger than themselves.*

- *Both men showed it's possible to live an ethically intelligent life, even under difficult circumstances.*

- *Both men sacrificed for what was right in the service of others.*

R2 Behavior	Cares for the Other	Trustworthy	Leads by Example	Respects Insignificance	Wisdom
Truthfulness	Altruism	Faithfulness	Transparency	Open and clear Worldview Window	Long Experience
Discernment	Benevolence		Honesty		Patience
Integrity	Compassion		Directness		Tolerance
Courageousness	Empathy				
	Kindness				
	Love				

In constructing our Roadmap for awakening an ethically intelligent life, we now know what that life looks like. Here is the profile of externally observable character traits of ethically intelligent people.

We now move to the next chapter, where I'll show you my way to awaken your ethical intelligence. I say "my way" because your way may be different. As we go forward, I ask that you keep an open mind and a receptive heart. Some of this content may be completely foreign to you. Take heart. Much was foreign to me in the beginning. Now let's continue our journey.

YOU MAY BE ETHICALLY INTELLIGENT IF ...

- When gazing into a mirror, you see a servant instead of a master.
- Truth is your constant companion.
- You never "write off" anyone.
- You understand that always being right is overrated.
- You know that a single act of kindness can change the world.
- Saying "Thank you" is more important than asking "What's in it for me?"
- You can see the seeds of greatness in everyone you meet.
- Upon entering a room, your first thought is not "I am the smartest person in this room!"
- You guard your Heart Refuge with the same fervor as your 401(k).
- You understand that everyone can teach you something.
- You know that silence in the face of wrong is participation in the wrong.
- You continue doing the right thing when nothing but wrong is happening.
- You don't fight battles that don't matter.

- You understand that keeping your Worldview Window open and clear keeps you out of a prison of prejudice.
- Your most important mission in life is helping others.

Questions for You

- Are you ready for the journey to an ethically intelligent life?
- Can you maintain an open mind and a receptive heart?
- Do you like the idea of changing your slice of the world for the better?
- Can you walk away from something when you know it's the right thing to do, even if it hurts?
- Are you prepared to have some people leave you because they can't or won't go where you're going?
- Can you accept that sometimes perfection is the enemy of good?
- Are you open to believing that last time is not a predictor of this time?

Endnotes

1. Potter, T., Adolf Busch: The Life of an Honest Musician. 2010, Rochester, NY: Boydell & Brewer Incorporated.

2. Morrison, J.H., The Political Philosophy of George Washington. 2009, Baltimore, MD: Johns Hopkins University Press.

3. Lantzer, J.S., Washington as Cincinnatus: A Model of Leadership, in George Washington: Foundation Of Presidential Leadership And Character, E.M. Fishman, W.D. Pederson, and M.J. Rozell, Editors. 2001, Greenwood Publishing Group: Westport, CT. p. 33-52.

4. Seneca, L.A., Seneca's Morals by Way of Abstract. 60/1818, London, UK: Sherwood, Neely and Jones.

5. Fowler, C.H., Lincoln: A Speech Delivered in 1876 at the Centennial Celebration In Philadelphia, in Werner's Readings and Recitations No. 45: Lincoln Celebrations - Part I, S. Schell, Editor. 1910, Edgar S. Werner & Company: New York, NY. p. 88-89.

6. Nicolay, J.G. and J. Hay, Notes Taken at the March 29, 1861 Cabinet Meeting, in Abraham Lincoln: A History, the Full and Authorized Record

of his Private Life and Public Career - Volume III, J.G. Nicolay and J. Hay, Editors. 1886, The American Historical Foundation: Washington, DC.

7. Jaffa, H.V., Crisis of the House Divided: An Interpretation of the Issues in the Lincoln-Douglas Debates. 50th Anniversary ed. 2009, Chicago, IL: University of Chicago Press.

8. Lincoln, A., Letter Dated April 4, 1864 to A. G. Hodges, Esq., Frankfort, Kentucky, in Littell's Living Age, Volume 84, E. Littell, Editor. 1865, Littell, Son, and Company: Boston, MA. p. 428-429.

9. Fishman, E., Washington's Leadership: Prudence and the American Presidency, in George Washington: Foundation Of Presidential Leadership And Character, E.M. Fishman, W.D. Pederson, and M.J. Rozell, Editors. 2001, Greenwood Publishing Group: Westport, CT. p. 125-144.

10. Keats, J., Letter to George and Thomas Keats Dated December 22, 1817, in The Complete Poetical Works and Letters of John Keats, H.E. Scudder, Editor. 1899, Houghton Mifflin Company: Boston, MA. p. 276-277.

CHAPTER 10

$\diamond$

AWAKENING YOUR ETHICALLY INTELLIGENT LIFE

> When you are inspired...dormant forces, faculties,
> and talents become alive, and you discover
> yourself to be a greater person by far than you
> ever dreamed yourself to be.
>
> *Patanjali*

"Thank you, Mary, for that wonderful rendition of *Amazing Grace*. We continue with our memorial service, and I now invite Dr. Jim Williams to the podium."

"Thank you, Frank, all of us who knew him well recall that Dr. John taught us to begin at the end. As he always led by example, I'm going to read for you the epitaph that Dr. John wrote for himself some 36 years ago."

John Opincar, business practitioner, entrepreneur, educator and the "father" of ethical intelligence, left this life doing what he loved—teaching. Beginning with his first book, *Ethical Intelligence: The Foundation of Leadership*, published in 2009, Dr. Opincar wrote more than two dozen books and scores of articles as a relentless champion of ethical conduct and team-based corporate governance. His *Ethical Intelligence Mosaic* is now the accepted standard measure of an individual's ethical intelligence, and an ethical portrait is a fixed credential of every leader.

During his seven-decade professional career, Dr. Opincar was a certified public accountant, consultant, CFO, CEO and, most important, a teacher. He taught and mentored thousands of students who now hold leadership positions in all areas of society. Dr. Opincar is a devout follower of Jesus Christ, and he believed we are all endowed at birth with a treasury of talents, dreams and a life purpose. Determined to exhaust his treasury, Dr. Opincar used every talent, followed every dream and achieved his purpose in this life. And, praise God, he left empty!

BEGIN AT THE END

I wrote that version of my epitaph nine years ago, in October 2007. I've presented it exactly as I wrote it. As you can see, I am a bit behind on my original anticipated schedule for publishing this book. But I am still on course. The dates aren't important. It's the outcomes that should hold our attention. As you begin your journey toward awakening your ethically intelligent life, I urge you to begin at the end. Knowing where we're going helps us get there.

I suggest that you write your own epitaph. Doing so transforms the ephemeral into the tangible. As you can see from my example, your epitaph is a grand statement about your life, with a few detailed milestones. It doesn't have to be perfect, but it should be meaningful to you. It should be a clear expression of intentions transformable into action. Your actions make it real. For the planners among us, at this stage, don't worry about a formal plan. We'll get to that in just a moment.

As you write your epitaph, I want you to "put yourself out there." Be willing to do something you've never done. You don't really know what's inside until you place a demand on yourself. Include the dreams you really *want* to fulfill, not just those you think you *can* fulfill. If you never tire, your dreams are too small.

> Be willing to do something you've never done.

Unleashing your ethical intelligence empowers you to achieve goals you now think are impossible and to conquer mountains that currently appear unscalable. As you take this journey, you'll discover talents and capabilities you never knew you had. But—*it is a journey*.

> You don't really know what's inside until you place a demand on yourself.

Once you know what the end looks like, you're ready to begin. Many of us type-A personalities like to create milestones and establish time frames within which we want certain things accomplished. My advice to you is—don't do that. It creates unnecessary stress, and artificial deadlines serve no useful purpose. This is your personal journey from where you are now to an ethically intelligent life. Everyone is different. Some of us have a lot to learn, and we might be stubborn, as I am. I began my journey more than 12 years ago. Although I've made great progress, I'm still an unfinished work. You will be also.

> If you never tire, your dreams are too small.

My Roadmap to an ethically intelligent life has 13 life lessons. You'll recognize most of the content of these life lessons because we've discussed the underlying ideas throughout this book. The Roadmap provides an organized way to plan your journey. I've arranged the life lessons in the order that makes sense to me. Some life lessons build upon previous life lessons. I suggest you complete one life lesson and then move to the next. Because some life lessons require an extended period for completion (or will be incomplete your entire life), it makes sense to move on to others and work simultaneously. For example, working on always telling the truth and being grateful can require an extended effort and can proceed simultaneously. How you advance is up to you. My most important admonition is to take the first step and get started.

Here are a few tips and words of wisdom that I discovered along the way that may help smooth, inform and enhance your journey.

- *You need eagles in your life. Eagles soar with eagles.*
- *Don't engage in every battle, only those that move you closer to your destiny.*
- *You will never change what you tolerate.*
- *What you are unwilling to walk away from holds you back.*
- *If you have to knock, it's probably the wrong door.*
- *Don't let the "facts" become an impossible wall.*
- *Don't let the last time curse this time.*
- *Not everyone will celebrate your success.*
- *Some cannot go where you're going.*

Now let's begin *your* journey to an ethically intelligent life. A life that will change your slice of the world for the better. Prepare to become the solution—a Warrior of Hope.

ROADMAP TO AN ETHICALLY INTELLIGENT LIFE

This is a Roadmap to a better life. It's a set of critical life lessons. Although it may resemble a course syllabus, there are no assignments, and there is no grading. You determine whether you've successfully completed a life lesson or not. There is no time limit. I've been at this more than 12 years, and I continue to learn and progress every day. It's my hope that you'll make this your map. It's your journey.

As you move forward, I suggest you use our discussion from Chapter 9 as a companion along your journey. The content I presented in Chapter 9 will not only help you in self-evaluation but also will provide motivation. I also suggest that you designate a guru. No, this doesn't mean you have to go find some holy or ascended person as a guide. (Although, if that helps you, have at it.) What I'm suggesting is to select one of the ethically intelligent Masters, and ask them rhetorical questions.

Lau Tzu observed: "A journey of a thousand miles begins with the first step." Believe and begin. There will never be a better time than today!

For example, you might ask what would Socrates say about this? Or, what might The Prophet or Buddha recommend in this situation? Or, how would Jesus or Confucius react in this circumstance? In my case, I've used multiple gurus, including Jesus, Socrates, Confucius, Dr. Martin Luther King, Jr. and George Washington. All of these Masters have been special guests in my Heart Refuge. Some even have their own rooms!

Before we get started working through these life lessons, I want you to know there are resources available to help you with each one of these. I'll mention some during our discussion. The website for this book, **www.ethicalintelligence.com**, contains a much more comprehensive list of resources to help you work through this journey.

Now, let's get started. Here are the 13 life lessons. We'll discuss each of them in order.

1. **TRUTH**
2. **GRATITUDE**
3. **PURPOSE**
4. **HEART REFUGE**
5. **WORLDVIEW WINDOW**
6. **PRIMAL RELATIONSHIP**
7. **INTERNAL COMPASS**
8. **ETHICAL FENCE**
9. **EMOTIONS**
10 **SWEAT**
11. **THINKING**
12. **OTHERNESS**
13. **WISDOM**

We start with truth because it's single the most important characteristic of an ethically intelligent person. Living a life of truth-telling is the foundation upon which all else is built.

Truth. Telling the truth was one of the most difficult parts of this journey for me. As I mentioned previously, I was a practicing alcoholic for too much of my life. Alcoholics are consummate liars. I can detect liars and lying from a mile away. Unfortunately, we live in a culture of deceit. Lying has become an art form. Our culture even praises really good liars. So this is your first step: become a person of truth. Refuse to tell even a so-called "white" lie. Whether white, gray, or black, it's still a lie.

Yes, I know. We tell "white" lies so that we don't hurt people's feelings. That's just an excuse for laziness. Instead, learn patience, discernment and tact. Telling someone the truth is an investment. When done tactfully, it adds value to the person.

Telling someone the truth is an investment. When done tactfully, it adds value to the person.

For example, when I'm grading a student's paper, and the paper is terrible, I don't tell the student, "This paper sucks!" Instead, I convey the same message through constructive and helpful criticism. It takes more time and effort, but I'm making an investment in improving the student's writing ability. I'm adding value.

Sometimes, you might say, telling someone the truth could diminish their self-esteem. If telling someone the truth diminishes their self-esteem, it's the fault of the truth-teller. Most of us have become so comfortable with telling "soft" lies, we do it unconsciously and justify our truth-telling incompetence with this bogus self-esteem argument. Contrary to that famous Jack Nicholson movie line, people *can* handle the truth. What people can't handle are incompetent truth-tellers. An ethically intelligent person tells the truth effortlessly and gracefully. To do otherwise is a theft.

Yes, you heard that right. Lying to someone steals their freedom. When you lie to someone, you're eliminating choices in that person's life, which limits their freedom to take beneficial actions. If we return to the example of the terrible student paper, telling the truth allows them to choose an avenue of improvement. If I don't tell the truth, the student won't see any need for improvement and will make the false choice of the status quo. Healing comes from honesty. Lying doesn't add value to anyone or anything.

This is especially important for managers and leaders. Telling lies to the people you're entrusted to manage and lead destroys the trust that is the bedrock of the leader/follower relationship. I understand that in some organizational cultures, this is

> Managers and leaders who ask you to lie are inevitably going to lie to you. You can't trust those who lie to you.

a tall order. Most of us have been in situations where we've been instructed to lie to the people who rely on us. This is especially true when organizations are restructuring or downsizing. It's not easy. But find a way to tell people the truth. Then, if managers and leaders ask you to lie, actively look for an exit from the organization. If they ask you to lie, they're inevitably going to lie to you.

When I began this journey 12 years ago, I promised God and myself that I would stop lying, which included lying in all of its forms—omission, commission, obfuscation, cover-up and strategic silence. Stop lying in all of its various combinations and permutations. If I could do it, I'm positive you can. Pick a date and a time, and begin a life of truth-telling. It takes lots of heavy lifting. But the rewards are priceless.

Gratitude. Gratitude is an emotion expressing appreciation for what you have. The dictionary defines gratitude as the quality of being thankful, including a readiness to show appreciation for and to return kindness.

Gratitude has long been an emotion associated with religious practice, and all of the world's religions encourage gratitude as an essential element of moral practice. Since antiquity, philosophers have studied, theorized and recommended the virtue of gratitude. Gratitude has also been associated with spirituality. And, during the past decade, psychologists and others have begun studying gratitude.

Those studies have demonstrated that grateful people are happier, less depressed, less stressed and more satisfied with their lives and relationships. So, if you want to experience more positive emotions, feel more deeply alive, sleep better and even strengthen your immune system, be intentionally grateful for even the smallest things that you have. Neuroscientists have demonstrated that intentional gratitude rewires our brains in positive ways. As you might imagine, in our gadget-centric world, there are even apps for this purpose.

Our human nature is not hardwired for gratitude. In my experience, it's just the opposite. Our human nature is hardwired to complain. For every grateful and happy person we're blessed to meet, we encounter five complainers and unhappy individuals. I once worked for a CEO who prided himself with what he called finding the "hole" in the donut. His approach to life was to look for what was wrong rather than what was right in every situation. I noticed that he was an unhappy man. I also noticed that those who worked for him also became unhappy and complainers over time. Incidentally, he didn't have any long-term staff members.

So why is gratitude a key to living an ethically intelligent life? Being grateful requires humility and mindfulness. It requires us to respect insignificance. When we're grateful for the small things in life, gratefulness opens our minds and spirit so that we can "see" the people in our lives the world considers insignificant. Gratitude helps us maintain an open and clear Worldview Window.

I must confess, I am a testament to the assertion that we are not hardwired for gratitude. Being grateful is a recently acquired behavior for me. I once took all I had for granted almost to the point of seeing my gifts as entitlements. When one of those gifts is suddenly absent, you become keenly aware not only of its loss, but it's importance. How many times have you heard someone say "I wish I would've told her how important she was?" Or, "I always meant to thank him for how well he did his job." Don't wait. Grateful people rarely have these regrets because thankful acknowledgment is a way of life to them.

Gratitude is a learned behavior. Using whatever method works for you, I encourage you to intentionally express gratitude for something at least twice a day. I also suggest maintaining a log or journal. Record your gratefulness. Did I mention there are apps for this? Intentionality is important, but significance is not. You don't have to wait for that "big" event to express gratitude. Be grateful that you have a car to drive or that you have clothes to wear. Be grateful that you have a place to live. Or, next time the elevator is out of order, be thankful that you can climb the stairs. At my age, I'm thankful for waking up every morning. Being able to get out of bed without assistance is an added bonus.

Cicero said, "Gratitude is not only the greatest of virtues, but the parent of all the others." Here are a few special truths I've learned along the way.

- *Until you're grateful for what's not enough, more than enough will never come.*
- *You will never get to where you want to go as long as you complain about where you are.*
- *Walk in humility.*
- *No one likes complainers.*
- *One of the few things we can control in life is our attitude.*
- *Attitude is a choice—choose gratitude.*

Ethically intelligent people are humbly grateful, especially for knowing their purpose in life and pursuing it.

Purpose. Everything has a purpose. That includes you and me. We're not just a convenient collection of molecules existing to soak up resources and expel waste. We are greater than the sum of our material parts. All of us are designed to serve a purpose greater than ourselves. No one else exactly shares your purpose. It's extraordinarily personal to you. And only you are uniquely gifted to fulfill that purpose. When you understand this, the curse of

> All of us are designed to serve a purpose greater than ourselves.

jealousy and envy dissolves from your life. You get to run your race. No one else can run it like you. Your purpose is a gift. Seek and discover it.

There are excellent resources available to help you with this part of your journey. Rick Warren's *The Purpose Driven Life* has sold multiple millions of copies and is a good first step.[1] You choose what's best for you. Don't become discouraged if it takes a while. Life-altering changes don't happen overnight. But one day you'll know what it is, and a compelling peace will descend into your life. Spending significant quality time in your Heart Refuge, however, may accelerate your quest.

Heart Refuge. If you're estranged, fall in love all over again with your Heart Refuge. It's your sacred space. Only you can enter, and you have complete control over what happens there. If you haven't intentionally visited in a while, it's time. Your Heart Refuge is the source of your strength and power. Fill it with goodness and peace. Maintain it with great diligence, paying special attention to the poison dripping into it from your collective unconscious. When you feel its tug, go visit, because it's where you'll hear that still small voice with resounding clarity.

You can envision your Heart Refuge any way you like. Mine is a serene garden containing a bubling brook flowing into a small lake. It also includes a horse and numerous dogs, all wonderful life memories. But in addition to the structures we discussed previously, I have a well of joy in my Heart Refuge. I draw from that well frequently because it's a reliable source of power. The quietness and stillness that permeates my Heart Refuge is my strength. Yours should be also. Protect your Heart Refuge as you would great wealth. It's worth much more.

When you're in the midst of the storm, don't let the storm into your Heart Refuge. It's your most intimate place. It's where the real you dwells. Don't allow people into this intimate place who haven't earned it. Ethically intelligent people spend quality time there because it's where ethical judgments are made. Entering and spending time there is neither complicated nor difficult. The simplest way to begin is find a physical space that's quiet. Take slow deep breaths and relax. Close your eyes, and enter. The more time you spend there, the more you'll want to visit. It's addictive in a very good way.

I'll share my daily practice with you. Remember, this is my way. You'll need to find your way. The God I worship asks for our first fruits, time, energy, resources. So the first item on my agenda every morning is to enter into my Heart Refuge and spend about 30 minutes in prayer and meditation. My ritual is a combination of practices taken from all the major religions and several spiritual traditions. I listen to music that resonates with me and helps me enter into a meditative state. While I am in my Heart Refuge, I check my Worldview Window for clarity, and I clear any trash that's accumulated since my last visit. The trash includes any droppings from my collective unconscious, leftover spent emotions from previous ethical judging sessions and any unforgiveness that may be present.

Unforgiveness is toxic to you. After the toxic poison dripping from your collective unconscious, unforgiveness is the most common pollutant of your Heart Refuge. Unforgiveness is the single most misunderstood emotion. We mistakenly believe that not forgiving someone or something is a potent way to exact revenge. Nothing is further from the truth. Harboring unforgiveness destroys your peace and steals your joy. In the presence of unforgiveness, the well of joy in your Heart Refuge becomes

Unforgiveness never hurts the intended target, but it exacts a terrible toll on you.

a well of despair, resentment and pain. Unforgiveness never hurts the intended target, but it exacts a terrible toll on you. I know you're asking yourself why have I suddenly airdropped this complex subject here? The answer is simple.

Your Heart Refuge is the epicenter of ethical judging. Anything that affects the environment you find there directly affects your ethical judging. Unforgiveness blocks the flow of life. If your Heart Refuge is not a place of peace, rest and contentment but, instead, is a battleground of strife, stress and discontent, your ethical judging will be anything but just and equitable. And, your desire to visit will dissolve into dread and avoidance. Don't let your Heart Refuge become as inhospitable as a prisoner of war camp. Unforgiveness is a learned behavior. Unlearn and forgive. You may not forget. That's okay. But for your own personal well-being and freedom—forgive. It's the ethically intelligent thing to do.

As your journey winds through these life lessons, you'll visit your Heart Refuge frequently because it's where the Worldview Window, Internal Compass, Ethical Fence, comfort zone and the Sweatbox are located. Your Heart Refuge is the doorway to your mind. Guard and protect it zealously. Become an intimate friend and visitor to this place, It's your oasis of respite from a demanding world that fogs your Worldview Window.

Worldview Window. Grow into a steely eyed, ethically clear-sighted person. Clean and maintain your Worldview Window. Destroy legacies of hate. Drop preconceived notions. Demolish traditions of prejudice. Resist the blindness of the destructive mores of popular culture. See the Other for who they are, not for who you or your culture say they are. Your window should *never* become a mirror! When forming ethical judgments, you may consciously exclude the Other for good reasons, but only after you've first "seen" them. This takes hard work, a commitment to respecting insignificance and a willingness to stand alone on the island of truth and understanding when everyone else is not. The task is made easier if your *Primal Relationship* is a green and flourishing field.

Primal Relationship. Relationships are where your ethical intelligence manifests and blooms. The *Primal Relationship* is the model for all relationships. In its pristine condition, the *Primal Relationship* is comprised of love, trust, empathy, caring, respect, sympathy, compassion, altruism and intimacy. It's designed as an intimate, nonjudgmental and nourishing fluid bonding between and among human beings. During infancy and into childhood, the *Primal Relationship* retains these conditions. We call this child-like innocence.

As we mature and experience the acculturation of a particular worldview, the purity of the *Primal Relationship* is slowly contaminated. In our increasing interactions with other humans, we experience deceit, betrayal, and perceived or real injustice. Our Worldview Window slowly clouds over with learned prejudices. And gradually, almost imperceptibly, our once-fertile green field turns brown. You must make it a fertile garden once again. Ethically intelligent people meticulously tend this metaphorical garden as they would any real-world garden.

Relationships are treasures. Treat them accordingly. Part of tending your *Primal Relationship* garden is continually evaluating your Internal Compass.

> Relationships are treasures. Treat them accordingly.

Internal Compass. Constantly challenge your values and principles. Most of us have deeply held values and principles that govern the way we live our lives. They're not only essential to ethical judging, but they permeate and penetrate the whole of our existence, mostly in unseen ways. Your values and principles affect your life in much the same way as your autonomic nervous system governs the operation of your body. For example, you don't have to think about breathing. Breathing is automatic. We also don't think about the thousands of value judgments we're making every day. They just happen in the background.

Something of this importance cries out for our attention. We should frequently ask ourselves *Why do I believe what I believe? What's the source of those beliefs? How reliable is that source? Can I trust that source? Does that source have a hidden agenda? Would I still believe in what the source tells me if I were privy to that agenda?*

Maintain a healthy skepticism about what you believe. This doesn't mean that what you believe is wedded to the changing winds of popular culture. But keep in mind that most of our values and principles are rooted in our worldview. Is your worldview rooted in ancient traditions that haven't withstood the test of time? If you don't know, find out.

Remember, worldview is a *commitment and orientation of the heart.* Our worldview is like the original software governing our thought life. Just like the software that operates your computer or other devices, it should be updated periodically. Don't let outdated and perhaps inappropriate values and principles rooted in a past worldview poison your future. Update that software. Know what you believe and why, because your Internal Compass establishes the location of your Ethical Fence.

Ethical Fence. Using the guidance of your Internal Compass, stake out the location of your Ethical Fence. Build the fence. Drive its posts deeply into the ground. If you've challenged the contents of your Internal Compass and found those contents valid, the location of your Ethical Fence should be fixed and not easily moved.

Your Ethical Fence marks a line in the sand you will not cross. It's solid, unmistakable and immovable. You know in your heart and in your mind that crossing that fence is wrong and a serious mistake. When you build your fence, that's your commitment.

Building a solid, unmistakable and immovable Ethical Fence will bring peace and serenity to your spirit. It's an assurance to your chattering left brain that you know the boundaries, and you've laid them out clearly. Creating a life built upon such an ethical structure shows in your behavior. People will read your behavior and see and understand your commitment to that solid line in the sand. It will give them comfort and assurance. It will build trust in your leadership, as they will know your commitment to that fence is consistent, constant and continuous. Incidentally, the first post that you drive in the ground for that fence should be *truth.*

Once your Ethical Fence is locked in place, stake out your comfort zone. The size of your comfort zone will depend on how well you know yourself. You should equip your comfort zone with flashing lights and warning sounds. On the unlikely occasions that you're unsure of how close to the Ethical Fence you are, the flashing lights and warning sounds will *guide you.* The flashing lights and warning sounds are metaphors for that still small voice within that tells you when you're getting too close. Once your comfort zone is established, *stay within it!* This is the one comfort zone you should *never* challenge.

As we've seen throughout the stories contained in this book, your comfort zone is indispensable because ethical judging is drenched in powerful behavior-altering emotions.

Emotions. Learn to feel again. Embrace your emotions. Recognize that passion drives greatness. Emotions are the source of a meaningful life. Understand how your emotions drive your behavior, often in unpredictable and seemingly irrational ways. Study and embrace the family of five fears. You can't run, and you can't hide from them. They're real, and they overwhelm your rationality. Work on becoming emotionally intelligent. Start out with Daniel Goleman's books and branch out from there. Since Goleman introduced the idea of emotional intelligence in 1995, it has become an industry unto itself.[2,3,4] I'm sure you can find accessible and sufficient resources.

Emotions are powerful forces. Use them to your advantage. Understand, also, that emotions are the source of your sweat.

Sweat. Sweating is useful. It cools and cleanses the body. It's also an outward sign of hard work and physical exertion. We must sweat for our body to remain healthy. We also must sweat for our ethical intelligence to remain healthy and functional. We sweat when our emotions are highly engaged and aroused. Public speakers sweat when delivering an emotionally charged speech. We sweat when having sex. We sweat when our anger is aroused. Sweating naturally accompanies an amplified limbic system.

Visit your Sweatbox frequently. As your ethical intelligence develops and matures, you'll spend an increasing amount of time there. If you would like to have an experience in a physical sweatbox, I encourage you to engage in that ritual at an appropriate venue. I realize that some of you are mystified by this commentary because you can never recall an instance of occupying *any* sweatbox. This is because most ethical dilemmas don't require a sweat, as they are easily resolved within one of the other structures. If you've ever had to render a heartbreaking ethical judgment, though, you were in your Sweatbox but were unaware of its special place within your psyche.

As we've seen in many of the stories in this book, especially in Truman's sweat, the Sweatbox is a highly emotionally charged environment in which you argue with yourself because you're the judge, jury, defendant and prosecutor. The Sweatbox is where you adjudicate the "gray" cases. Rendering an ethical judgment about stealing is easily dispatched by your Internal Compass. Rendering an ethical judgment about taking a client to a high-end illicit poker tournament should easily fit into your comfort zone, or not. Choosing who lives and dies when there are two near-death heart patients but only one donor heart is available is a Sweatbox dilemma. You won't have to appear there often, but prepare yourself for when you're summoned and the sweating is profuse.

Thinking. Your thinking is a significant factor in awakening, nurturing and maturing your ethical intelligence. But I'm not talking about thinking in general. I'm talking about the *type of thinking* that occupies your mind. Please don't be offended, but most people are small thinkers. Their thoughts are focused on the minutia. Their mind is overrun with details. Small thinkers make their way through this minutia much like someone who is hiking through a forest walks through and among the trees. All they see are the individual trees and the surrounding details. Don't get me wrong, there is nothing wrong with this kind of thinking, but it's *not* the kind of thinking that leads to an ethically intelligent life.

In addition to the ability to engage in small thinking, ethically intelligent people are big thinkers. Big thinkers are strategic thinkers. They disengage from the details and look at the big picture. It's the classical 30,000 foot metaphor we use when we describe CEO thinking. Big thinkers are able to construct the context and connect the dots. They see the gems in the coal dust. Big thinkers can see the miracle in the mess. Big thinkers are what we call general systems thinkers[5] or, using the more modern terminology, holistic thinkers. We used to believe this was left-versus right-brain thinking. I'm not so sure of that simple answer anymore. I prefer to call it whole brain thinking. Why is this important?

It's important because ethical dilemmas occur within relationships—often a mosaic of relationships. In many cases, those relationships overlap and create subsets of equitable claims. The ethically intelligent person must be able to grasp the entirety of the situation and be able to connect dots of information that, on the surface, seem unrelated. As I've mentioned throughout this book, I presented students with ethical dilemmas embedded within complex cases and asked them to simply define the stakeholders and their interests in the outcome. In 100% of the cases, the students would enumerate only the most visible and obvious. That kind of superficial analysis is insufficient for rendering equitable ethical judgments.

Think back to Truman's decision to use atomic weapons. You witnessed his sweat. You heard the various arguments and considerations. Truman knew all of those details, and he was able to assemble them into a complete mosaic. He understood the big picture, and it helped him drill down, isolate and focus on the one single important consideration—minimizing the loss of any additional American lives. This is holistic thinking. It's something I want you to learn as you develop and nurture your ethical intelligence. It's an essential capability. Some people have it naturally as a gift. Everyone else has to learn how to do it. The sooner you get started, the better.

Otherness. Otherness is everything that isn't you. Over the millennia, we have forever lost our trust in innocent Otherness. For demonstrably valid and practical reasons, most of us rightfully distrust any Otherness. This cannot continue. We must rise to the occasion and thoughtfully love and respect Otherness. Simply because several people have screwed you over in business deals doesn't mean that *everyone* will screw you over in a business deal. We've all been betrayed. It doesn't mean *everyone* is a betrayer. Although we may have lost trust in leaders at all levels in society, that doesn't mean there aren't leaders we can trust. We need to learn and engage in discernment. How do we do this?

I know this is going to sound self-serving, but we become ethically intelligent. Changing your life by learning and living these life lessons provides the tools necessary for discernment. Visiting, purifying and opening your Heart Refuge is the first step. Cleansing your Worldview Window is the second. You must "see" the Other before any discernment occurs. Restoring your *Primal Relationship* to its ideal pristine green-field condition burns off the fog that hampers our clear perception of the Other. Jesus counseled us to be innocent as doves and wise as serpents. That is the ethically intelligent way of thoughtfully loving and respecting Otherness, for which Wisdom is our guide.

Wisdom. Wisdom is … I'll let you finish that sentence. We all understand wisdom within a thousand shades of gray. We've discussed wisdom in many places in this book. Throughout the millennia and within numerous religious and spiritual traditions, wisdom has been personified. The Greeks knew wisdom as Athena, the Romans, Minerva. Get to know wisdom. Become best friends. Wisdom is an enabler and a product of ethical intelligence. Learning and living the first 12 life lessons predisposes you to becoming wise. Wisdom is the fitting crown of your journey to an ethically intelligent life.

> Wisdom is the fitting crown of your journey to an ethically intelligent life.

Passionately living these 13 life lessons everyday of your life is the way to an ethically intelligent life. These life lessons don't exist in a vacuum. They spring from the knowledge and wisdom contained in this book. I encourage you to cross-reference each life lesson with its sustaining knowledge in the book. Although we've provided additional resources on the website, don't hesitate to tap into other outside resources that you find meaningful, including our Ethical Intelligence Research Center.

It's your future. It's your life. I am confident that you'll join us and become part of the solution. I leave you with some helpful daily practices and reflections.

DAILY PRACTICES AND REFLECTIONS

As we saw in the lives of our ethically intelligent exemplars, there are practices that should become part of our daily lives. As you journey along this Roadmap to an ethically intelligent life, engaging in these activities reinforces and reifies your victories along the way. Here are some daily practices and reflections that have been helpful to me.

- *Encourage someone today.*
- *Live a life that enables others to win.*
- *Help others win. It lifts you closer to winning.*

- *Forgive every morning.*
- *Don't let the sun go down on your anger.*
- *Treat everyone like they are the key to your destiny.*
- *People remember how they feel when they meet you.*
- *Believe in others more than they believe in themselves.*
- *Become someone's miracle today.*
- *Get good at letting things go today.*
- *Kind words work wonders every day.*
- *Be thankful for something every day.*
- *Celebrate someone today.*
- *Do something artistic today.*
- *Believe in people before they succeed.*
- *Give someone what you need today.*
- *Understand there will never be another you.*

Do You Know...

- What drives you?
- Where your Ethical Fence is?
- The boundaries of your ethical comfort zone?
- Your fear factor?
- Your breaking point?
- Your value?
- What to give?
- Where to turn?
- What everyone needs?
- Why you're here?
- There's hope?

Endnotes

1. Warren, R., The Purpose Driven Live: What on Earth Am I Here For? 2012, Grand Rapids, MI: Zondervan.

2. Goleman, D., Emotional Intelligence. The 10th Anniversary ed. 1995, New York, NY: Bantam Books.

3. Goleman, D., Working With Emotional Intelligence. 1998, New York, NY: Bantam Books.

4. Goleman, D., R. Boyatzis, and A. Mckee, Primal Leadership: Realizing the Power of Emotional Intelligence. 2002, Boston, MA: Harvard Business School Press.

5. von Bertalanffy, L., The History and Status of General Systems Theory. Academy of Management Journal, 1972. 15(000004): p. 407-426.

CHAPTER 11

---◆---

ETHICALLY INTELLIGENT ORGANIZATIONS

An ounce of prevention is worth a pound of cure.

Benjamin Franklin

Buzz ... buzz ... buzz ... buzz. The vibrating phone on the night stand finally stirred Jim from a deep sleep. He reached over and grabbed the phone to see who was calling at this hour of the night. It was Fred Carrington, the head of his board's audit committee. Jim answered the phone.

"Hi, Fred. This must really be important for you to call me at this time of night."

Fred responded in a somber tone of voice Jim has rarely heard. "Jim, sorry to wake you up. I hope I didn't also wake Cara."

Jim glanced over at his wife, who was sleeping peacefully. He said, "Not a problem. Cara could sleep thorough a rock concert. What's so important that you're up at this time of night? Your tone of voice tells me it's not good news."

"I just got off the phone with Roger Pinkett, the audit partner in charge of our audit this year. Roger is a college fraternity brother, and he gave me a courtesy heads up call a few minutes ago. We're going to receive an interim internal control report tomorrow implicating our Mystic Controls operation in a substantial accounting fraud."

Jim was accustomed to receiving bad news, but accounting fraud—not on his watch!

"How high does it go?" Jim asked.

"You're not going to want to hear this," Fred said, "but all the way to the top."

"So, is Kurt involved?"

"Roger tells me that Kurt is the moving force behind the fraud," Fred said. "And it gets worse. Kurt has been siphoning money through a number of front companies in order to pay gambling debts and support his mistress."

"That miserable bastard!" Jim's outcry woke Cara.

"Jim, what is it?" Cara turned on the bedside light and saw tears trickling down her husband's cheeks.

"How much theft are we talking about?" Jim asked.

"At least $20 million," Fred said, "maybe a lot more. You're not going to like this, either. There is also evidence of money laundering on behalf of some very bad actors. It seems Kurt's mistress has some close ties to the drug trade. Jim, I'm sorry to bring you this news at this hour. But I figured a heads up was better than a bolt out of the blue in the morning. We'll talk more tomorrow."

"You're not going to like this either. There is also evidence of money laundering on behalf of some very bad actors."

Jim ended the conversation and sat in silence for several minutes.

"Jim, you're scaring me," Cara said. "What is going on?"

"Our little girl and our two granddaughters are about to pass through a very long valley of sorrows," he said. "I should never have allowed her to marry Kurt. There was always something about him ..."

This story eventually ended with long prison sentences, hundreds of millions of lost shareholder value, many business and professional reputations tarnished and a shattered family. Suppose we could prevent these types of scandals? Or, if not prevent, at least maintain a heightened awareness of high risk managers and leaders?

LOCK THE BARN DOOR

Let's stop locking the barn door after the horse is gone. We must end our reactionary response to ethical failures like this one. We have an eight-decade-long history of *responding and reacting* to ethical scandals, beginning with the passage of the enabling legislation for the Securities Exchange Commission in 1934 and 1935. Since that watershed moment, we've added hundreds of federal and state laws, and thousands of federal and state regulations, and we've sentenced thousands of managers and leaders to prison. Yet we've hardly made any progress in preventing the problem because every time we close one fraudulent door, another unforeseen and unexpected door opens. There's a better way.

As I've previously mentioned, this book is the product of a research project that began in the spring of 2006. During the years since then, I've assembled a large and growing body of actionable knowledge, some of it presented in this book. The research technology I used for this book is applicable to the real world. Using that technology, I can produce Heart-Mind Maps for organizations and individuals. These maps show the influencers behind ethical judgments—a glimpse into hearts and minds. They show us what's going on when that person is in the Sweatbox. Why is this useful?

> Yet we've hardly made any progress in preventing the problem because every time we close one fraudulent door, another unforeseen and unexpected door opens. There's a better way.

Heart-Mind Maps are useful because they show us what's going on behind the scenes when someone is making an ethical judgment. For example, a Heart-Mind Map would show us whether an executive was motivated more by fear or the organizational culture when resolving ethical dilemmas. Most organizations would prefer the organization's culture as the prime driver behind ethical conduct. How might this work? Here are some sample maps taken from my research data. As we review these illustrations, please keep in mind that, although I've chosen pie charts as a presentation format, this data can be presented in any number of ways.

Also, this technology is still in its infancy. There is much more to learn about how to reliably generate, interpret and *ethically* use these Heart-Mind Maps. This sample, however, provides a glimpse into the promise of this hermeneutic-phenomenological technology—prevention and/or interdiction rather than postmortem horrified reactions, regret and remonstration. Here is our illustration.

XYZ CORPORATION'S HEART-MIND MAP

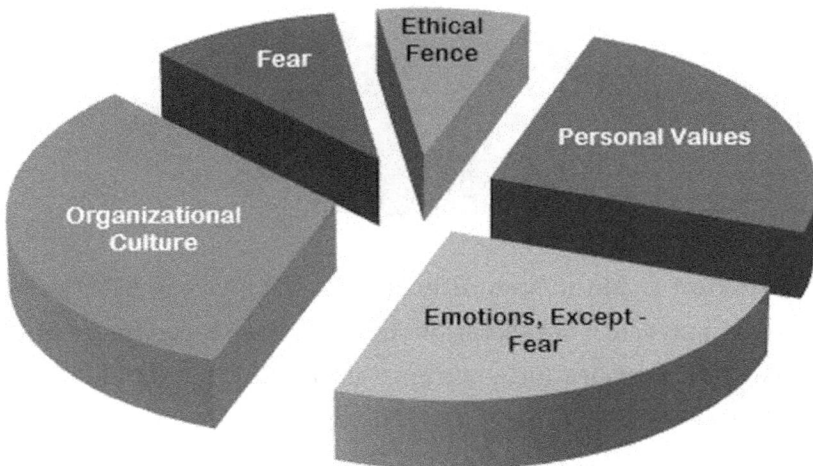

XYZ CEO HEART-MIND MAP

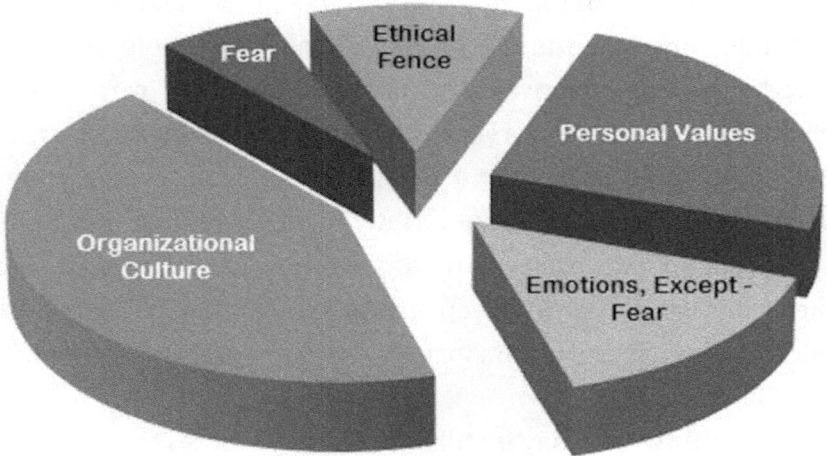

XYZ CFO HEART-MIND MAP

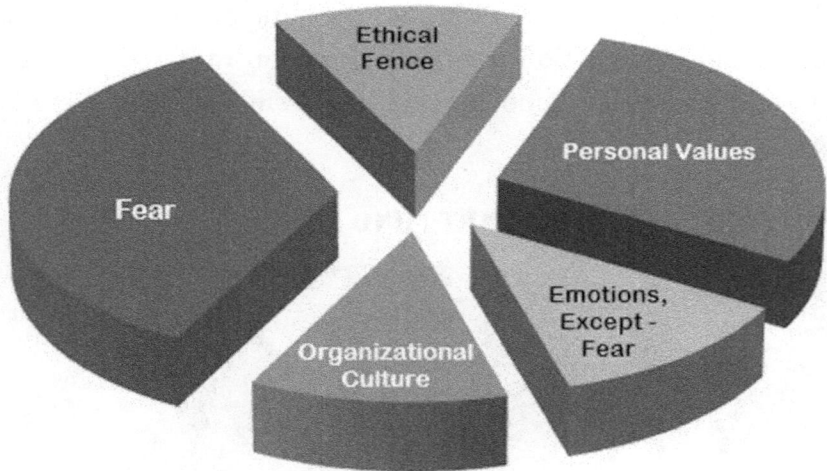

Illustration Explanation. Although the data is real, XYZ Corporation is a mythical organization. Here we have three Heart-Mind Maps—XYZ Corporation's composite, the CEO's individual map and the CFO's individual map. The composite map is a consolidated view of XYZ's 21 individual Heart-Mind maps, which I created by merging all 21 maps into a single view. Each map shows the type and weight of ethical judging influencers present in the Sweatbox during ethical judging.

What it Means. Heart-Mind Maps convert the ephemeral and subjective into a form more easily grasped and understood. These Heart-Mind Maps incorporate the theory and real-world experience I've discussed in this book into something concrete. If we look at the composite Heart-Mind Map, as an example, we see that more than a third of the influencers are emotions. We can also note that the personal and the organizational cultural influencers are about equal. If you look at all three Heart-Mind Maps, it's noteworthy that the Ethical Fence and comfort zone are approximately equal in all three maps.

> Heart-Mind Maps convert the ephemeral and subjective into a form more easily grasped and understood.

Now let's take a look at some interesting comparisons. The CEO's Heart-Mind Map shows a reduced influence of emotions during his or her ethical judging. We also note that the personal values take a back seat to organizational culture in this executive's ethical judging. This tells me that the CEO is a bit calmer and cooler during ethical judging than the organization as a whole.

If we now consider the CFO's Heart-Mind Map, we see a much different story, which is not surprising given the public company CFO's professional balancing act.

In this case, we see that nearly half of the ethical judging influencers are emotional, with fear a notable standout. It's significant how organizational culture plays a much diminished role in the CFO's ethical judging as compared to the CEO, meaning this CFO may be less of a "team player" than his or her contemporaries. Having been a CFO of a public company, the composition of the CFO's Heart-Mind Map is not surprising. In this case, we can see that personal values and emotions represent nearly 70% of the influencing factors in this executive's ethical judging.

Let's dive into this dilemma a bit more deeply.

In a public company, the CFO serves two masters—the company and its stakeholders *and* the public in the person of regulators—regulators who can put you behind bars. Although the Sarbanes-Oxley Act of 2003 equalized CEO and CFO liability in cases of fraud, regulators routinely view the CFO as the police officer on the beat, especially if the CFO is also a licensed professional, such as a CPA.

In many public companies, the CFO comes under significant pressure from the remainder of the C-Suite team to "hit" the right number every quarter. As a result, CFOs are often less influenced by organizational culture and rely more on their Internal Compass, Ethical Fence and ethical comfort zone when in the Sweatbox. This CFO's Heart-Mind Map illustrates that real-world experience. If we were to look at the Heart-Mind Map of the Chief Compliance Officer, we might find similar results.

Let's consider a slightly different scenario.

These days, we have diverse multicultural organizations. These organizations can have members with very different worldviews. We've seen the profound effect worldview has on an individual's Internal Compass. Suppose we find a senior executive within an organization whose individual Heart-Mind Map reveals that his or her Internal Compass plays a much larger role in ethical judging than the organization's culture. In such a case, we might conclude that such an executive, when in the throes of the Sweatbox, is more likely to make ethical judgments contrary to the organization's culture. Do we work to change his or her worldview? If so, where do we go with this powerful tool?

Moving Forward. As is usually the case, new tools and technology are often two-edged swords. Such tools and technology can do much good but also, when used inappropriately, can cause great harm. I think, in the case of this technology and tool, it's appropriate to invoke the Hippocratic oath: First, do no harm. There is still much to learn about using this new technology. In our Ethical Intelligence Research Center, we're continuing and expanding that research. As we move forward, we can make great strides in understanding and interdicting unethical behavior. It's my pledge that this new tool and the underlying technology will be used for good and not harm.

> I think, in the case of this technology and tool, it's appropriate to invoke the Hippocratic oath: First, do no harm.

ROADMAP TO AN ETHICALLY INTELLIGENT ORGANIZATION

In the previous chapter, I presented a detailed Roadmap to an ethically intelligent life. Here, I'm presenting a Roadmap to an ethically intelligent *organization*. There are some similarities but mainly differences between the two Roadmaps. Although organizations are living creatures (organism is the root word for organizations), they are very different from human beings. As a result, our Roadmap reflects that dissimilarity. It's more generic and lacks the specificity of the human Roadmap.

The ethically intelligent organization Roadmap possesses all of the organizational lessons presented here, but those lessons must be tailored to fit each organization. Here are the general organizational lessons of the Roadmap to an ethically intelligent organization.

1. **TRUTH**
2. **PEOPLE**
3. **RIGHT-THINKING-RIGHT-ACTING (R^2 BEHAVIOR)**
4. **ACTING**
5. **CULTURE**
6. **CLOISTER**
7. **OTHERNESS**

Before we start working through these organizational lessons, I want you to know there are resources available to help you. The Boardroom Partners (www.boardroompartners.com) website contains an array of resources available to help you work through this journey. And, of course, we're available for consultations.

As we discuss these organizational lessons, please keep in mind that these are not stand-alone unrelated lessons. They are intrinsically intertwined, symbiotic and synergistic. For example, creating a right-thinking-right-acting (R^2) organization is dependent upon truth-telling. The more truth-telling that occurs within an organization, the easier it becomes for people to consistently do the right thing, which contributes to the organization's R^2 Culture.

> Lying is an insidious poison to any organizational culture. It corrodes the very essence of trust.

Now, let's get started. Here are the seven organizational lessons.

Truth. As I've said before: Stop lying! Creating an ethically intelligent organization begins at the same place that awakening an ethically intelligent human life begins— telling the truth. Truth-telling is *the* essential foundation for not only creating an ethically intelligent organization but any organization that effectively fulfills its purpose.

Lying is an insidious poison to any organizational culture. It corrodes the very essence of trust. Lying corrupts decision-making, and it promotes a perverse Darwinian culture where the fittest liar survives. Lying organizations seldom succeed.

I've seen these effects firsthand. As an auditor, employee, officer and consultant, I've worked in and observed hundreds of organizations and their respective cultures. Organizations that tolerate lying underperform those that don't. I've seen some organizations where lying was considered a high art form, and people were praised for creatively deceitful skills. Every one of those organizations eventually failed, some in spectacular public implosions. Why is this important?

It's simple: lying steals freedom. I've made this point once before, and I emphasize it again because most people don't understand this aspect of lying. Lying steals your freedom to choose right actions. Let's consider a simple example.

Many organizations tolerate so-called "budget padding," which is a common form of organizational deceit. Managers and leaders justify this practice because forecasting is imprecise, and budget overruns can be costly to your career. So they add a little "fudge" factor that will enable them to either hit or come in a little under budget, something that always looks good. At the micro level, this may seem shrewd and acceptable.

At the senior leadership level, however, this is a potential disaster. Let's say that there are three levels of consolidation contained within the forecast. If each of those levels added even a 6% padding factor, the padded consolidated budget would be 18% higher than a truthful budget. That 18% difference could be a decisive factor in not launching a new product. Or it might influence the choice of health insurance provider with expanded benefits. Because of the 18% difference, senior leadership would be deprived of positive project selection. As a senior manager or leader, it means you've lost an element of your freedom to correctly choose.

Lying is anathema to creating an ethically intelligent organization. Managers and leaders should demand the truth, tell the truth to others and themselves, and live a life based on truth. One of the best ways of accomplishing this goal is to hire the right people.

> Organizations are created by and for people. Organizations contain people. Organizations reflect the people who populate them.

People. Hire and nurture ethically intelligent people. I know this seems obvious, but it's impeccable advice. Organizations are created by and for people. Organizations contain people. Organizations reflect the people who populate them. If someone is not ethically intelligent when they walk through your front door (and most won't be), make sure you provide a welcoming environment that supports them on their journey to an ethically intelligent life.

There is an important symbiosis and synergy neatly interlaced into this second organizational lesson. Organizational members self-select in or out of organizations. Once you've set the organization on its ethically intelligent growth journey, every ethically intelligent person who comes on board increases the incentive for those who are not ethically intelligent (or on the journey) either to begin their journey or leave the organization. This creates a virtuous self-reinforcing loop. Your job as a manager or leader is to get it started and nurture its growth. You give it life and love until others join you. Success is in multiplication, not addition!

Ethically intelligent organizations are places where telling the truth is the number one value. Members of ethically intelligent organizations don't lie, don't tolerate those who lie and respectfully admonish those who do. Such organizations don't mislead customers, even when it's more profitable to do so. They shoot straight with their employees. Such organizations admit mistakes when they occur, take responsibility for those mistakes and equitably compensate anyone damaged from such mistakes. These are the organizations that create an R^2 Culture and have a bright future.

R^2 Behavior. Create a culture of R^2 Behavior or an R^2 Culture. We defined R^2 Behavior as right-thinking-right-acting behavior. It's an expression that aptly describes a virtuous practice, colloquially called "doing the right thing." We know from our discussion in Chapter 5 that R^2 Behavior is timeless and has three parts: truthfulness, discernment and integrity. We also know that most managers and leaders want to lead a team of R^2 people executing a vision and a mission within an R^2 organization. How do we get there?

We've already covered the first two steps. An R^2 Culture is grounded in truthfulness. As I mentioned previously, in all of my interviews with senior business leaders, telling the truth was always considered the right thing to do. That's step one.

Hiring ethically intelligent people is step two. People who do what's right in all circumstances are the backbone of an R^2 organization.

Steps three and four are a bit more challenging to describe—a discerning organization acting with integrity. Crafting a discerning organization acting with integrity requires not only hiring discerning people possessing integrity but also an organizational structure whose decision-making and judging processes are intrinsically discerning and reflect integrity. I know this sounds a bit complicated and esoteric because we're ascribing human characteristics to something that isn't human. It's both possible and necessary, however, to create an R^2 organization with these characteristics. Let's consider an example that will help illustrate my point.

Most business organizations have internal decision-making and judging processes designed to maximize profit and the return on investment to shareholders. There is nothing wrong with this orientation. Let's consider a plant manager who is deciding on modernizing certain aspects of the plant's manufacturing infrastructure. The modernization would add years of competitive productivity to the plant. The existing internal decision-making process is driven by the plant's projected discounted cash flow. In addition, the plant manager's annual bonus is tied to the plant's profitability.

On the surface, this decision-making process seems straightforward. We project the additional future cash flows of the plant after the improvements and decide if those improvements result in an appropriate return on our shareholders' investment. There is, however, an internal conflict in this process. Investing in the current year reduces not only the plant's profitability and cash flows but also the plant manager's bonus. Our non-discerning internal process is challenging our plant manager's integrity because the right thing to do is make the investment this year. As someone who has been compensated under this kind of arrangement, I can tell you that today's bonus is much more important than next year's. I might not be around next year!

How do we fix this? We change the process to make it more discerning of the inherent contexts. We allow the plant manager to share in future projected results even if the plant manager is not around to see future results. This incentivizes decision-makers to do the right thing which, in this case, is to do what's appropriate for the long-term health of the organization and return on investment to its shareholders.

This is a simple example, but it demonstrates how organizations sabotage themselves internally with non-discerning decision-making and judging processes. Discerning organizations acting with integrity don't have these internal conflicts. Organizational members should see R^2 Behavior as the force that animates the organization. They will see it only if organizational managers and leaders act well.

Great managers and leaders are great actors. They show us. They lift us with their example. They inspire us with actions. They walk the talk.

Acting. Great managers and leaders are great actors. They show us. They lift us with their example. They inspire us with actions. They walk the talk. My pastor says we act out more sermons than anyone will ever preach.

The application of this wisdom is universal. Faith-based pursuits is just one arena of success. Without right actions, your words are empty, producing scant outcomes. Great managers and leaders are great actors. The rest of us, not so much. This is one of the few leadership skills that I strongly advise you to work on. If you're not an effective actor, you won't be an effective manager or leader. Acting skills are important for managers and leaders, but they're not a substitute for sincerity. I'm not suggesting that you acquire acting skills so that you can feign false concerns and an artificial attitude. Whatever you do as a manager or leader must come from an internal sincerity. Otherwise, you'll become known as a fake or a phony. Let me offer a few examples.

Many years ago when I was offered my first "formal" leadership assignment, my manager taught me what I'm teaching you.

I was having a difficult time leading my team. I didn't have the respect of my team members, and they were not receptive to my leadership. My team was in chaos. I went to my manager for advice. He told me what I'm telling you. I was not acting like a leader. My actions were tentative, and I showed that I was unsure of what I was doing. My response was, "That's all true. I'm *not* sure I know what I'm doing. I'm afraid of making mistakes, especially in front of my team members."

His response was, "Fake it 'til you make it." That advice rings in my ears to this day.

Here's another example. I was once mentoring a young aspiring professor. After several weeks spent in the classroom, she came to me and said teaching in a physical classroom wasn't for her. She was going to concentrate on teaching only online. Knowing how bright and capable she was, I asked her why she was entertaining such a foolish notion. What she told me is instructive. "I feel so inadequate when I'm standing in front of the class. Many of the students are more experienced and older than I am. When they ask me a question that I don't know the answer to, I freeze and look foolish. In an online environment, the students can't see me. So I have time to research the question and provide an answer. I never look like I'm not in control."

I told her what I'm telling you. When you're asked a question to which you don't know the answer—and this can happen frequently in a technical and evolving subject like accounting—act like you know the answer and think logically. Use the question as a teaching opportunity and solicit responses from the other class members. They may know the answer, and you may learn something. And there is nothing wrong with saying you don't know the answer off the top of your head, but you surely know where to find it. Act the role until you *are* the role.

There are many other examples I could offer. Think back to Chapter 6 and our discussion of Dr. Martin Luther King, Jr., when he first became leader of the bus boycott group. He didn't want the job. He was scared to death of it. But he stepped up and acted like a leader until he became one. There is nothing deceptive or underhanded about acting. Acting is a noble profession. Combine it with excellent leadership skills, and it can move mountains. Embed this idea into your organizational culture.

Culture. Culture is a force as fierce as fire. Harness the fire. Culture is to an organization as emotions are to individual humans. Emotions are the energy of life. They provide the passion for great achievements. Culture is the life force that animates organizations. It transforms ephemeral missions and vision into reality. Culture is the conduit for transfusing ethical intelligence into your organization. Cultural transfusion permeates and infuses your organization just like an injection fills a living organism with medication. Culture is the bloodstream of your organization. Before you can use it wisely and purposefully, you must understand it. How much do you know about your culture? Have you ever had a cultural audit or assessment? Can you describe your organizational culture in a single sentence? Can you list some of the key traditions of your organizational culture? Is there any wet work going on? Do you have termites?

These are important questions relevant to not only the CEO and the C-Suite but also every organizational member. If are going to change and improve organizational culture, you have to know where you are so you can assess the length and breadth of your journey to your desired destination.

Culture will make or break any effort at transforming your organization into an ethically intelligent organization. Find out if you have the Sick Six cultural dysfunctions. Satisfy yourself that your values statements translate into values behaviors. Please know that posting a survey on Survey Monkey and having your team members respond is not going to answer the questions I've posed. A doctor is needed to diagnose illness in people. Likewise, a doctor is needed to diagnose organizational cultural illnesses. We can help. Just ask.

Cloister. In Chapter 8, we discussed the Captivity Cloister and Innocuous Imperial Box, metaphorical structures within which we confine members of the C-Suite. As much as is practical, dismantle those structures. As enticing as the idea of squeezing every nanosecond of productivity out of your highly paid C-Suite leaders may be, there are serious downsides, as I described in Chapter 8. Yes, provide all of the assistants and tools necessary for maximizing productivity, but tear down the walls of isolation and captivity. Get your C-Suite members out into the organization. Everyone might be surprised at what they learn. Spread the same practice into other areas of the organization.

… tear down the walls of isolation and captivity. Get your C-Suite members out into the organization.

I once consulted with the CEO of a manufacturing organization about commercialization of engineering ideas or, in their case, the lack thereof. This CEO, who was an engineer, described an elaborate internal process for moving newly discovered engineering breakthroughs into the marketing arena for commercialization. Unfortunately, there was little commercialization because the marketing group always found a reason why the "breakthroughs" wouldn't succeed in the marketplace. After some investigation, I discovered the engineering group was sequestered in an engineering lab located some miles from headquarters, where the marketing group was situated.

When I asked the CEO the reason for the separation of these two groups, he was surprised that the logic of it had escaped me. His response was, "I want to keep those guys [the engineers] focused on their jobs. I don't want them wandering around the halls of headquarters wasting their time. I especially don't want them talking to the marketing guys. They would just fill the heads of my engineers with all their cockamamie ideas. No, it was a stroke of genius on my part keeping my engineers away from all those harebrained marketing types. I want my sales and marketing people focused on selling, and my engineers focused on research and development."

Do you recognize the problem?

This organization needed collaboration, not segregation. I recommended that the marketing organization and the engineering group communicate frequently, even working together on projects. Imagine the time that was saved when an engineer with an idea ran it by a marketing or sales person who either validated it or killed it before the organization wasted substantial resources. Organizations that create walls and stovepipes will not survive the relentless competition of the 24/7/365 21st century business environment.

I had another client that did the same thing with their information technology group. At great expense, the information technology group was relocated, in this case, across town from the users they were supporting. Over time, help-desk response times increased, and the user-friendliness of applications degenerated. After talking to the information technology folks and the users, it was clear the separation was responsible for the problems.

When everyone was together in one location, informal conversations and day-to-day activities created a symbiotic relationship between the information technology group and users. The physical separation had built walls of ignorance and indifference that previously didn't exist.

Tear down those walls. Yes, there are instances where secrecy and information must be compartmentalized and released only to those with a need to know. But unless you lead a spy agency or a team creating the next cutting-edge weapons system for the Department of Defense, those walls and stovepipes are costing you dearly. Insist on horizontal as well as vertical communications.

Spend some time walking around and talking to people in your manufacturing plant or call center. Go on some sales calls with your sales team and find out what your customers are actually saying about your organization and your products and/or services. You may learn that Otherness is not necessarily hostile.

Ethically intelligent organizations engage in strategic openness rooted in wisdom.

Otherness. Test your assumptions about others. Keep your Worldview Window clear. Ethically intelligent organizations engage in strategic openness rooted in wisdom. Think back to our discussions of Violative Paranoia and Hostile Otherness. That paranoia and hostility is real. I understand the defensive reactions to it. But not everyone is out to get us. Not every interaction with our external environment is fraught with great danger. Strategic openness is something all living organisms use to survive. With non-sentient organisms, it's autonomic. Instinctual interactions with the external environment are saturated with caution and fear. But they, nonetheless, occur. With humans, strategic openness must be interwoven with acknowledged fear, informed caution and learned wisdom.

Strategic openness must permeate your organizational culture. Almost everyone in your organization is going to interact with your external environment. Not all of those interactions can be monitored or screened by your legal department. Well, I take that back. It's possible for your legal department to monitor and screen every external interaction, but you'll go out of business waiting for something to happen.

I understand there are risks in encouraging organizational members to engage in strategic openness. I've worked in one of the most highly regulated industries in the country. But with proper training and supervision, strategic openness can work to your benefit. A companion solution is reform.

REFORM

There is much in business and government needing reform, none more urgently than the Foreign Corrupt Practices Act and Regulation Full Disclosure. I've already addressed both of these well-intentioned but harmful responses to real-world problems. There are some additional points I want to address and amplify others.

Foreign Corrupt Practices Act (FCPA). The FCPA is a source of civic corruption and an enabling force for foreign competition. The FCPA was an ill-fated attempt to export our view of pristine business competition to the rest of the world. I'll let you decide if that is a noble enterprise or not. But despite FCPA promoters' claims that it's working because our view is slowly being recognized and adopted worldwide, the reality is that FCPA not only restrains United States-based companies' ability to compete effectively in worldwide markets but also aids and abets our foreign competitors. Our senior business leadership won't criticize the law for fear of political repercussions. I'll dare to speak for them and make the politically incorrect statement—this is nuts! Companies headquartered in the United States spend untold billions of dollars complying with FCPA and its accompanying regulations. This law has taken management of the foreign operations of United States companies out of the hands of experienced operational leaders and transferred it to lawyers. Legal counsel for these companies are paranoid about this law and its regulations. As result, they go to extreme measures hoping not to violate its Byzantine mosaic. This law is suffocating the foreign operations of our domestic companies with scant return on investment.

Here's an example. I was recently talking to an executive of a Fortune 100 company domiciled in the United States. We were reminiscing about how much easier it was to do business overseas 25 years ago. In those days, if a country manager needed $500 to ease the passage of machinery through customs, you would simply approve with no questions asked. This executive told me that, these days, he wouldn't even attempt the $500 payment because he would incur over $5,000 in compliance expense trying to make the $500 happen. His firm would simply put up with the foreign "bureaucratic delays" and eat the cost of the wasted time as a cost of doing business. Incidentally, the cost of the wasted time was far in excess of the $500 "passage" payment.

As I said at the beginning, this is not only nuts, but it's also hypocritical. Foreign executives look at what we do, and they think we're crazy. We're not only less competitive by tying our own hands behind our back, but we also think we're furthering our pristine view of competitive practices in foreign cultures.

Nothing could be further from the truth. Foreign executives look at our domestic practices when dealing with governmental agencies and see nothing superior to the practices in their own cultures. They pay to grease the wheels of commerce, and we call it bribery. We pay to grease the wheels of commerce in the United States, and we call it political contributions. Foreign business executives call that hypocrisy.

> They pay to grease the wheels of commerce, and we call it bribery. We pay to grease the wheels of commerce in the United States, and we call it political contributions.

The FCPA and its ensnaring regulations need to be thrown into the dustbin of history. Let our companies compete when operating in foreign markets. We have no business trying to forcibly export our business practices into other cultures. If our business practices are superior, that superiority should be revealed on the field of competition, not in the bowels of government bureaucracies and courtrooms. Don't get me wrong, I'm not advocating bribing government officials. But we need to recognize that, in some cultures, the income of low-level government bureaucrats is like the income of wait staff in the United States. The salary is low, but the difference is earned in tips. Our business leaders should be able to pay those tips without the fear of going to prison.

The FCPA, among many other laws and regulations, is corroding and corrupting the relationship between government and business. It has caused a corrosive cloud of hostility to descend into our domestic business environment, birthing a commonly held view of government as the hostile Other. Our businesses have reacted by forming political action committees that make billions of dollars of political contributions in an attempt at allaying the hostility. When organized crime engages in this sort of activity, we call it a protection racket and label it a crime. We must find an ethically intelligent solution to this sordid consequence. Regulation Full Disclosure, another well intended law, has had similar unintended consequences.

Regulation Full Disclosure (FD). Because I covered Regulation Full Disclosure (FD) in some detail in Chapter 8, I'm not going to repeat that discussion here. My purpose here is to make the case for reforming this regulation in a way that permits senior business leaders a well-defined exit from their solitary confinement. The intent of Regulation FD is noble. It was aimed at reducing insider trading. The jury is still out whether this objective has been obtained. There is no doubt, however, about the serious undesirable unintended consequences of this regulation. We've made it nearly impossible for senior business leaders to have practical and meaningful outside lifelines.

There have been some accommodations offered. Senior business leaders have a narrow safe harbor of individuals with whom they can have "privileged" conversations. For many of the reasons we have already discussed, the safe harbor is too narrow. The limited audience with whom a senior business leader is permitted to have conversations is impractical and unworkable. Why? Lawyers are rightly paranoid. Although the regulation permits certain types of conversations, out of an abundance of caution: Most corporate legal counsels would prefer *no* conversations. The contents of a conversation can't be misconstrued if the conversation never takes place. I completely understand that logic. Corporate legal counsels are only doing their jobs.

The real solution to this problem is a generous safe harbor along the lines of the secret meeting I described at the beginning of Chapter 8. These illicit meetings are now taking place. We should make them legal. There are plenty of public-minded social organizations that could easily host these types of meetings.

Senior business leaders are serious and responsible members of the community. The probability of any of them trying to profit from the sort of intimate information shared in these meetings is very low. On the other hand, potential rewards to society at large are huge. As the percentage of senior business leaders carrying the Essential Credential grows, the rewards would be even greater.

ESSENTIAL CREDENTIAL

In the final chapter of this book, we'll discuss why ethical intelligence is the foundation of leadership. Managers and leaders should not presume to lead others until they have shown they are ethically intelligent, or at least on the journey to becoming ethically intelligent.

Leadership is a sacred bond. It's a special relationship between leader and follower that is grounded in mutual trust and respect. We should demand the highest ethical standards from our managers and leaders. In that regard, I have a dream and a vision for the future of leadership.

I have a vision that one day every manager and leader will possess a Heart-Mind Map and certificate demonstrating a fluent ethical intelligence—an Essential Credential. As we gather more data and create hundreds, perhaps thousands of Heart-Mind Maps, we'll be able to statistically create and validate a "normal" or "standard." The point is, those who seek to manage and lead others must show, in some way, that they possess the ethical intelligence to deserve our trust. *You cannot lead without it.*

———————◆———————

Chapter Highlights

- Let's stop locking the barn door after the horse is gone.
- Hermeneutic-phenomenological analysis shows great promise.
- Heart-Mind Maps convert the ephemeral and subjective into a form more easily grasped and understood.

- Lying is an insidious poison to any organizational culture. It corrodes the very essence of trust.
- Hire and nurture ethically intelligent people.
- Ethically intelligent organizations are places where telling the truth is the number one value.
- People who do what's right in all circumstances are the backbone of a right-thinking-right-acting organization.
- Great managers and leaders are great actors. They show us. They lift us with their example. They inspire us with actions. They walk the talk.
- Culture is the life force that animates organizations. It transforms ephemeral missions and vision into reality.
- Culture is the conduit for transfusing ethical intelligence into your organization.
- Ethically intelligent organizations engage in strategic openness rooted in wisdom.
- Foreign business executives pay to grease the wheels of commerce, and we call it bribery. Domestic business leaders pay to grease the wheels of commerce in the United States, and we call it political contributions.
- One day every manager and leader will possess a Heart-Mind Map and certificate demonstrating a fluent ethical intelligence—an Essential Credential.

Questions for You

- Is your organization ethically intelligent?
- Is truth-telling the number one value in your organization?
- Can you describe your organizational culture in one sentence?
- When was the last time you just showed up at an operating unit?
- Are your internal processes discerning?
- When was your last cultural assessment?
- Is your board ethically intelligent?

CHAPTER 12

---◆---

YOU CANNOT LEAD
WITHOUT IT

Ethical behavior lies at the heart of leadership.

Joanne Ciulla

We're going to listen in on one of my MBA leadership class discussions of the classic "Was Hitler a leader?" argument. This was a class of 14 students split about evenly between men and women. All of the class members were working adults ranging in age from early 30s to the late 50s. Some of the students owned their own businesses. The remainder worked for medium to large-sized organizations in managerial or high-level leadership positions. Four of the students were retired military. Let's listen in on the discussion.

Professor: "Okay everyone, let's get started. Tonight we're going to join an age-old argument over whether Adolph Hitler was a leader. By a show of hands, who believes Hitler was a leader? Wow! It's rare to get any group to completely agree. So, everyone here believes Hitler was a leader?"

Class: "Yes."

Professor: "Okay. We're going to make a list of reasons you all believe Hitler was a leader. Yes, Sarah?"

Sarah: "I've had enough classes with you to know when you think we're wrong. I see that faint grin on your face!"

Rich: "I think Sarah is onto something. Are we wrong? You don't think Hitler was a leader?"

Professor: "I have my thoughts, but I am more interested in your thoughts right now. So, who wants to go first? Yes, Jim."

Jim: "I believe Hitler was a leader because he had followers."

Professor: "Okay. We'll put 'Had followers' on our list. Go ahead, Sinead."

Sinead: "Hitler was a leader because he had a vision and got people to buy into it and follow him."

Professor: "Excellent point. We'll add 'Had a vision' and 'Convinced others to see his vision and pursue it with him.' Marissa, did you want to add something?"

Marissa: "Well, I'm not sure. But wasn't he considered a leader because he accomplished his objectives by using others?"

Professor: "I am interested in your terminology, 'used others.' I'll add it to the list, 'Accomplished objectives by using others.' Okay, Wendy, you're next."

Marissa: "Wait! Maybe it should say, 'through others?'"

Professor: "'Using' was a little harsh?"

Marissa: "A little."

Professor: "Okay, Wendy."

Wendy: "I think Hitler was a leader because he changed the world."

Professor: "Okay, I'll add it to the list, but does it matter how?"

Wendy: "Wow. I didn't consider that."

Professor: "Yes, Shawn."

Shawn: "I don't see how Hitler wasn't a leader. He created a plan. Recruited a team to implement the plan and changed the world forever. We may not agree with his plan or his tactics, but he certainly implemented it. How can he not be a leader? Besides, we're still talking about him. I think we need more leaders like him."

Amy: "Are you crazy? Look at the damage and death Hitler caused. I just don't get that!"

Shawn: "You just said it. He caused something. He moved the needle. What else do you expect from a leader?"

Ralph: "I agree with Shawn. At least Hitler did something. Unlike these worthless politicians we have today."

Professor: "Shawn and Ralph, I take it that your criterion is 'Got results?'"

Shawn: "Yeah. We don't pay leaders to be nice. If you don't get results, you aren't a leader in my book."

Amy: "So, let me get this straight. As long as you get some kind of results, that qualifies you as a leader? You've gotta be kidding me."

Ralph: "Yep."

Amy: "Now I know you're crazy! Doctor John, what do you think about this?"

Professor: "I'm loving this discussion. Keep going! Maria, did you have something?"

Maria: "Now I'm beginning to understand how men keep getting us into wars. Shouldn't the results be good? Look at what Castro did to Cuba. My grandfather barely escaped with his life from Castro. I think you guys are all wrong. Real leaders should produce something good."

Wendy: "I'm with Maria on this one. I don't want a leader forcing me to do something I consider wrong. This is exactly what Hitler did. Most of his 'recruits' were forced into serving."

Jim: "The question wasn't whether Hitler was a good or bad leader. It was, was he a leader, period. I agree with Ralph and Shawn."

Krystal: "I think Jim is right. I saw President Obama on stage last night with a group of world leaders. There were people in that group who are dictators, and they treat their people terribly. But the news media calls all of them leaders. So who are we to say they aren't?"

Amir: "Wow. You actually believe the news media?"

Krystal: "You know what I mean!"

Amir: "Well, in my country you wouldn't even be allowed to speak. Just kidding, of course. I find this discussion, shall we say, strange. In my country, my part of the world, anyone man enough and strong enough to seize power is a leader. There is no doubt. Strength and power define leadership."

Ann: "That brings up a good question, Doctor John. Is the definition of leadership different in different cultures?"

Professor: "What do you think? Is someone a leader because of position? If someone calls you a leader, are you a leader?"

Ann: "I don't think it should be, but I'm confused."

Professor: "You're in good company. Many are confused by the idea of leadership. Sylvester, you've been silent. Please sum up for us."

Sylvester: "Hitler was a leader. Maybe, not so great, but a leader."

Professor: "That's all you've got?"

Sylvester: "That's it! Can we take a food break?"

Professor: "Okay, let's take a break."

So, there you have it. A small portion of an hour-long discussion with adult MBA students studying leadership. I've taught this course dozens of times. And I've held this discussion dozens of times. The result is always the same. Students believe that leadership is defined by position and results regardless of the nature of those results.

The world at large holds many of these same beliefs. In fact, until the last few years, leadership experts engaged in the "Hitler-leader" discussion and arrived at essentially the same conclusions—leadership is tied to position and outcomes. The quality or nature of the outcomes is irrelevant to the definition of leadership.

But our understanding of leadership has evolved over the past five decades. How do I know? I've lived it!

My Leadership Journey

I am humbled by my unique opportunity to experience the last 50 years of leadership theory and practice evolution. When I began my business career, most business leaders were members of the greatest generation. They had come of age during the war years and served either in World War II or the Korean conflict. Whatever leadership training these men (there were few women) possessed came from the military—think George Patton and Douglas MacArthur leadership styles.

That style was what you might expect. It was authoritarian, positional and highly structured. You were a cog in a machine. You did what you were told, kept your nose clean and aspired to the next level on the organization chart. We were the "organization men," discussed in the best-selling book of a similar name.

On second thought, perhaps "organization man" is a bit strong, because most of us hadn't "sold" our soul to the organization. I sometimes marvel at the stark differences between that era of leadership and that which we find today. As an example, I was blessed with the opportunity of working at Ford Corporate Headquarters a few years after Rob-

> You did what you were told, kept your nose clean and aspired to the next level on the organization chart.

ert McNamara became John Kennedy's secretary of defense. Mc-Namara's Ford legacy was obvious in the machine-like precision with which the corporate finance staff operated. Our opinions, however, were rarely sought and never offered. We did what we were told.

We learned that style of leadership and found it effective and efficient. We later learned, however, that our industrial successes of that era were probably linked more to factors unrelated to the leadership styles of those organizations. In fact, many of those organizations lost their competitiveness, with many going bankrupt—bankruptcies that could have been avoided with a more modern, inclusive and open leadership style. I know how difficult that transition was. Those of us who "made our leadership bones" during that era had a lot to learn about the true nature of leadership, including almost losing jobs because of our stubbornness.

I still vividly remember the first consulting project I was assigned to lead. I was hired by a Big 4 (Big 8 at that time) consulting practice as a manufacturing "guru" because of my manufacturing background, including at the Ford Motor Company. My team consisted of two men and one woman. After about three weeks at the client site, the partner who had hired me and to whom I reported, Phil, paid us a visit. Phil was a retired naval captain, and he ran a tight ship.

Not one to beat around the bush, Phil said, "We need to talk about how you're running this job."

I was surprised and defensively said, "What do you mean? We're on schedule and on budget. And the client is pleased with our progress. I just talked to the COO yesterday."

Phil said, "The job is fine, but Myra doesn't like your leadership style. She's called me several times and said you're acting like a dictator."

Now I was confused and, frankly, starting to get angry.

Phil continued, "You can't just order people around! I understand how difficult that is because I have a lot of experience ordering people around. When I told people what to do, I expected them to do it without comment or complaint. That's not the way it works here. Myra also said you told her that you don't have to listen to her."

To which I blurted out, "What! Do you mean I have to listen to her? She's a junior consultant, and she knows nothing about manufacturing. Her background is in banking!"

Phil got this "Phil" look on his face and said, "Opincar, for as bright as you are, you sure miss some important shit! You're a great technician, but you've got to learn some of these soft skills if you want to move up in this organization. I deliberately put Myra on this project so that you could teach her something."

> "Opincar, for as bright as you are, you sure miss some important shit!"

Phil's words were like a punch in the nose. All I could muster was a weak, "Oh."

That was my first encounter with the idea of adding value to team members. It certainly wasn't the last.

Phil was a great guy and my first mentor. Even though he'd come out of the military, he'd learned a lot about real leadership somewhere along the way, and he showed me that you can *learn* leadership skills. These days, I chuckle under my breath every time I hear the term "natural born leader." You may be born with raw natural leadership talents, but leaders raise up other leaders. You don't learn it from reading books or self-help articles in

> You may be born with raw natural leadership talents, but leaders raise up other leaders.

Fortune or the *Wall Street Journal.* Sure, you can study leadership. I have a doctorate in it. But you learn how to be a leader from another leader, someone who takes the time to invest in you like Phil did me.

Since that fortunate first encounter with a mentor/leader, I've had the privilege of leading dozens of teams and organizations. I've seen many leadership styles come and go, including charismatic, transactional, situational, transformational, authentic and servant, just to name a few. I think you can discern some of what I've learned from the contents of this book. There's more I have yet to learn about leadership, but one thing I already know for certain—leadership is all about relationships.

LEADERSHIP AND RELATIONSHIPS

This is where the rubber meets the road. And, this is where leadership and ethical intelligence are inextricably bound together. Your ethical intelligence lives in your consciousness, but it manifests in your relationships. Leadership lives in your relationships, but it manifests in your followers' outcomes. Leadership is a fellow traveler with your ethical intelligence. The two are synergistic partners. Ethical intelligence amplifies your leadership's efficacy. Your leadership's privilege draws its legitimacy and goodness from your ethical intelligence.

Leadership is a privilege. It draws its power and authority from those who

Your ethical intelligence lives in your consciousness, but it manifests in your relationships. Leadership lives in your relationships. It manifests in better outcomes for your followers.

Leadership is a privilege. It draws its power and authority from those who are being served by the leader.

are being served by the leader. Yes, that's right—from those who are being served. This is the exact opposite from the leadership style I first learned as a young professional. Back then, as a follower, I was the servant, and an unhappy one at that. It was wrong then. It's wrong now. Leaders must relish the opportunity to add value to those they lead. And, although it's important, I'm not just talking about financial value. I've led dozens of organizations where my leadership added financial value. That's the CEO's—or any leader's—job, but it's not the only job. It's just the starting point.

> Ethical intelligence amplifies your leadership's efficacy. Your leadership's privilege draws its legitimacy and goodness from your ethical intelligence.

Leaders are called to serve a purpose higher than themselves. Generating financial wealth for yourself or others doesn't qualify as that higher purpose. Don't get me wrong, everyone needs financial sustenance, some of us more than others. But that sustenance is just the floor. It's the minimum. It's just the first step in your climb to success as a leader. You must serve others by helping them better their lives and the lives they touch. You can do this only within green-field relationships. Ethically intelligent leaders understand such relationships because they have restored the original pristine condition of their *Primal Relationship*.

I want to illustrate this point using an experience that touched me very deeply. I view teaching as a leadership position. Several years ago, after I had been teaching for only a couple of years, I had a class of freshmen students taking a course on personal financial management, the third course in the curriculum. The class consisted of adult students ranging in age from their late 20s through their mid-50s. Most of these students held GEDs and were the first generation of their families to attempt college. As an ethically intelligent leader, I keep my Worldview Window clean. It helps me to "see" everyone, regardless of their background.

One of the students in this class—we'll call her Tasha—was in her late 40s. Tasha had lived a hard life. She had several estranged children and male friends. She'd recently lost her job and decided that furthering her education was the key to a better life.

Tasha was interactive in class, and I was impressed with her intellectual and practical skills. In team activities, she became a leader and was maintaining an excellent grade. Suddenly, she stopped coming to class. It was very unlike her. I decided to try and find her and offer whatever assistance I could.

After sending several emails and calling numerous phone numbers, some of which were disconnected, I reached a number where I could leave a voicemail message. In my message, I told Tasha I was concerned about her because she had missed class. I also told her how gratified I was to see her excelling in the class.

I offered my thoughts that she truly was "college" material. I encouraged her to come back to class as soon as possible and offered her the opportunity of making up the work she had missed. I hung up the phone, hoping to see her in the next class.

The next day Tasha called me. I could tell by the sound of her voice that she had had a terrible night, and she was crying. What she told me forever etched in my mind the importance of relationships in leadership.

Tasha said she'd heard me call but didn't answer the phone. Instead, she listened to me leaving the voicemail.

She said, "I was going to kill myself last night. I had lost all hope. I couldn't pay my rent. My car had broken down. Then one of my kids called asking for money, and I didn't have any to give. My daughter yelled and screamed at me. She told me how worthless I was and how I'd ruined her life. So I had the pills ready, and I was just trying to get up the courage to do it. Then you called."

Tasha continued, "You're the first person to say they cared about me in a very long time. When you said I was college material, something happened on the inside of me. I thought maybe I wasn't worthless after all. Maybe you saw something in me I couldn't. I thought about it all night, and I decided maybe there was hope after all. I threw the pills into the toilet and flushed them away. I'll be back in class this week. Thank you for saving my life!"

I don't tell this story very often because it seems self-serving and makes me appear better than I am. But it taught me several important lessons that I hope you learn and take to heart.

- *No one is worthless.*
- *Keep your Worldview Window clear. You need it to "see" every one.*
- *The power of a few simple words of encouragement is amazing. Those words didn't cost me anything except for a few minutes of my time.*
- *Look for the good, and call it forth.*
- *Our highest calling as leaders is to add value to those we lead.*
- *Leaders are called to serve a purpose higher than themselves.*
- *That purpose finds its fulfillment in green-field relationships.*

> … leaders are called to serve a purpose higher than themselves. That purpose finds its fulfillment in green-field relationships.

THE FUTURE OF LEADERSHIP IS GARDENING

Leaders are gardeners. We sow. We fertilize. We water. We cultivate. We weed. We prune. Then, one day, we give thanks and celebrate our harvest—a new ethically intelligent leader who will make their slice of the world a better place. So, where is the garden?

Leaders are gardeners. We sow. We fertilize. We water. We cultivate. We weed. We prune.

The garden is wherever you have a relationship. For those of us who visualize our Heart Refuge as a garden, it's the first garden we tend. The second is the *Primal Relationship*. After that, most of us have numerous other gardens.

For leaders, every leader/follower relationship is a garden. Into that garden we sow seeds of hope, recognition and expectation. We fertilize those seeds with teaching and direction. We water with encouragement and understanding. We cultivate with a vision of our destination. We weed with assessment and feedback. We prune by allowing mistakes. Through it all, we set clear expectations for a bountiful harvest.

Those who master this new art of relationship gardening will become the great ethically intelligent leaders who change the world.

Those who master this new art of relationship gardening will become the great ethically intelligent leaders who change the world.

FINAL WORDS OF WISDOM

- *Ethical intelligence—you can't lead without it.*
- *A leader is never too big or important to do something small.*
- *If you have to tell someone you're a leader, you probably aren't.*
- *What we do after we make a mistake defines our legacy as leaders.*
- *You can't trust selfish people.*
- *One word can change a life.*
- *It doesn't matter what you say, it's what you do.*
- *Don't ever fight battles with small people.*

- *When people fall, cover them, gently restore them. It's what leaders do.*
- *Greatness is reaching back and helping someone reach greatness.*
- *Let the secret die with you.*
- *Be positive or be quiet.*
- *Growth is not automatic. It's intentional.*
- *Celebrate unfinished people, including yourself.*

Questions for You

1. Was Hitler a leader? I'll answer that for you: No! True leaders take their followers to a better place. True leaders change the lives of those they lead for the better.

ABOUT THE AUTHOR

Dr. John Opincar, CPA, CGMA, serves as President and CEO of Boardroom Partners, a board-level consultancy. He is a college professor and President and CEO of the Ethical Intelligence Research Center, a not-for-profit research and educational institute. His current professional pursuits are all directed toward making the world a better place through research, writing, speaking and teaching about team-based corporate governance and human ethical intelligence— one person and one organization at a time.

Previously, Dr. Opincar served as Campus and Academic Director for the University of Phoenix in Iowa. Since joining the University of Phoenix in 2003, he also served as Director of Academic Affairs in Iowa, Lead Faculty/Area Chair in Houston, and Associate Faculty member in Iowa, Houston, and Online Campuses. Dr. Opincar continues his role as a University of Phoenix associate faculty member. He previously held teaching posts at Belhaven University and Our Lady of the Lake University.

Prior to entering higher education, Dr. Opincar built a successful multi-decade career in business with large enterprises such as Deloitte Touche, PriceWaterhouseCoopers, and Ford Motor Company. He also founded and led several startups, the last of which was housed in the Technology Incubator at the University of Texas at Austin.

During his career, Dr. Opincar served in numerous business and higher educational leadership positions, including Chief Academic Officer at the University of Phoenix, CFO of a NYSE energy company, managing director of an international software consortium, board member and advisor, senior consultant to a select group of Fortune 500 clients and their directors and CEO of a number of privately held companies.

Dr. Opincar earned degrees from the University of Detroit Mercy, Michigan State University and the University of Phoenix. He is a lifetime member of Alpha Sigma Nu, Beta Alpha Psi, Beta Gamma Sigma and Delta Mu Delta honor societies. Dr. Opincar is a Certified Public Accountant in Michigan and a Chartered Global Management Accountant. He is a certified John Maxwell Team leadership coach, trainer and speaker. His non-professional pursuits include gourmet cooking, music, politics, gardening and Standard Poodles.

Author's Contact Information
Boardroom Partners, Inc.
john.opincar@boardroompartners.com

www.ingramcontent.com/pod-product-compliance
Lightning Source LLC
Chambersburg PA
CBHW020911210326
41598CB00018B/1832